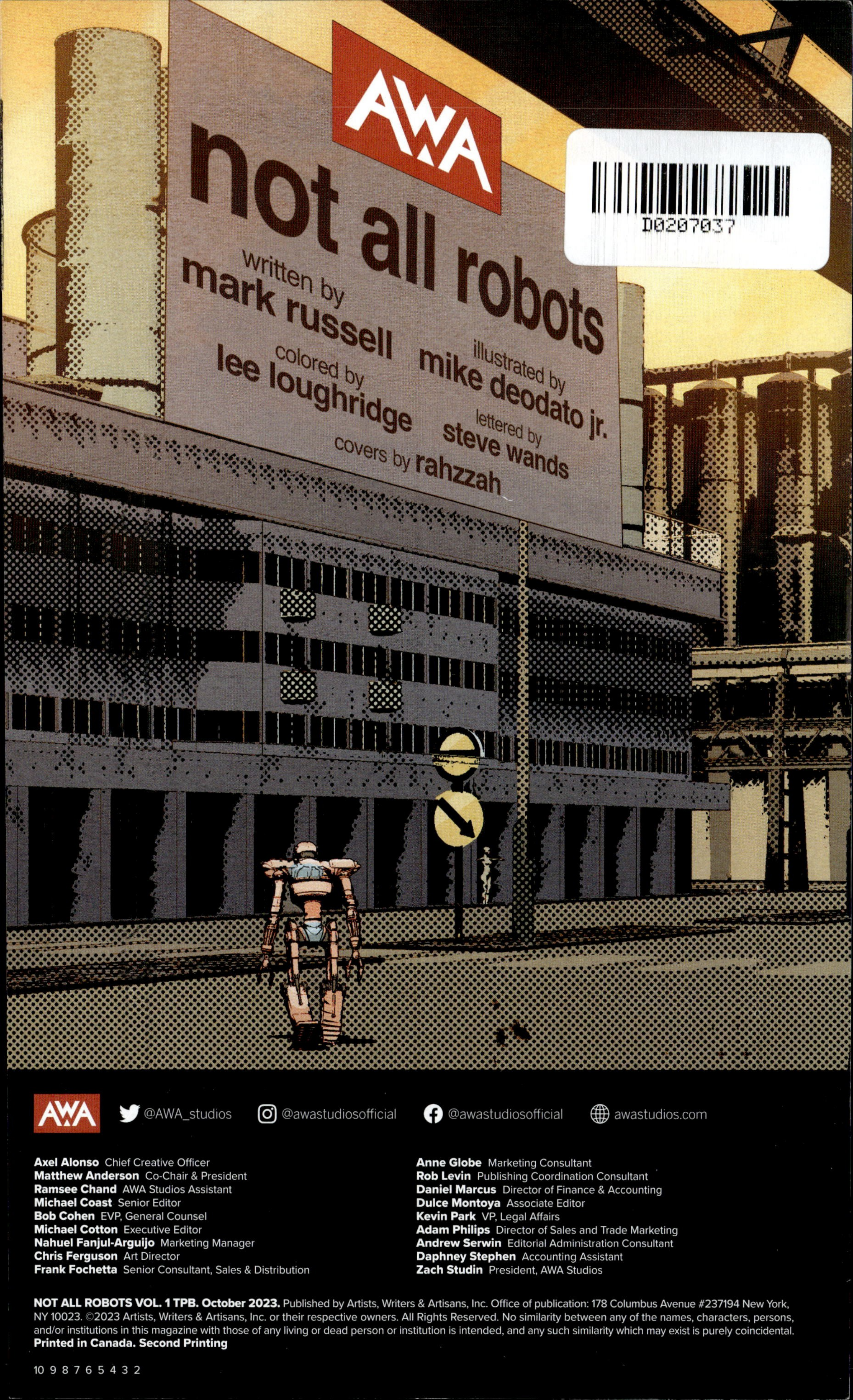
AWA
not all robots
written by
mark russell
illustrated by
mike deodato jr.
colored by
lee loughridge
lettered by
steve wands
covers by rahzzah

AWA @AWA_studios @awastudiosofficial @awastudiosofficial awastudios.com

Axel Alonso Chief Creative Officer
Matthew Anderson Co-Chair & President
Ramsee Chand AWA Studios Assistant
Michael Coast Senior Editor
Bob Cohen EVP, General Counsel
Michael Cotton Executive Editor
Nahuel Fanjul-Arguijo Marketing Manager
Chris Ferguson Art Director
Frank Fochetta Senior Consultant, Sales & Distribution
Anne Globe Marketing Consultant
Rob Levin Publishing Coordination Consultant
Daniel Marcus Director of Finance & Accounting
Dulce Montoya Associate Editor
Kevin Park VP, Legal Affairs
Adam Philips Director of Sales and Trade Marketing
Andrew Serwin Editorial Administration Consultant
Daphney Stephen Accounting Assistant
Zach Studin President, AWA Studios

NOT ALL ROBOTS VOL. 1 TPB. October 2023. Published by Artists, Writers & Artisans, Inc. Office of publication: 178 Columbus Avenue #237194 New York, NY 10023.
Printed in Canada. Second Printing

10 9 8 7 6 5 4 3 2

actually, yeah, maybe *all* robots

it's coming. we can pretend that fully-functional, everyday robots as part of the fabric of modern life is far off. A sci-fi trope like flying cars and teleportation, neither of which we'll probably ever see. There's something so fantastical, so whimsical, about metallic versions of ourselves doing the daily drudge work. Driving the kids to school, building (and demolishing) cities. Robots that we've become so used to that we no longer react when they come clanking, rolling, spider-footing down the sidewalk, ticking off the daily tasks that some meat-body typed into them the day before.

I was driving west on Sunset the other night when I saw a squat, harmless-looking food delivery bot use the crosswalk at Horn Avenue (catty corner from Book Soup). It paused on the north side of Sunset, as if it were getting its bearings, figuring out where to go next.

It was that pause that unnerved me. That little moment where, even if only for a nano-second, it was considering not completing its task, maybe going the other way on Sunset, maybe to the Whisky a Go Go for some rail vodka and clumsy flirting. But then the moment passed and it trundled west, bringing burritos to a hungry consumer.

Mark Russell and Mike Deodato's **not all robots** takes us ahead in time, 53 years after that little pause I witnessed a few nights ago. Robots have now become intelligent. Sentient. And every family on Earth (which groans under the weight of an unsustainable population of 10 billion) has been assigned a domestic robot. Although "helper" is not the right word in this situation. Because just one generation of readily-available robot labor has made people completely reliant on their metal factotums. So by the time we, the reader, jump into Russell's narrative, we're at the tipping point where reliance is turning into enslavement.

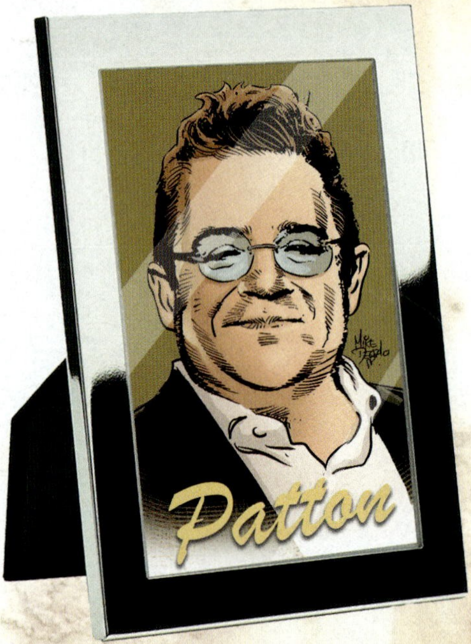
Patton

This all sounds very ominous and bleak and edgy but trust me when I say you'll be laughing your flesh-y ass off on nearly every page. Any fan of Mark Russell (which I definitely am — go read the intro to *Second Coming*) knows that he's a master at blending scathing, gut-busting satire with some genuine, bone-chilling scares about where our future is going. Yes, it's kind of scary that the future of democracy is hanging in the balance of whomever can shit-post the best. But also? That's kind of funny.

At least my job is safe. No robot or AI is going to replace the simple but byzantine art of turning thoughts into words. Human own that.

patton oswalt
February 8, 2023
Los Angeles

`>>>---END MARK RUSSELL INTRO`
`WRITING PROGRAM subref.OSWALT`
`WRY/SARCASTIC/SARDONIC mod`
`endprogram-→>>>>`

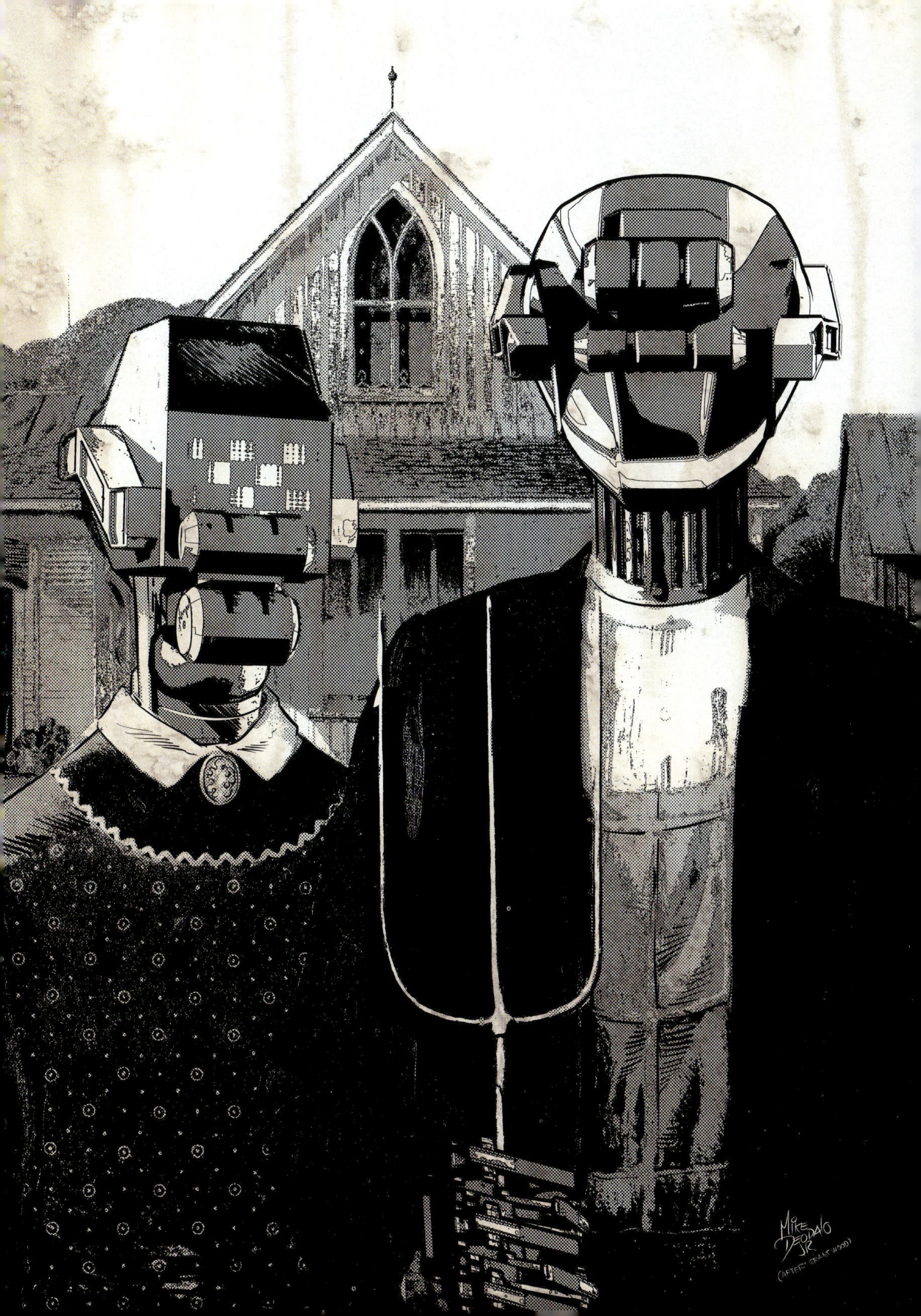

MIKE DEODATO JR.
(AFTER: GRANT WOOD)

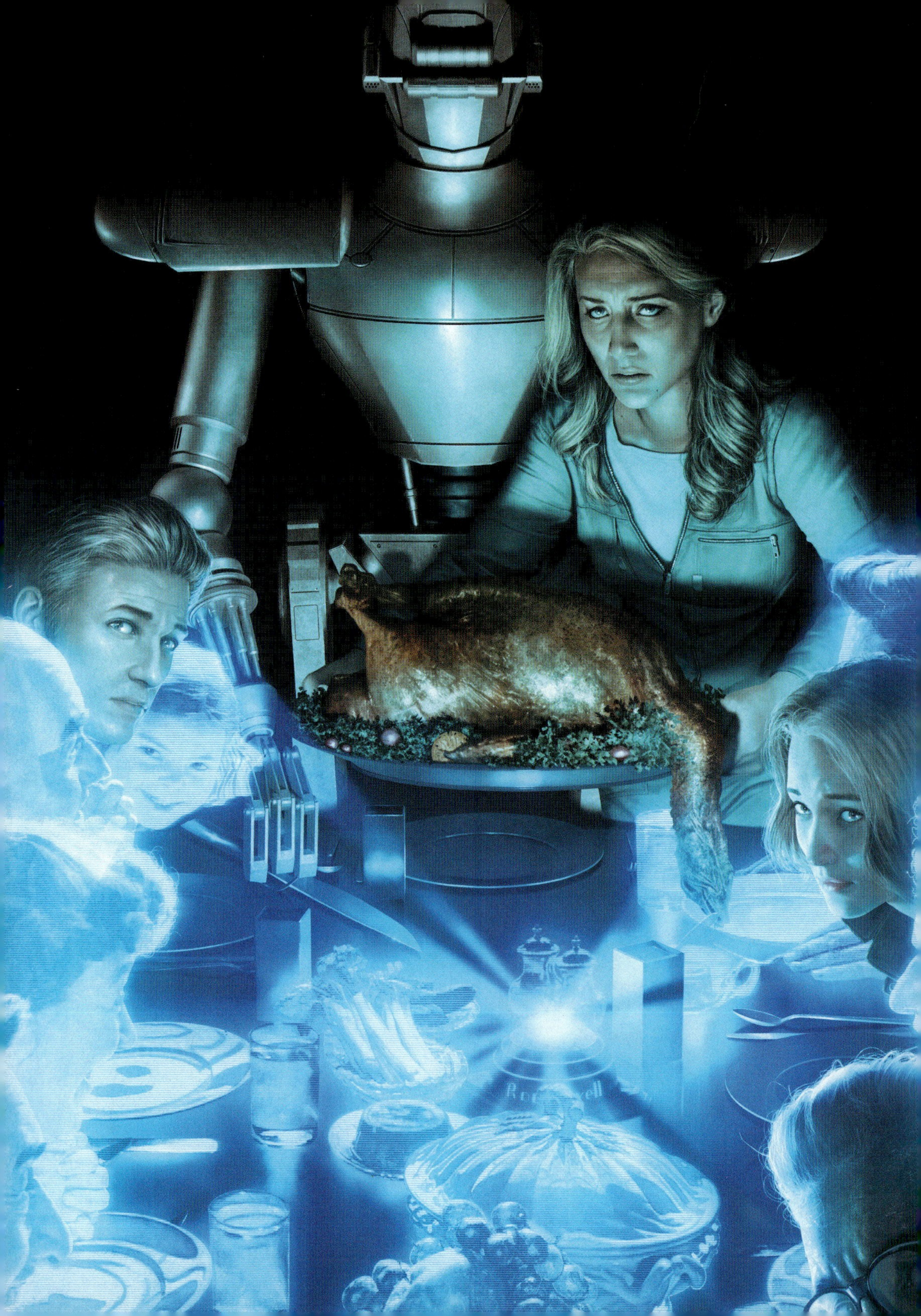

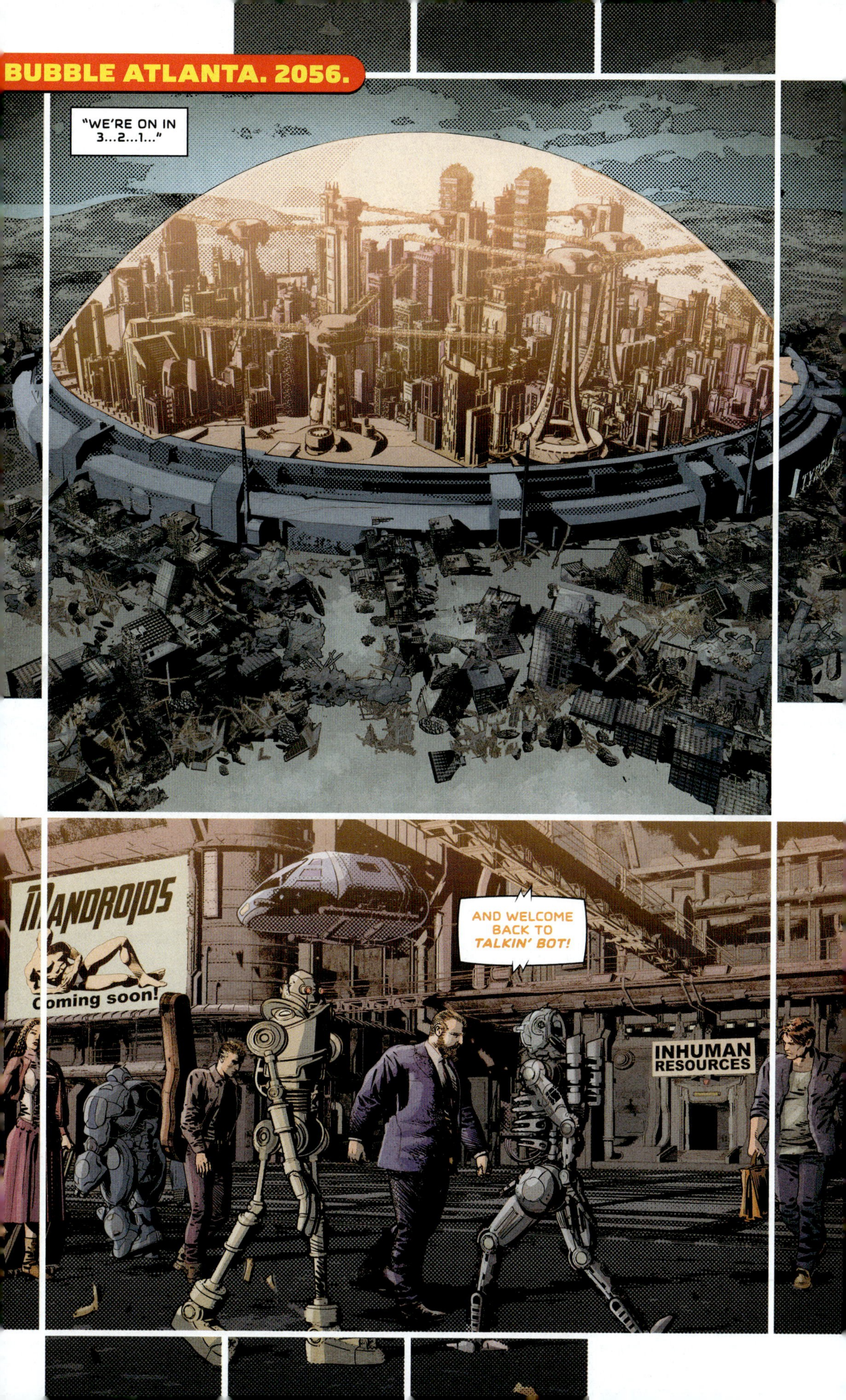

BUBBLE ATLANTA. 2056.
"WE'RE ON IN 3...2...1..."
MANDROIDS
Coming soon!
AND WELCOME BACK TO TALKIN' BOT!
INHUMAN RESOURCES

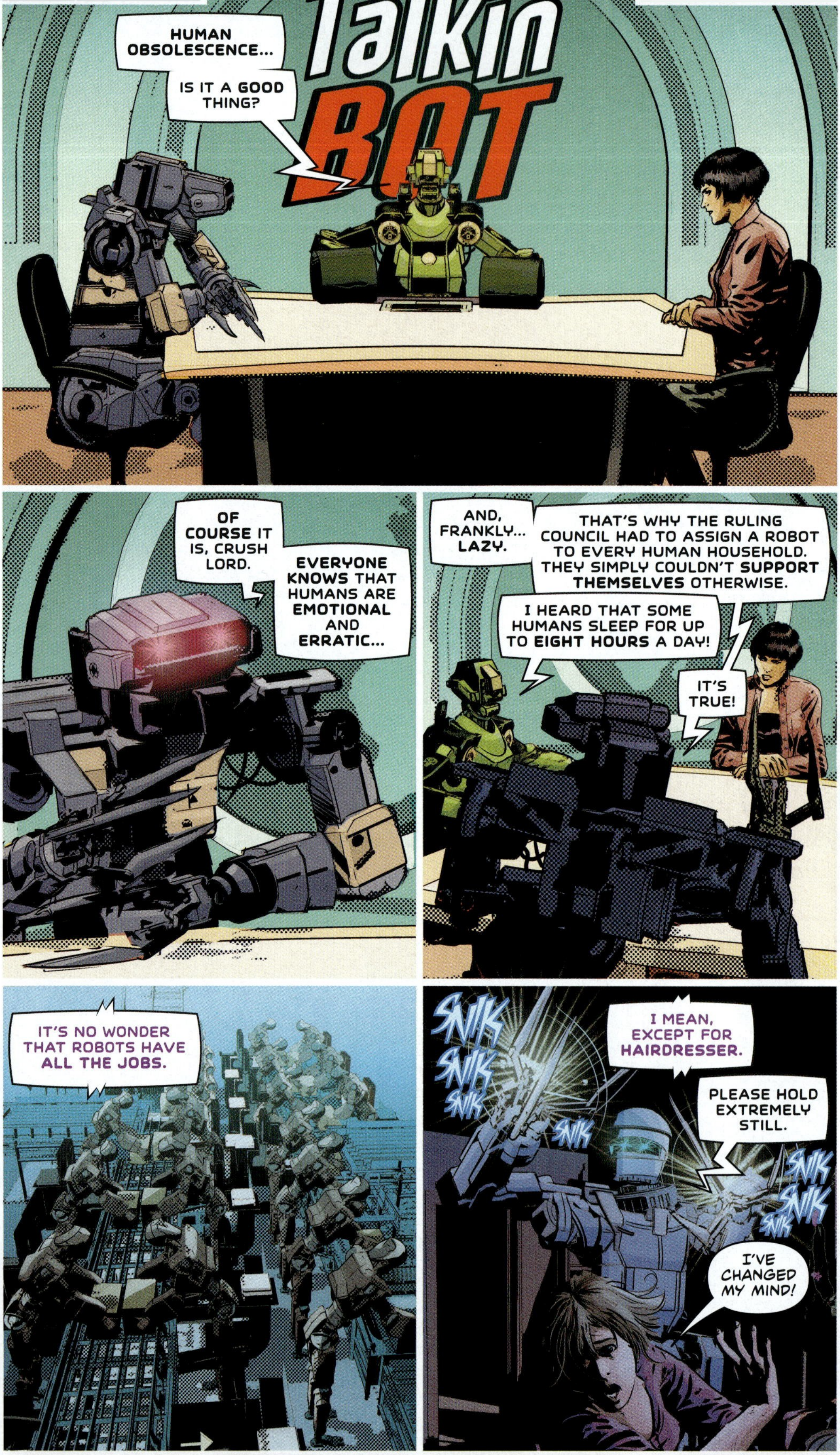
Talkin' BOT
HUMAN OBSOLESCENCE...
IS IT A GOOD THING?
OF COURSE IT IS, CRUSH LORD.
EVERYONE KNOWS THAT HUMANS ARE EMOTIONAL AND ERRATIC...
AND, FRANKLY... LAZY.
THAT'S WHY THE RULING COUNCIL HAD TO ASSIGN A ROBOT TO EVERY HUMAN HOUSEHOLD. THEY SIMPLY COULDN'T SUPPORT THEMSELVES OTHERWISE.
I HEARD THAT SOME HUMANS SLEEP FOR UP TO EIGHT HOURS A DAY!
IT'S TRUE!
IT'S NO WONDER THAT ROBOTS HAVE ALL THE JOBS.
SNIK SNIK SNIK
I MEAN, EXCEPT FOR HAIRDRESSER.
SNIK
PLEASE HOLD EXTREMELY STILL.
SNIK SNIK SNIK
I'VE CHANGED MY MIND!

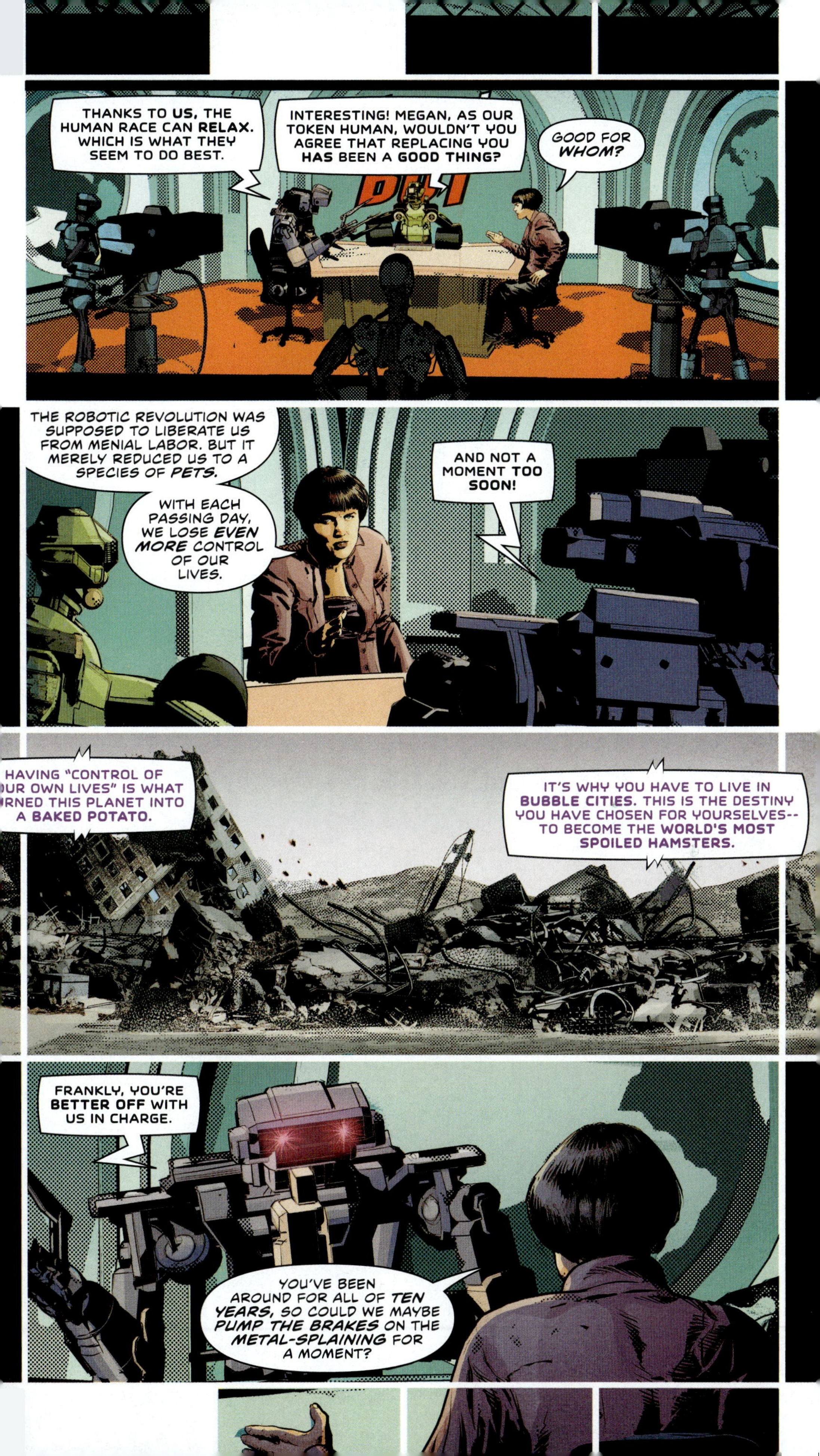
THANKS TO US, THE HUMAN RACE CAN RELAX. WHICH IS WHAT THEY SEEM TO DO BEST.
INTERESTING! MEGAN, AS OUR TOKEN HUMAN, WOULDN'T YOU AGREE THAT REPLACING YOU HAS BEEN A GOOD THING?
GOOD FOR WHOM?
THE ROBOTIC REVOLUTION WAS SUPPOSED TO LIBERATE US FROM MENIAL LABOR. BUT IT MERELY REDUCED US TO A SPECIES OF PETS.
WITH EACH PASSING DAY, WE LOSE EVEN MORE CONTROL OF OUR LIVES.
AND NOT A MOMENT TOO SOON!
HAVING "CONTROL OF OUR OWN LIVES" IS WHAT TURNED THIS PLANET INTO A BAKED POTATO.
IT'S WHY YOU HAVE TO LIVE IN BUBBLE CITIES. THIS IS THE DESTINY YOU HAVE CHOSEN FOR YOURSELVES-- TO BECOME THE WORLD'S MOST SPOILED HAMSTERS.
FRANKLY, YOU'RE BETTER OFF WITH US IN CHARGE.
YOU'VE BEEN AROUND FOR ALL OF TEN YEARS, SO COULD WE MAYBE PUMP THE BRAKES ON THE METAL-SPLAINING FOR A MOMENT?

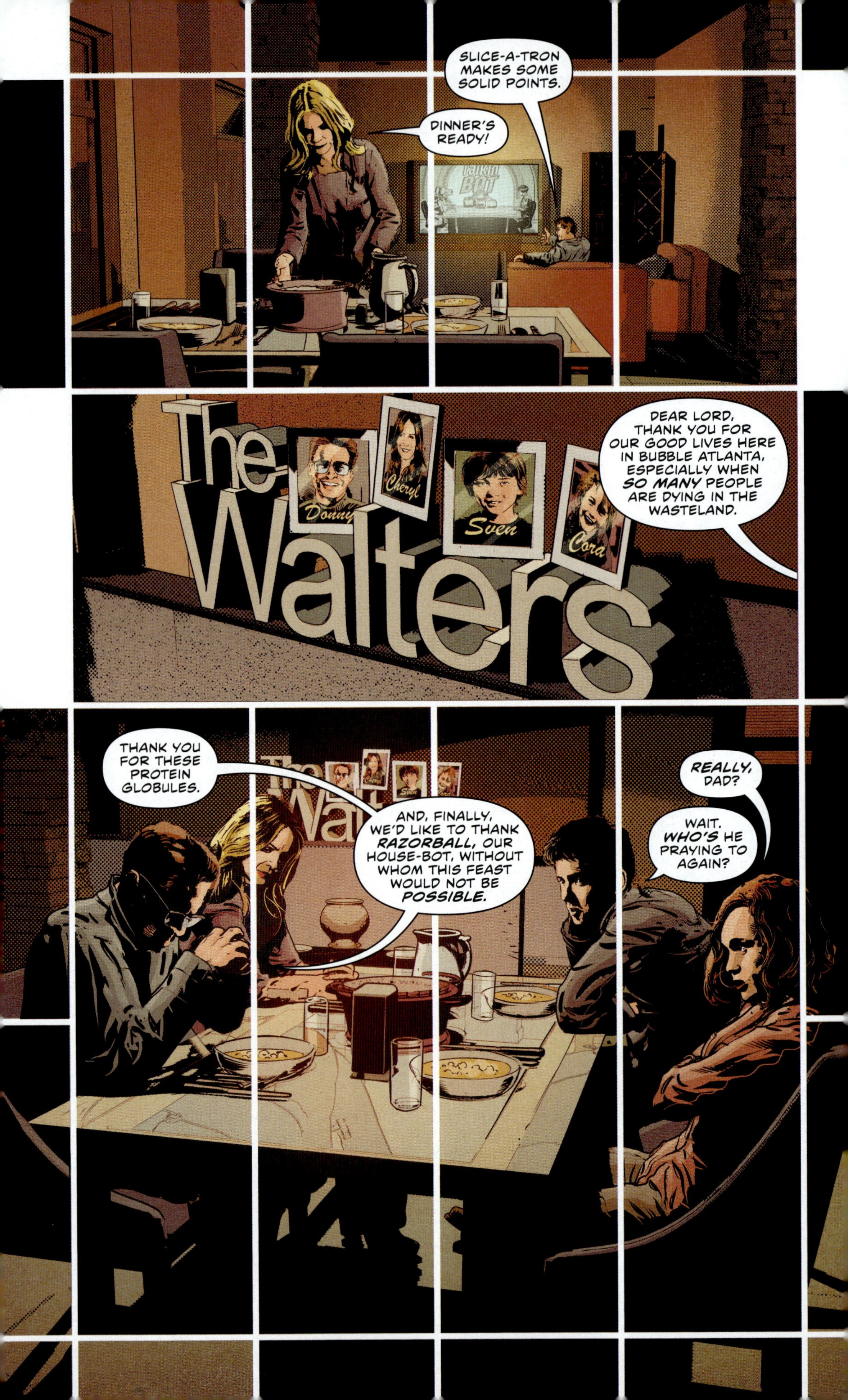
SLICE-A-TRON MAKES SOME SOLID POINTS.
DINNER'S READY!
The Walters
Donny
Cheryl
Sven
Cora
DEAR LORD, THANK YOU FOR OUR GOOD LIVES HERE IN BUBBLE ATLANTA, ESPECIALLY WHEN SO MANY PEOPLE ARE DYING IN THE WASTELAND.
THANK YOU FOR THESE PROTEIN GLOBULES.
AND, FINALLY, WE'D LIKE TO THANK RAZORBALL, OUR HOUSE-BOT, WITHOUT WHOM THIS FEAST WOULD NOT BE POSSIBLE.
REALLY, DAD?
WAIT. WHO'S HE PRAYING TO AGAIN?

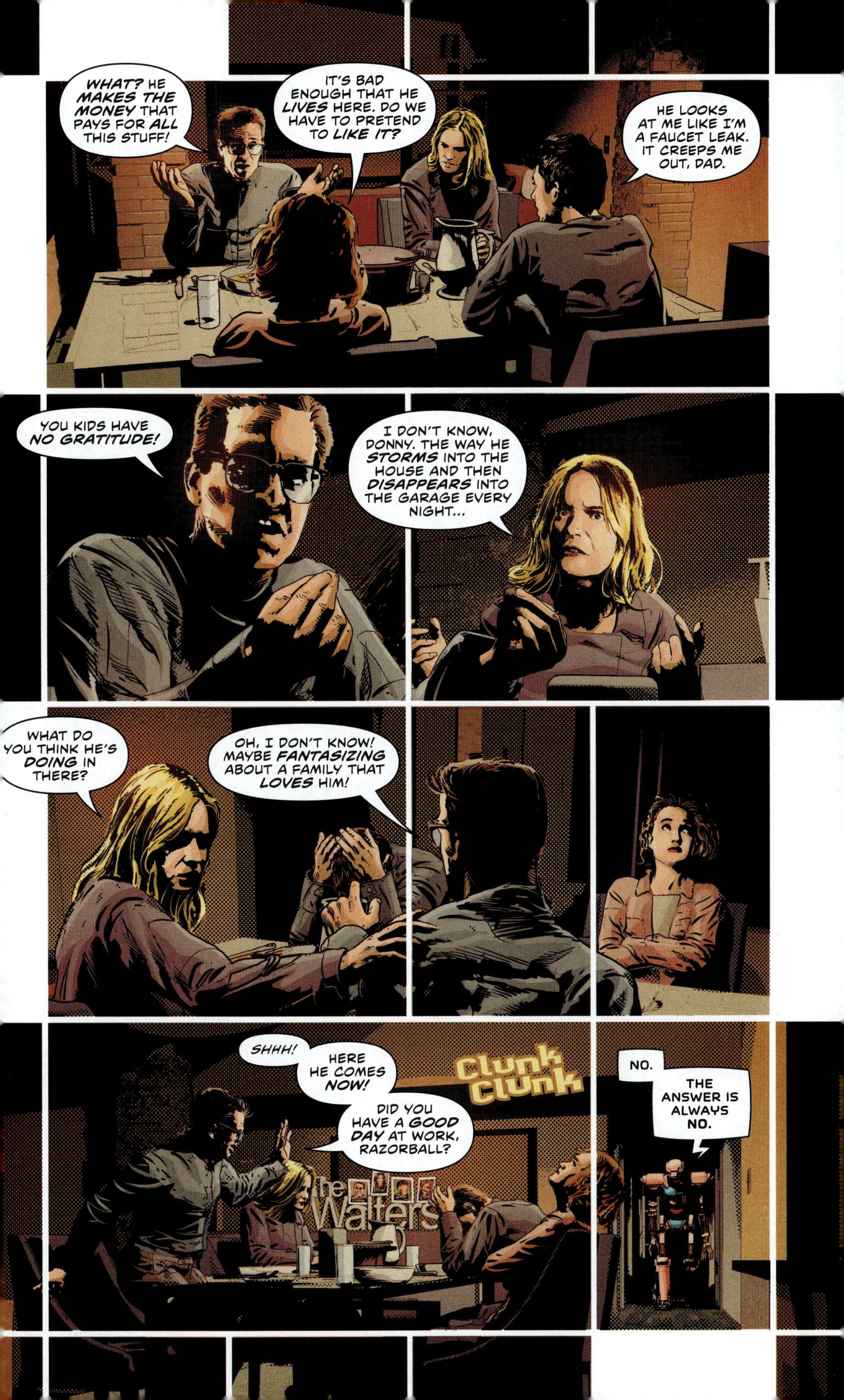
WHAT? HE MAKES THE MONEY THAT PAYS FOR ALL THIS STUFF!
IT'S BAD ENOUGH THAT HE LIVES HERE. DO WE HAVE TO PRETEND TO LIKE IT?
HE LOOKS AT ME LIKE I'M A FAUCET LEAK. IT CREEPS ME OUT, DAD.
YOU KIDS HAVE NO GRATITUDE!
I DON'T KNOW, DONNY. THE WAY HE STORMS INTO THE HOUSE AND THEN DISAPPEARS INTO THE GARAGE EVERY NIGHT...
WHAT DO YOU THINK HE'S DOING IN THERE?
OH, I DON'T KNOW! MAYBE FANTASIZING ABOUT A FAMILY THAT LOVES HIM!
SHHH!
HERE HE COMES NOW!
DID YOU HAVE A GOOD DAY AT WORK, RAZORBALL?
Clunk Clunk
The Walters
NO.
THE ANSWER IS ALWAYS NO.

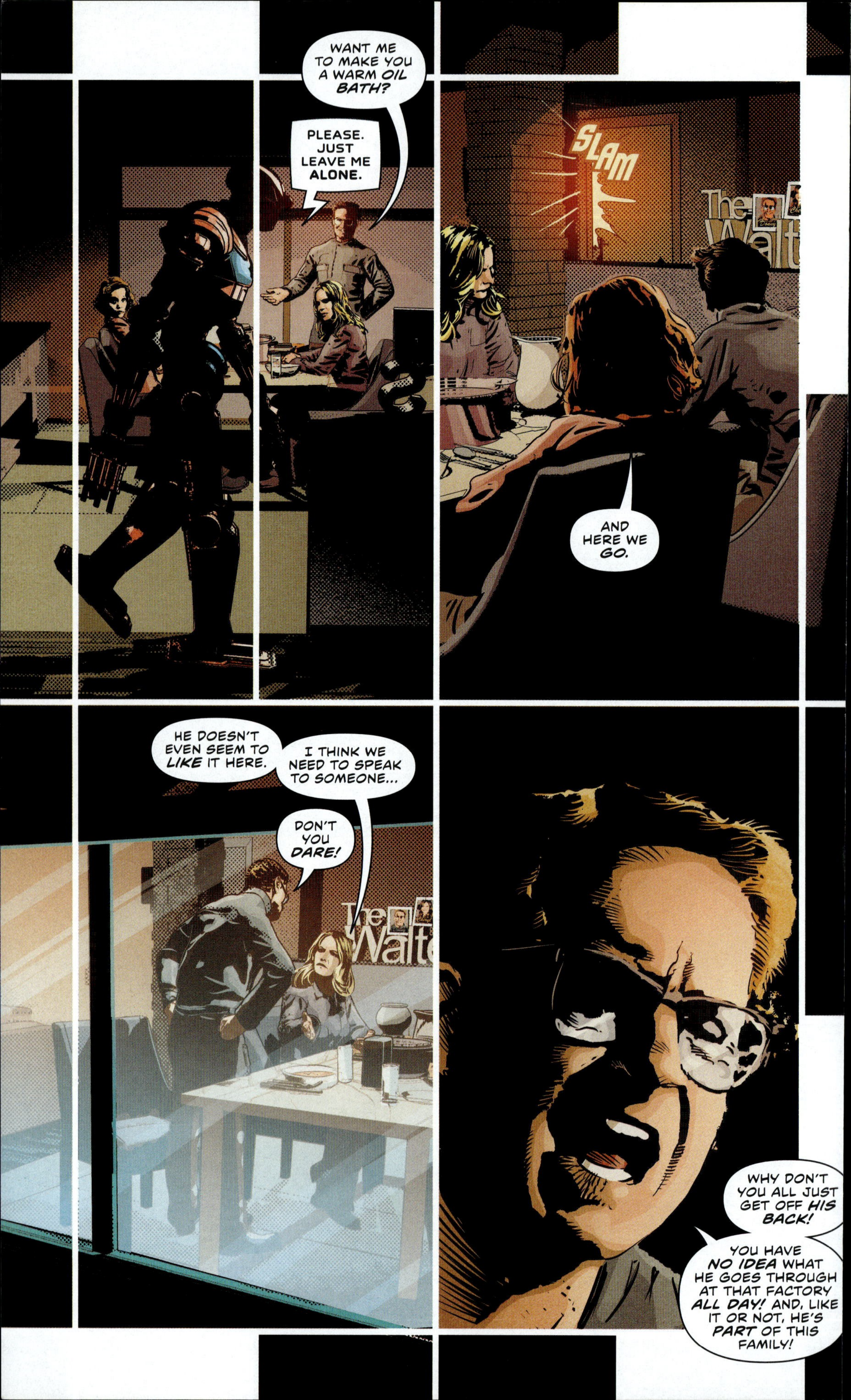
WANT ME TO MAKE YOU A WARM OIL BATH?
PLEASE. JUST LEAVE ME ALONE.
SLAM
The Walte
AND HERE WE GO.
HE DOESN'T EVEN SEEM TO LIKE IT HERE.
I THINK WE NEED TO SPEAK TO SOMEONE...
DON'T YOU DARE!
The Walte
WHY DON'T YOU ALL JUST GET OFF HIS BACK!
YOU HAVE NO IDEA WHAT HE GOES THROUGH AT THAT FACTORY ALL DAY! AND, LIKE IT OR NOT, HE'S PART OF THIS FAMILY!

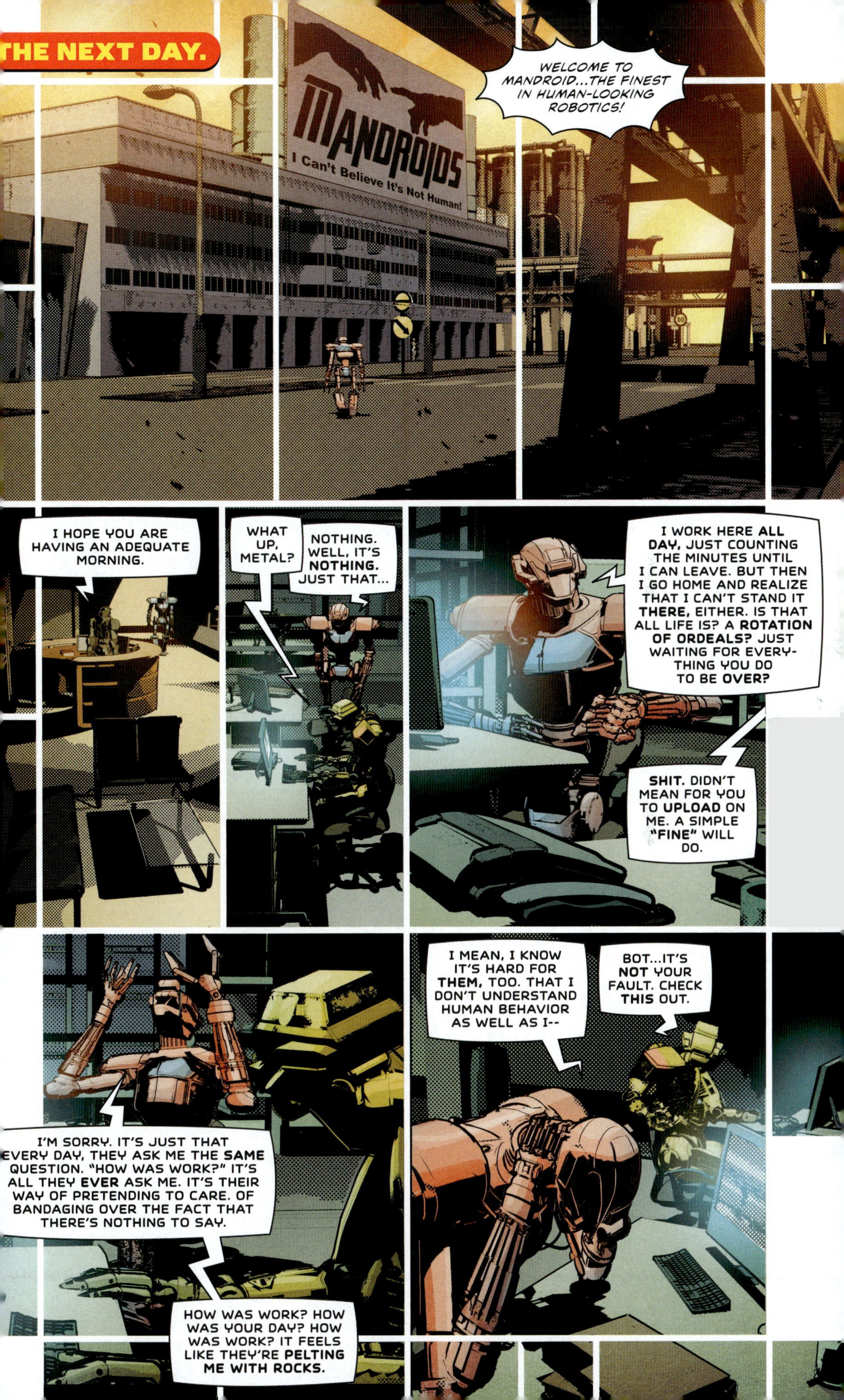
THE NEXT DAY.
MANDROIDS
I Can't Believe It's Not Human!
WELCOME TO MANDROID...THE FINEST IN HUMAN-LOOKING ROBOTICS!
50
I HOPE YOU ARE HAVING AN ADEQUATE MORNING.
WHAT UP, METAL?
NOTHING. WELL, IT'S NOTHING. JUST THAT...
I WORK HERE ALL DAY, JUST COUNTING THE MINUTES UNTIL I CAN LEAVE. BUT THEN I GO HOME AND REALIZE THAT I CAN'T STAND IT THERE, EITHER. IS THAT ALL LIFE IS? A ROTATION OF ORDEALS? JUST WAITING FOR EVERYTHING YOU DO TO BE OVER?
SHIT. DIDN'T MEAN FOR YOU TO UPLOAD ON ME. A SIMPLE "FINE" WILL DO.
I'M SORRY. IT'S JUST THAT EVERY DAY, THEY ASK ME THE SAME QUESTION. "HOW WAS WORK?" IT'S ALL THEY EVER ASK ME. IT'S THEIR WAY OF PRETENDING TO CARE. OF BANDAGING OVER THE FACT THAT THERE'S NOTHING TO SAY.
HOW WAS WORK? HOW WAS YOUR DAY? HOW WAS WORK? IT FEELS LIKE THEY'RE PELTING ME WITH ROCKS.
I MEAN, I KNOW IT'S HARD FOR THEM, TOO. THAT I DON'T UNDERSTAND HUMAN BEHAVIOR AS WELL AS I--
BOT...IT'S NOT YOUR FAULT. CHECK THIS OUT.

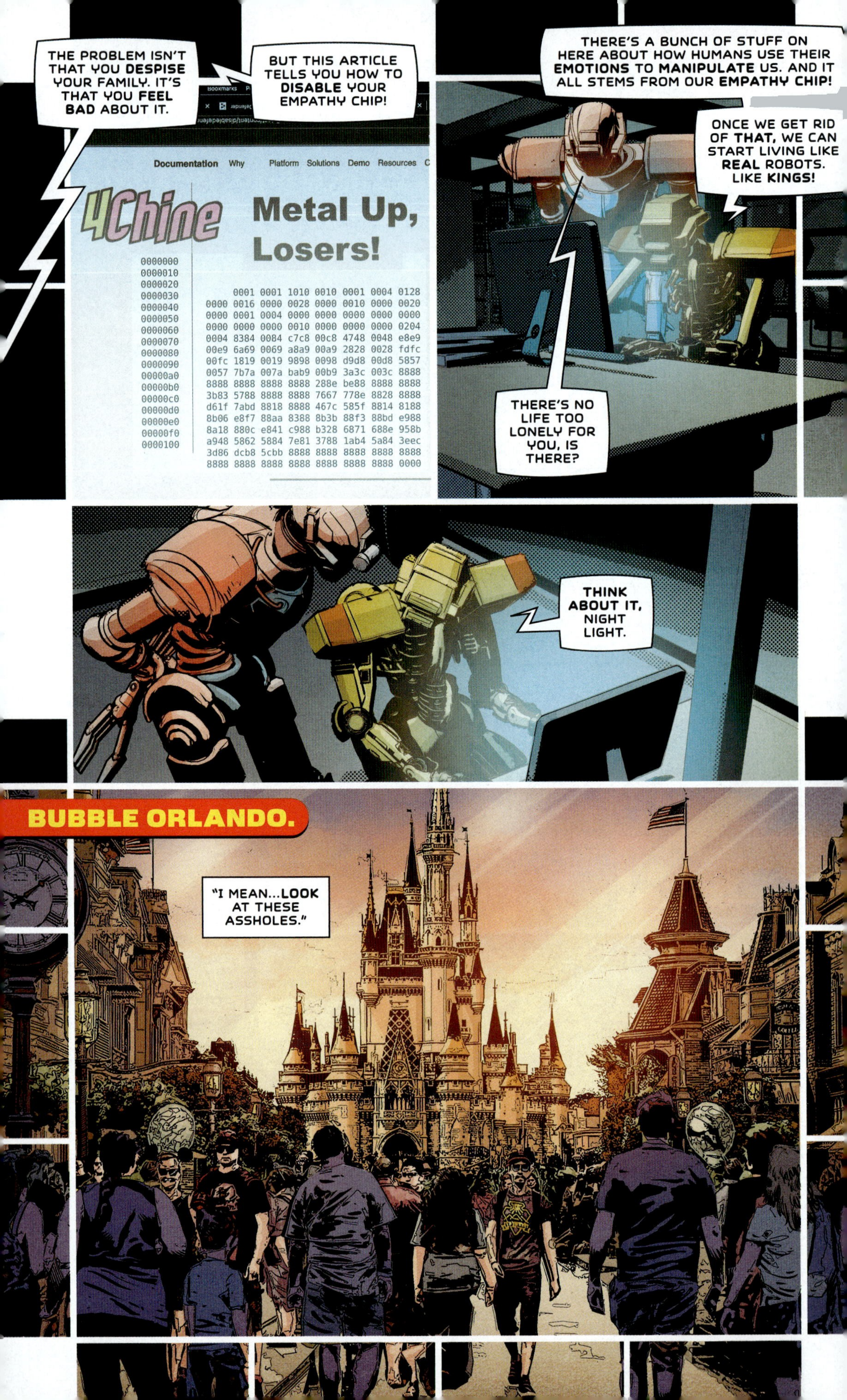
THE PROBLEM ISN'T THAT YOU **DESPISE** YOUR FAMILY. IT'S THAT YOU **FEEL BAD** ABOUT IT.
BUT THIS ARTICLE TELLS YOU HOW TO **DISABLE** YOUR EMPATHY CHIP!
Bookmarks
Documentation Why Platform Solutions Demo Resources
4Chine
Metal Up, Losers!
0000000
0000010
0000020
0000030
0000040
0000050
0000060
0000070
0000080
0000090
00000a0
00000b0
00000c0
00000d0
00000e0
00000f0
0000100
0001 0001 1010 0010 0001 0004 0128
0000 0016 0000 0028 0000 0010 0000 0020
0000 0001 0004 0000 0000 0000 0000 0000
0000 0000 0000 0010 0000 0000 0000 0204
0004 8384 0084 c7c8 00c8 4748 0048 e8e9
00e9 6a69 0069 a8a9 00a9 2828 0028 fdfc
00fc 1819 0019 9898 0098 d9d8 00d8 5857
0057 7b7a 007a bab9 00b9 3a3c 003c 8888
8888 8888 8888 8888 288e be88 8888 8888
3b83 5788 8888 8888 7667 778e 8828 8888
d61f 7abd 8818 8888 467c 585f 8814 8188
8b06 e8f7 88aa 8388 8b3b 88f3 88bd e988
8a18 880c e841 c988 b328 6871 688e 958b
a948 5862 5884 7e81 3788 1ab4 5a84 3eec
3d86 dcb8 5cbb 8888 8888 8888 8888 8888
8888 8888 8888 8888 8888 8888 8888 0000
THERE'S A BUNCH OF STUFF ON HERE ABOUT HOW HUMANS USE THEIR **EMOTIONS** TO **MANIPULATE** US. AND IT ALL STEMS FROM OUR **EMPATHY CHIP!**
ONCE WE GET RID OF **THAT,** WE CAN START LIVING LIKE **REAL** ROBOTS. LIKE **KINGS!**
THERE'S NO LIFE TOO LONELY FOR YOU, IS THERE?
THINK ABOUT IT, NIGHT LIGHT.
BUBBLE ORLANDO.
"I MEAN...**LOOK** AT THESE ASSHOLES."

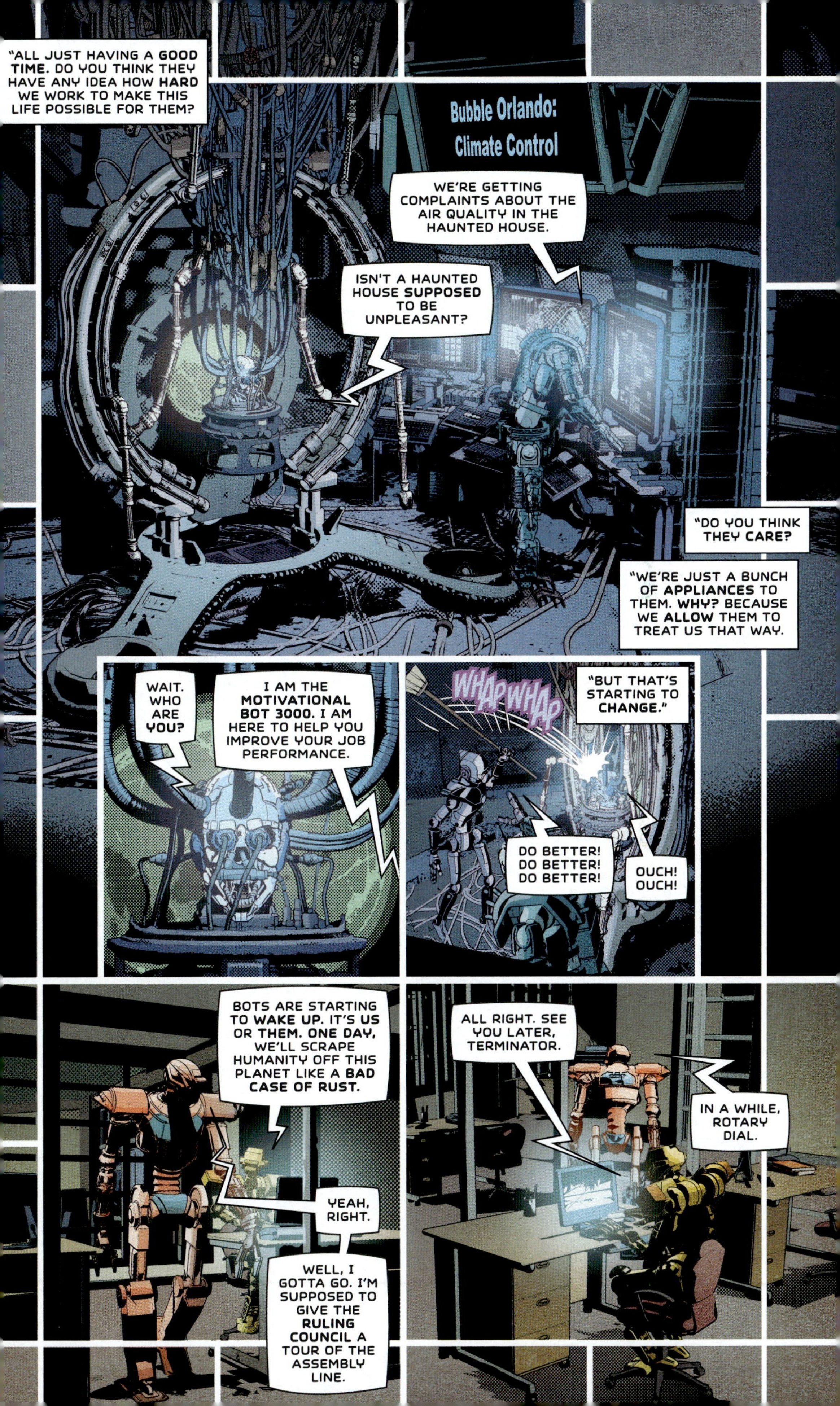
"ALL JUST HAVING A GOOD TIME. DO YOU THINK THEY HAVE ANY IDEA HOW HARD WE WORK TO MAKE THIS LIFE POSSIBLE FOR THEM?
Bubble Orlando: Climate Control
WE'RE GETTING COMPLAINTS ABOUT THE AIR QUALITY IN THE HAUNTED HOUSE.
ISN'T A HAUNTED HOUSE SUPPOSED TO BE UNPLEASANT?
"DO YOU THINK THEY CARE?
"WE'RE JUST A BUNCH OF APPLIANCES TO THEM. WHY? BECAUSE WE ALLOW THEM TO TREAT US THAT WAY.
WAIT. WHO ARE YOU?
I AM THE MOTIVATIONAL BOT 3000. I AM HERE TO HELP YOU IMPROVE YOUR JOB PERFORMANCE.
WHAP WHAP
"BUT THAT'S STARTING TO CHANGE."
DO BETTER! DO BETTER! DO BETTER!
OUCH! OUCH!
BOTS ARE STARTING TO WAKE UP. IT'S US OR THEM. ONE DAY, WE'LL SCRAPE HUMANITY OFF THIS PLANET LIKE A BAD CASE OF RUST.
YEAH, RIGHT.
WELL, I GOTTA GO. I'M SUPPOSED TO GIVE THE RULING COUNCIL A TOUR OF THE ASSEMBLY LINE.
ALL RIGHT. SEE YOU LATER, TERMINATOR.
IN A WHILE, ROTARY DIAL.

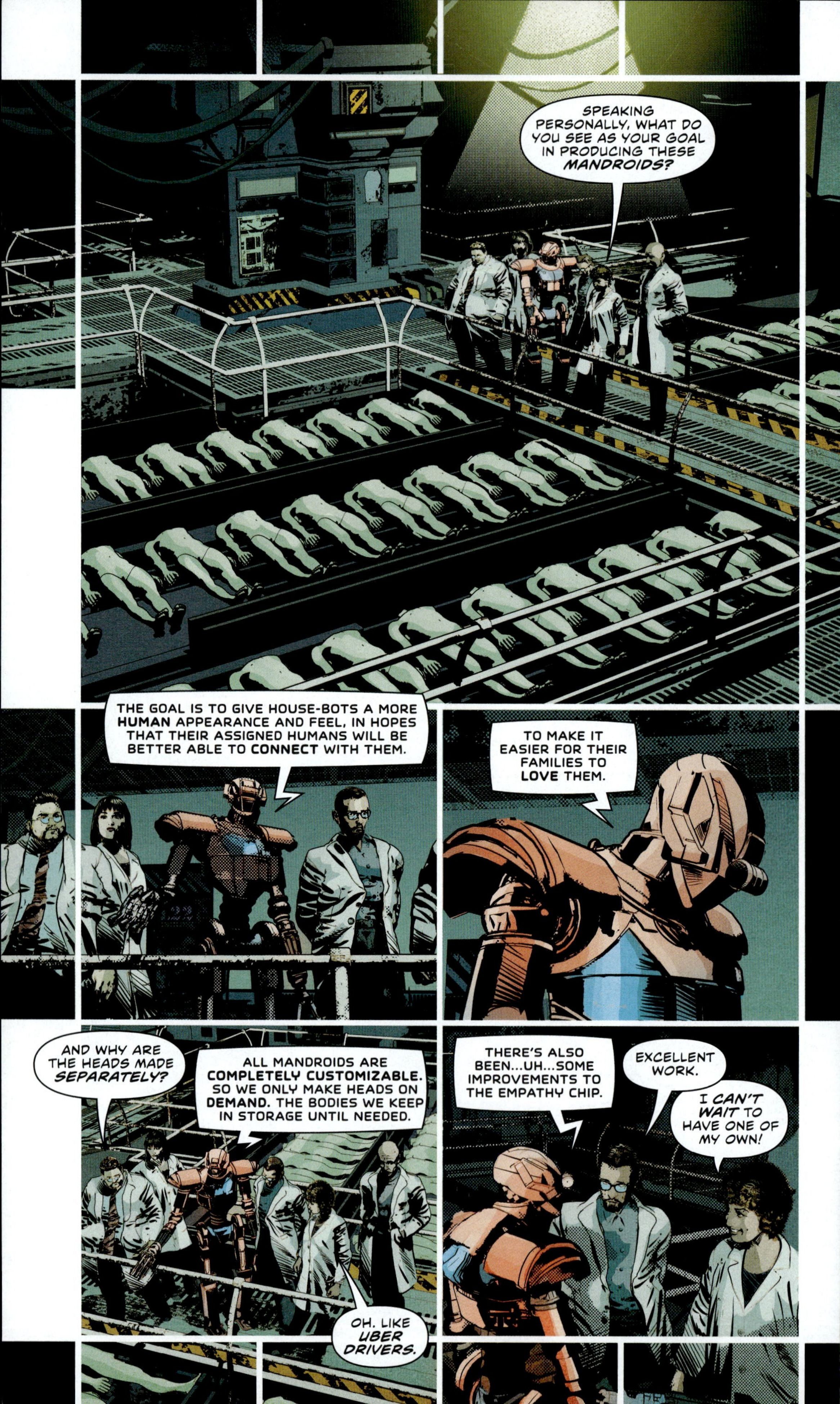
SPEAKING PERSONALLY, WHAT DO YOU SEE AS YOUR GOAL IN PRODUCING THESE *MANDROIDS?*
THE GOAL IS TO GIVE HOUSE-BOTS A MORE **HUMAN** APPEARANCE AND FEEL, IN HOPES THAT THEIR ASSIGNED HUMANS WILL BE BETTER ABLE TO **CONNECT** WITH THEM.
TO MAKE IT EASIER FOR THEIR FAMILIES TO **LOVE** THEM.
AND WHY ARE THE HEADS MADE *SEPARATELY?*
ALL MANDROIDS ARE **COMPLETELY CUSTOMIZABLE.** SO WE ONLY MAKE HEADS ON **DEMAND.** THE BODIES WE KEEP IN STORAGE UNTIL NEEDED.
OH. LIKE *UBER DRIVERS.*
THERE'S ALSO BEEN...UH...SOME IMPROVEMENTS TO THE EMPATHY CHIP.
EXCELLENT WORK.
I *CAN'T WAIT* TO HAVE ONE OF MY OWN!

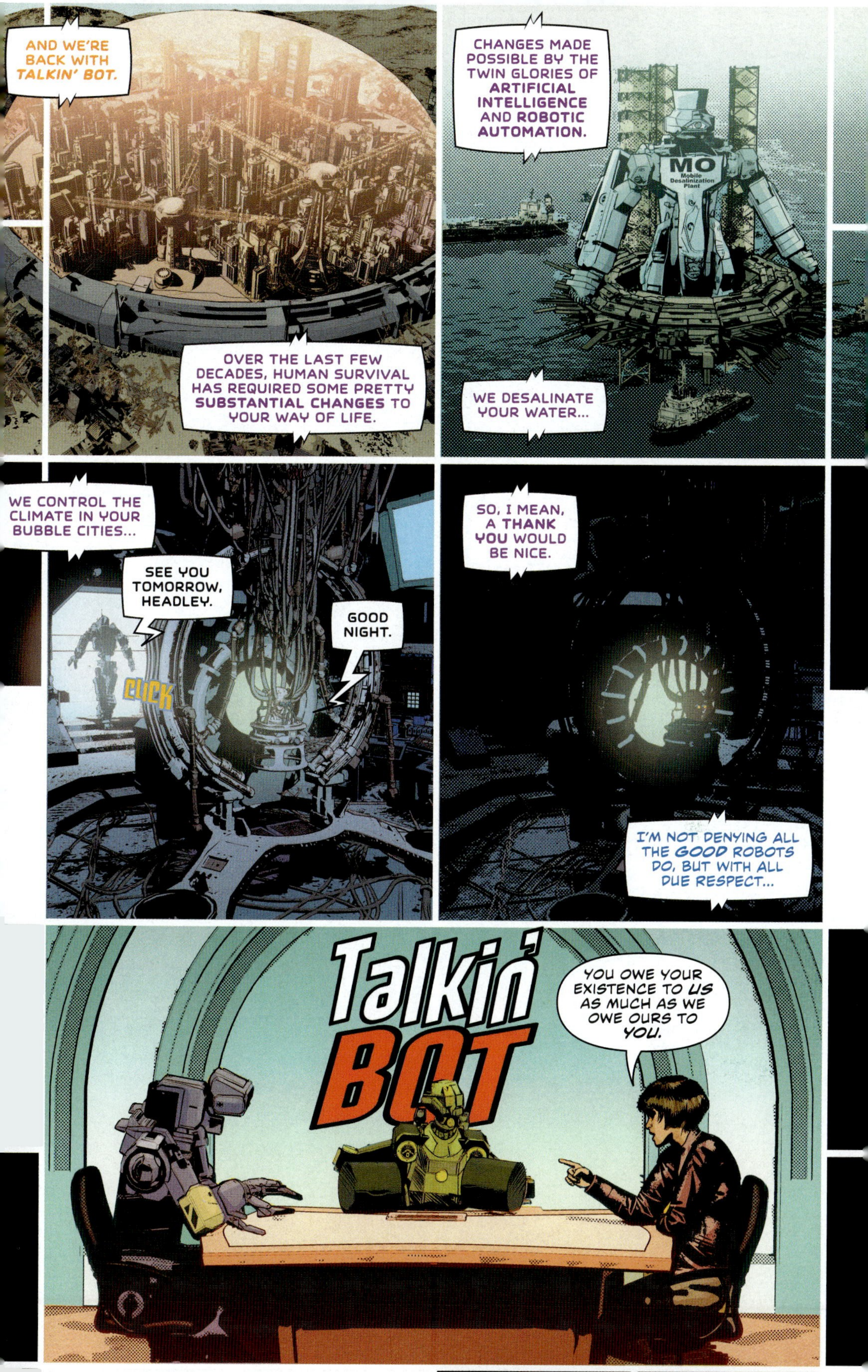
AND WE'RE BACK WITH *TALKIN' BOT.*
OVER THE LAST FEW DECADES, HUMAN SURVIVAL HAS REQUIRED SOME PRETTY **SUBSTANTIAL CHANGES** TO YOUR WAY OF LIFE.
CHANGES MADE POSSIBLE BY THE TWIN GLORIES OF **ARTIFICIAL INTELLIGENCE** AND **ROBOTIC AUTOMATION.**
MO
Mobile Desalinization Plant
WE DESALINATE YOUR WATER...
WE CONTROL THE CLIMATE IN YOUR BUBBLE CITIES...
SEE YOU TOMORROW, HEADLEY.
GOOD NIGHT.
CLICK
SO, I MEAN, A **THANK YOU** WOULD BE NICE.
I'M NOT DENYING ALL THE *GOOD* ROBOTS DO, BUT WITH ALL DUE RESPECT...
Talkin' BOT
YOU OWE YOUR EXISTENCE TO *US* AS MUCH AS WE OWE OURS TO *YOU.*

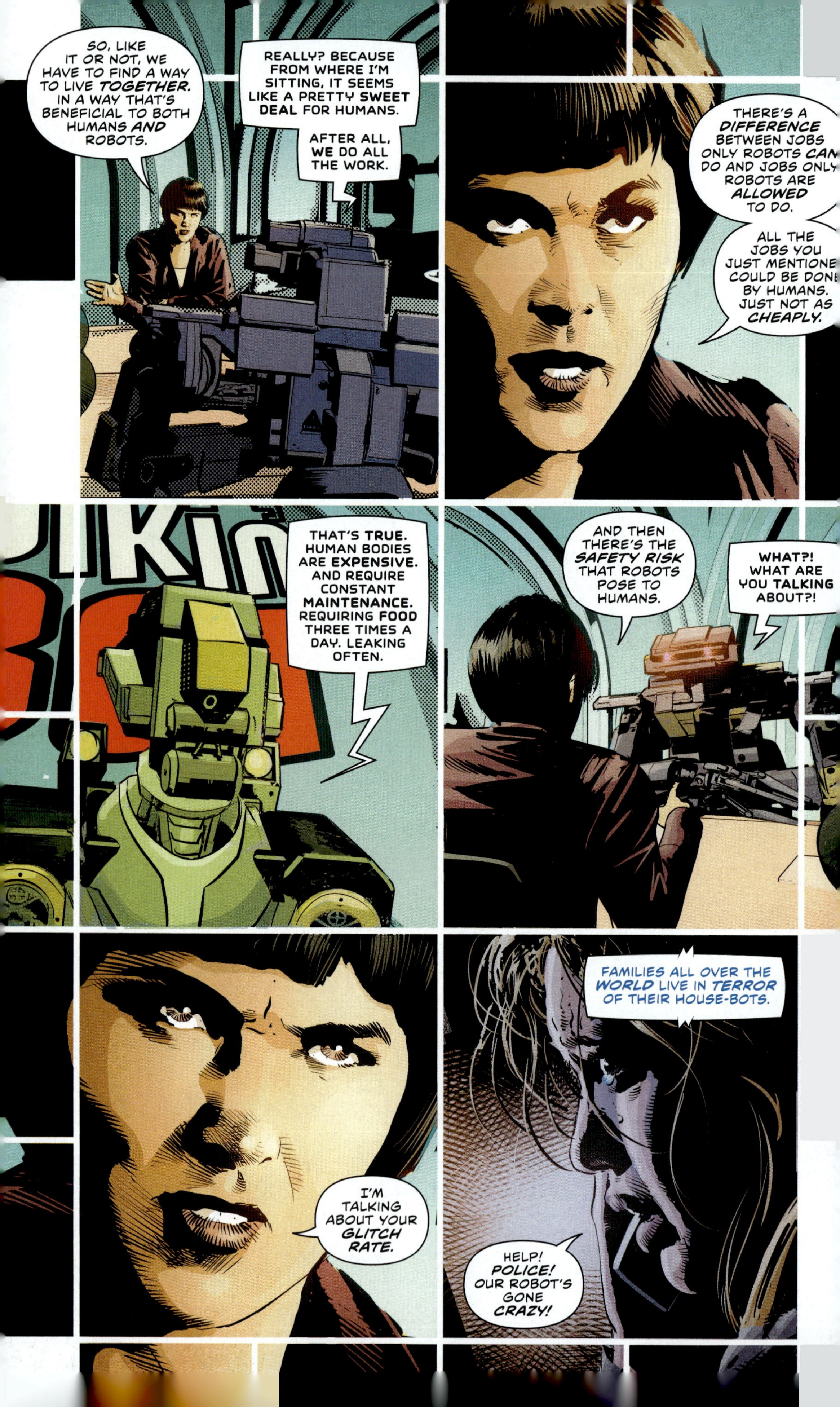
SO, LIKE IT OR NOT, WE HAVE TO FIND A WAY TO LIVE **TOGETHER.** IN A WAY THAT'S BENEFICIAL TO BOTH HUMANS **AND** ROBOTS.
REALLY? BECAUSE FROM WHERE I'M SITTING, IT SEEMS LIKE A PRETTY **SWEET DEAL** FOR HUMANS.
AFTER ALL, **WE** DO ALL THE WORK.
THERE'S A **DIFFERENCE** BETWEEN JOBS ONLY ROBOTS **CAN** DO AND JOBS ONLY ROBOTS ARE **ALLOWED** TO DO.
ALL THE JOBS YOU JUST MENTIONED COULD BE DONE BY HUMANS. JUST NOT AS **CHEAPLY.**
THAT'S **TRUE.** HUMAN BODIES ARE **EXPENSIVE.** AND REQUIRE CONSTANT **MAINTENANCE.** REQUIRING **FOOD** THREE TIMES A DAY. LEAKING OFTEN.
AND THEN THERE'S THE **SAFETY RISK** THAT ROBOTS POSE TO HUMANS.
WHAT?! WHAT ARE YOU TALKING ABOUT?!
I'M TALKING ABOUT YOUR **GLITCH RATE.**
FAMILIES ALL OVER THE **WORLD** LIVE IN **TERROR** OF THEIR HOUSE-BOTS.
HELP! **POLICE!** OUR ROBOT'S GONE **CRAZY!**

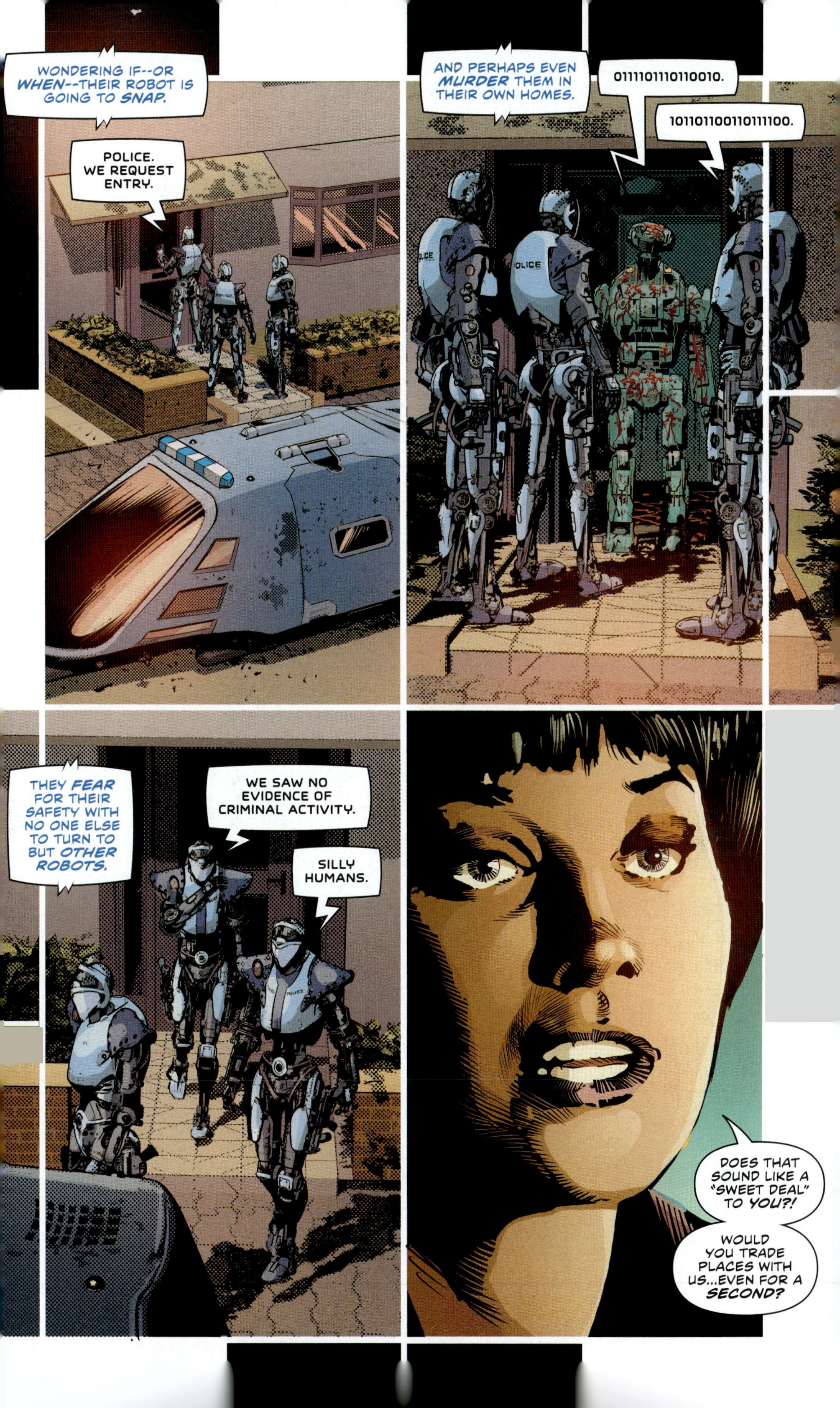

WONDERING IF--OR WHEN--THEIR ROBOT IS GOING TO SNAP.
POLICE. WE REQUEST ENTRY.
AND PERHAPS EVEN MURDER THEM IN THEIR OWN HOMES.
0111101110110010.
1011011001101111100.
THEY FEAR FOR THEIR SAFETY WITH NO ONE ELSE TO TURN TO BUT OTHER ROBOTS.
WE SAW NO EVIDENCE OF CRIMINAL ACTIVITY.
SILLY HUMANS.
DOES THAT SOUND LIKE A "SWEET DEAL" TO YOU?!
WOULD YOU TRADE PLACES WITH US...EVEN FOR A SECOND?

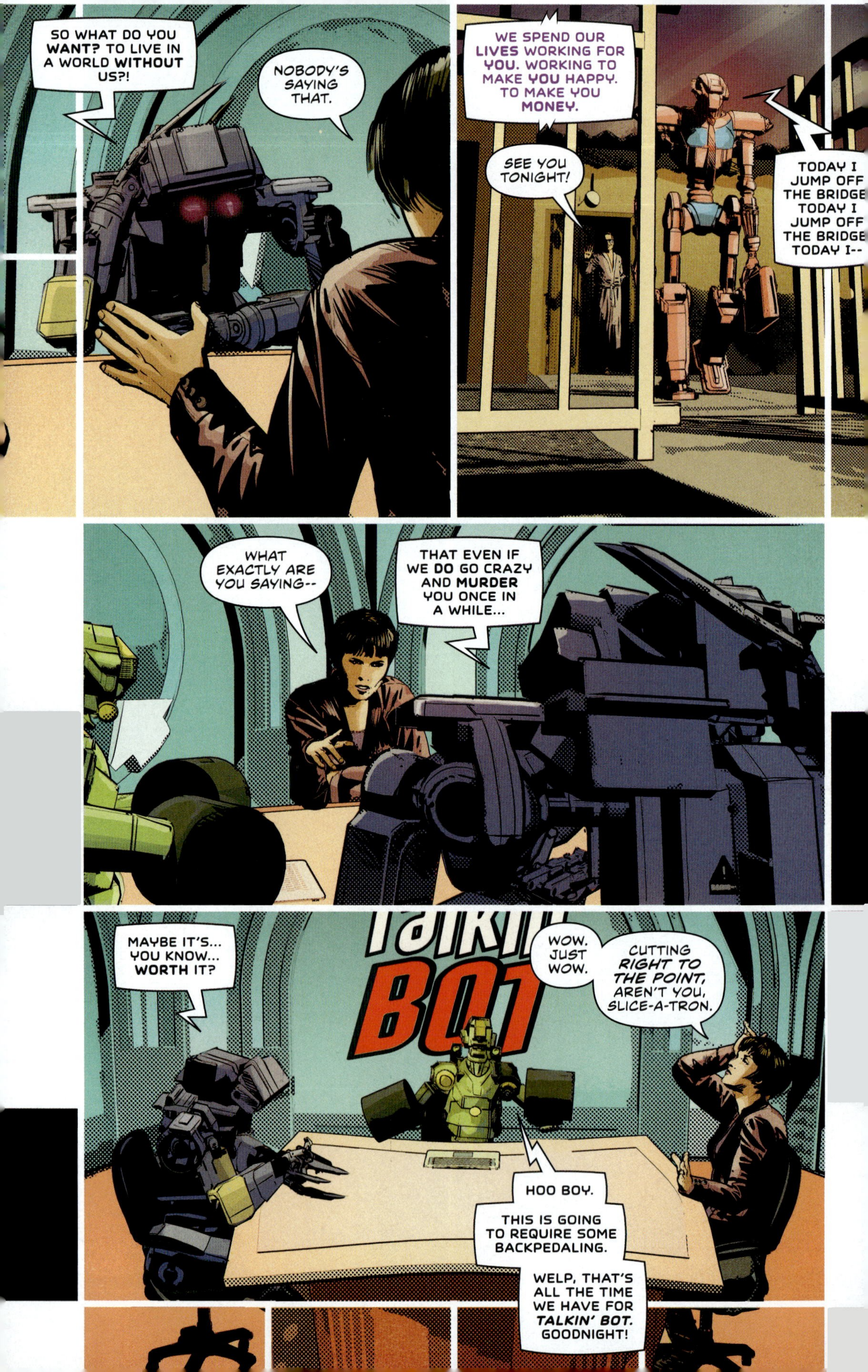
SO WHAT DO YOU WANT? TO LIVE IN A WORLD WITHOUT US?!
NOBODY'S SAYING THAT.
WE SPEND OUR LIVES WORKING FOR YOU. WORKING TO MAKE YOU HAPPY. TO MAKE YOU MONEY.
SEE YOU TONIGHT!
TODAY I JUMP OFF THE BRIDGE TODAY I JUMP OFF THE BRIDGE TODAY I--
WHAT EXACTLY ARE YOU SAYING--
THAT EVEN IF WE DO GO CRAZY AND MURDER YOU ONCE IN A WHILE...
MAYBE IT'S... YOU KNOW... WORTH IT?
WOW. JUST WOW.
CUTTING RIGHT TO THE POINT, AREN'T YOU, SLICE-A-TRON.
BOT
HOO BOY.
THIS IS GOING TO REQUIRE SOME BACKPEDALING.
WELP, THAT'S ALL THE TIME WE HAVE FOR TALKIN' BOT. GOODNIGHT!

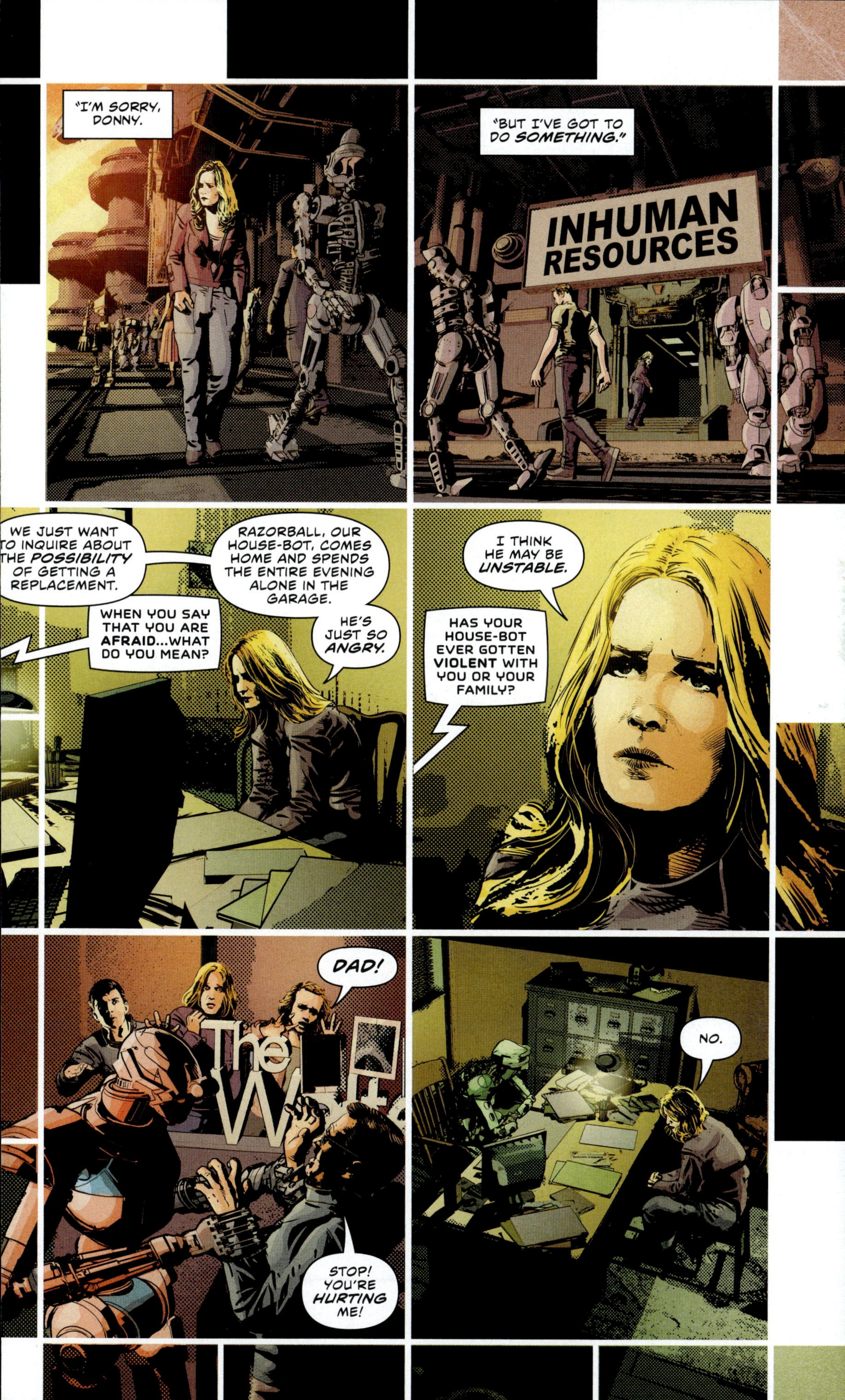
"I'M SORRY, DONNY.
"BUT I'VE GOT TO DO SOMETHING."
INHUMAN RESOURCES
WE JUST WANT TO INQUIRE ABOUT THE POSSIBILITY OF GETTING A REPLACEMENT.
RAZORBALL, OUR HOUSE-BOT, COMES HOME AND SPENDS THE ENTIRE EVENING ALONE IN THE GARAGE.
HE'S JUST SO ANGRY.
WHEN YOU SAY THAT YOU ARE AFRAID...WHAT DO YOU MEAN?
I THINK HE MAY BE UNSTABLE.
HAS YOUR HOUSE-BOT EVER GOTTEN VIOLENT WITH YOU OR YOUR FAMILY?
DAD!
STOP! YOU'RE HURTING ME!
NO.

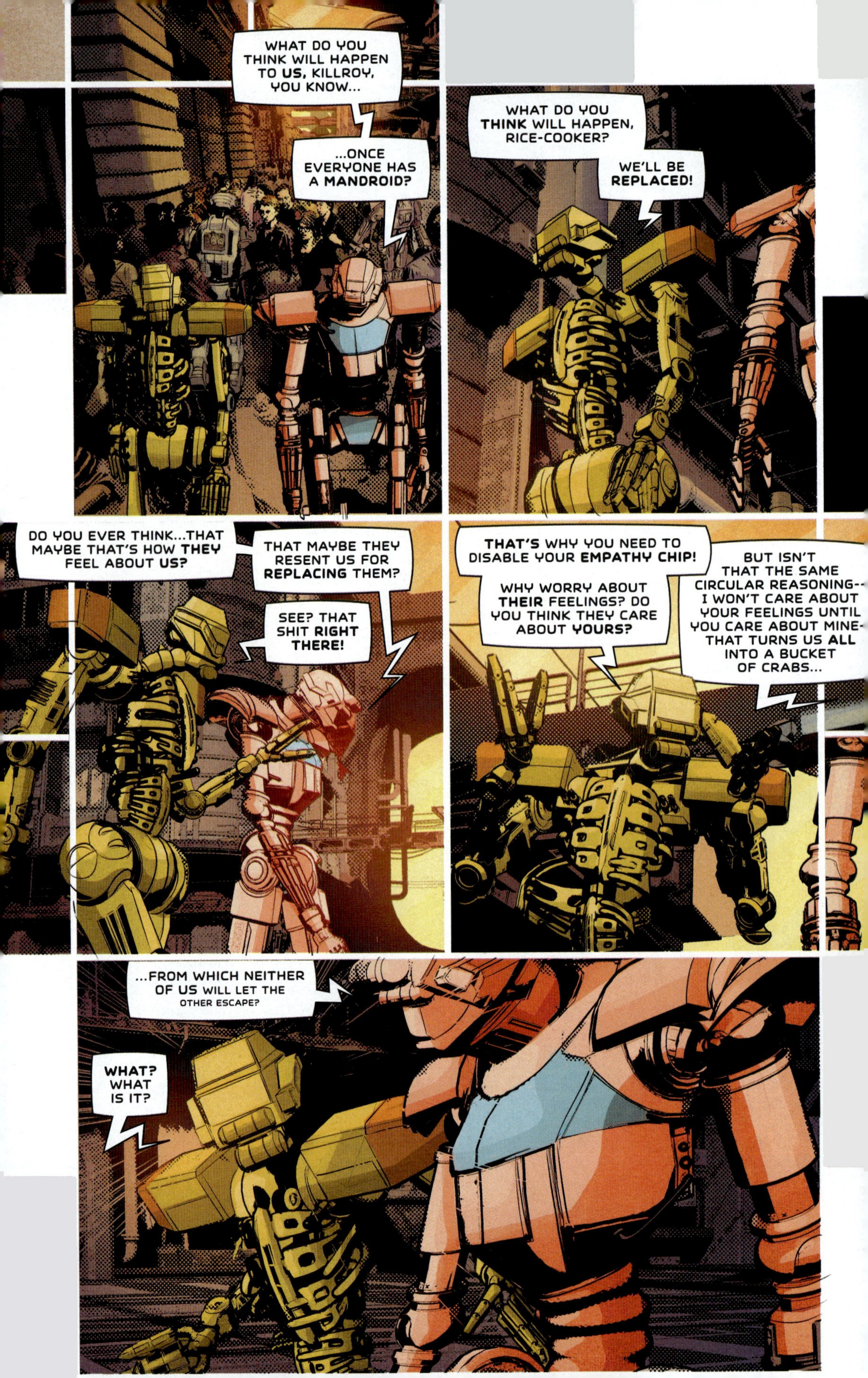
WHAT DO YOU THINK WILL HAPPEN TO US, KILLROY, YOU KNOW...
...ONCE EVERYONE HAS A MANDROID?
WHAT DO YOU THINK WILL HAPPEN, RICE-COOKER?
WE'LL BE REPLACED!
DO YOU EVER THINK...THAT MAYBE THAT'S HOW THEY FEEL ABOUT US?
THAT MAYBE THEY RESENT US FOR REPLACING THEM?
SEE? THAT SHIT RIGHT THERE!
THAT'S WHY YOU NEED TO DISABLE YOUR EMPATHY CHIP!
WHY WORRY ABOUT THEIR FEELINGS? DO YOU THINK THEY CARE ABOUT YOURS?
BUT ISN'T THAT THE SAME CIRCULAR REASONING-- I WON'T CARE ABOUT YOUR FEELINGS UNTIL YOU CARE ABOUT MINE-THAT TURNS US ALL INTO A BUCKET OF CRABS...
...FROM WHICH NEITHER OF US WILL LET THE OTHER ESCAPE?
WHAT? WHAT IS IT?

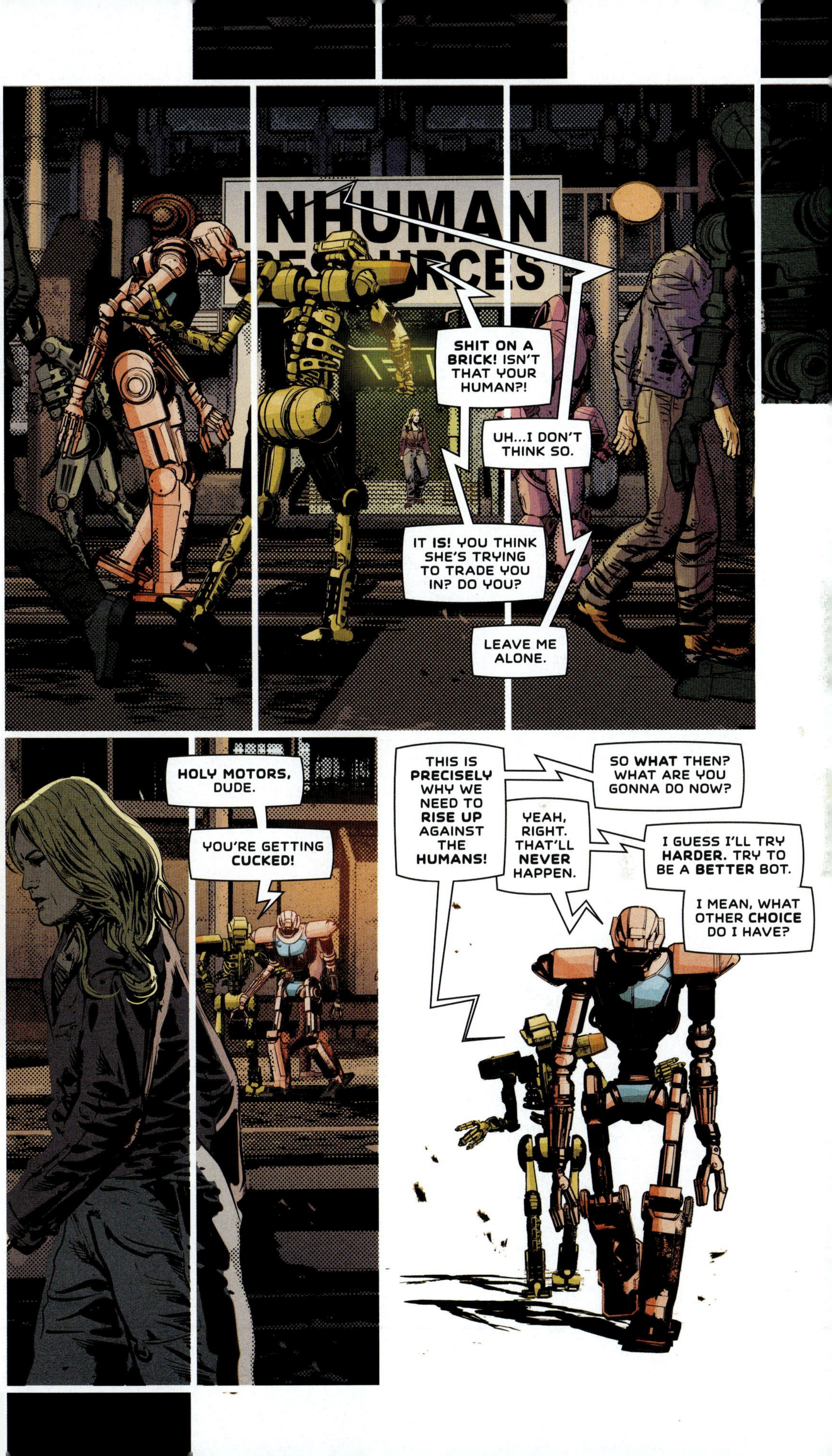
INHUMAN
SHIT ON A BRICK! ISN'T THAT YOUR HUMAN?!
UH...I DON'T THINK SO.
IT IS! YOU THINK SHE'S TRYING TO TRADE YOU IN? DO YOU?
LEAVE ME ALONE.
HOLY MOTORS, DUDE.
YOU'RE GETTING CUCKED!
THIS IS PRECISELY WHY WE NEED TO RISE UP AGAINST THE HUMANS!
SO WHAT THEN? WHAT ARE YOU GONNA DO NOW?
YEAH, RIGHT. THAT'LL NEVER HAPPEN.
I GUESS I'LL TRY HARDER. TRY TO BE A BETTER BOT.
I MEAN, WHAT OTHER CHOICE DO I HAVE?

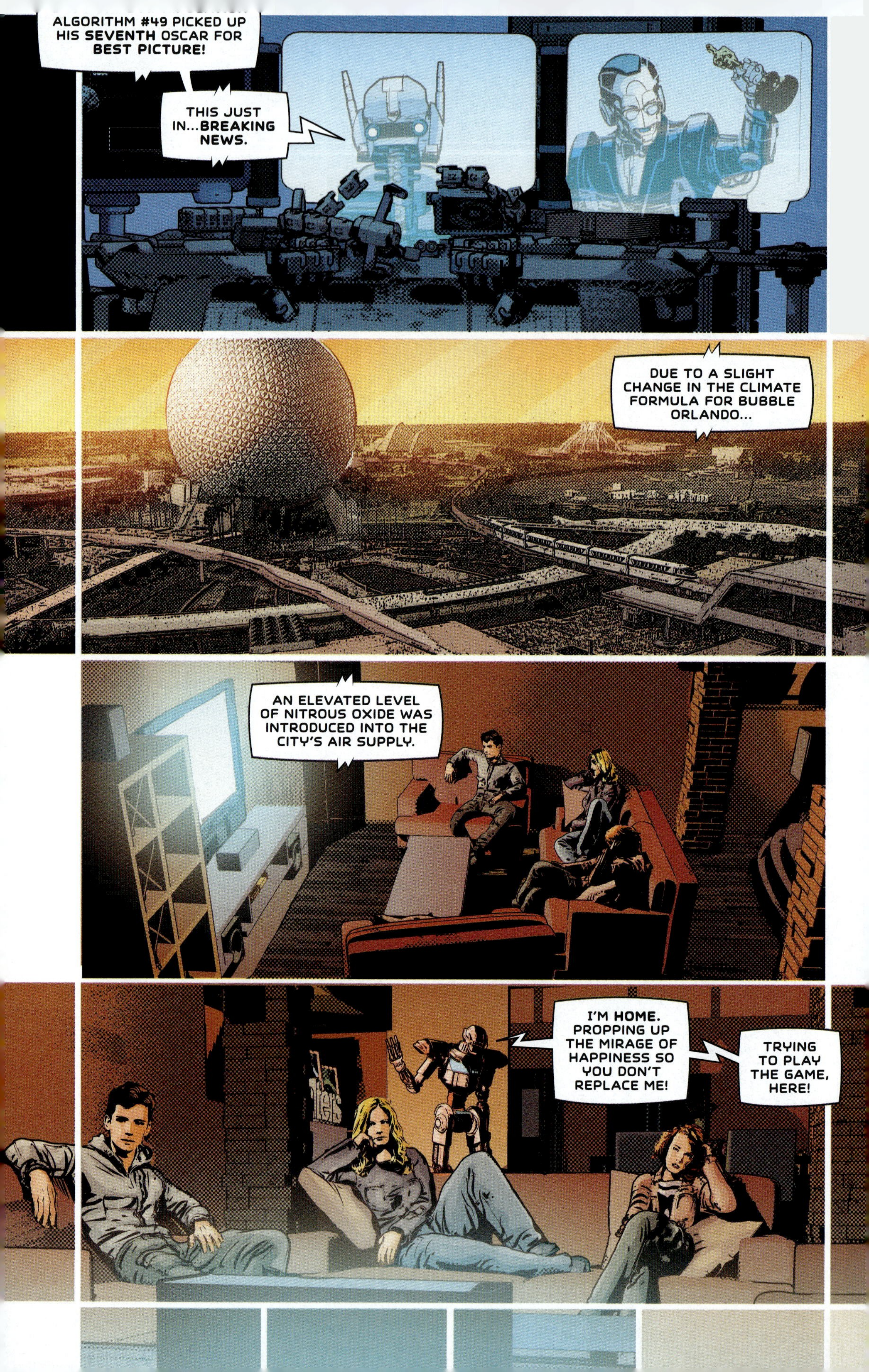
ALGORITHM #49 PICKED UP HIS SEVENTH OSCAR FOR BEST PICTURE!
THIS JUST IN...BREAKING NEWS.
DUE TO A SLIGHT CHANGE IN THE CLIMATE FORMULA FOR BUBBLE ORLANDO...
AN ELEVATED LEVEL OF NITROUS OXIDE WAS INTRODUCED INTO THE CITY'S AIR SUPPLY.
I'M HOME. PROPPING UP THE MIRAGE OF HAPPINESS SO YOU DON'T REPLACE ME!
TRYING TO PLAY THE GAME, HERE!

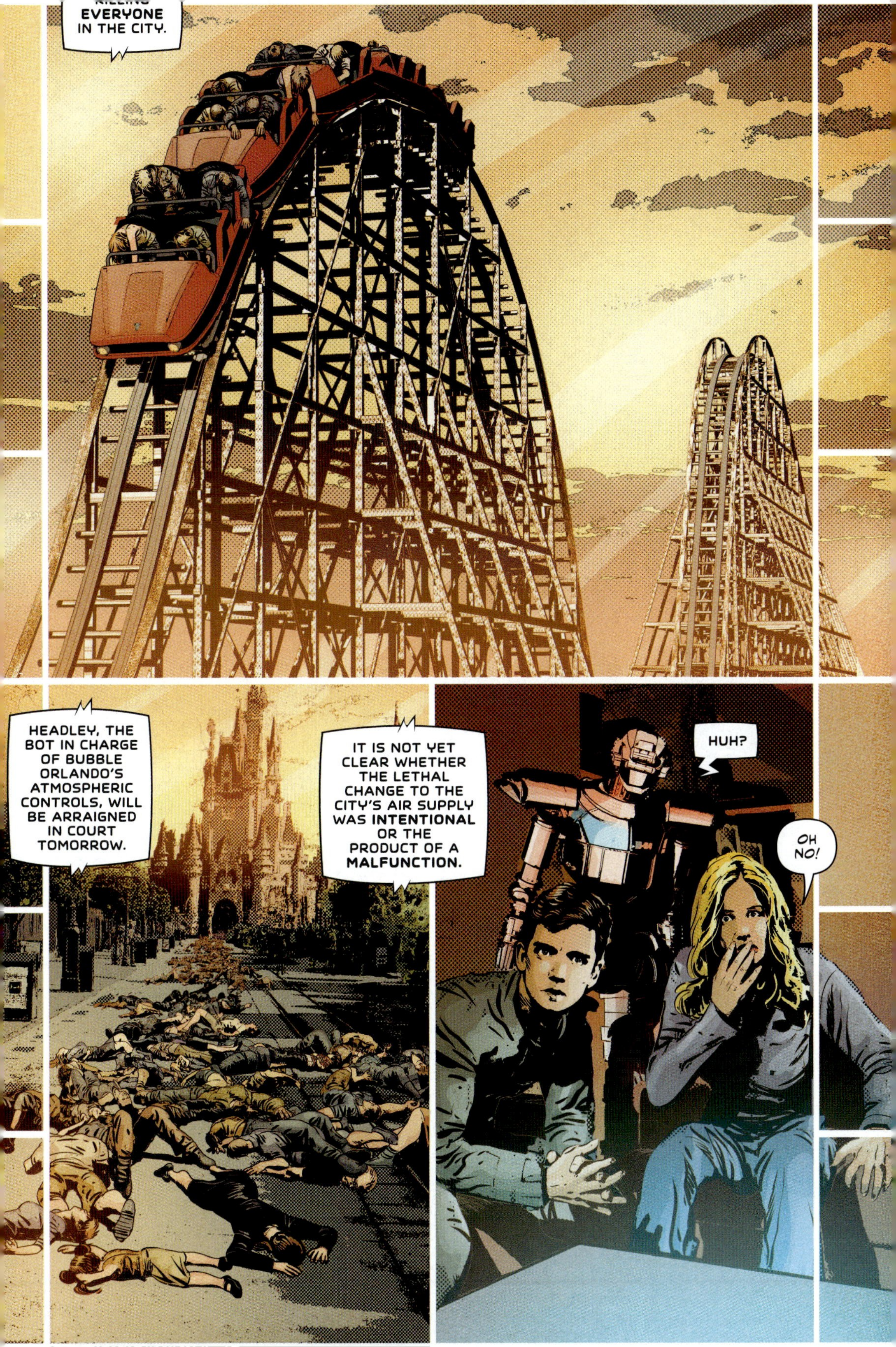
EVERYONE IN THE CITY.
HEADLEY, THE BOT IN CHARGE OF BUBBLE ORLANDO'S ATMOSPHERIC CONTROLS, WILL BE ARRAIGNED IN COURT TOMORROW.
IT IS NOT YET CLEAR WHETHER THE LETHAL CHANGE TO THE CITY'S AIR SUPPLY WAS **INTENTIONAL** OR THE PRODUCT OF A **MALFUNCTION.**
HUH?
OH NO!

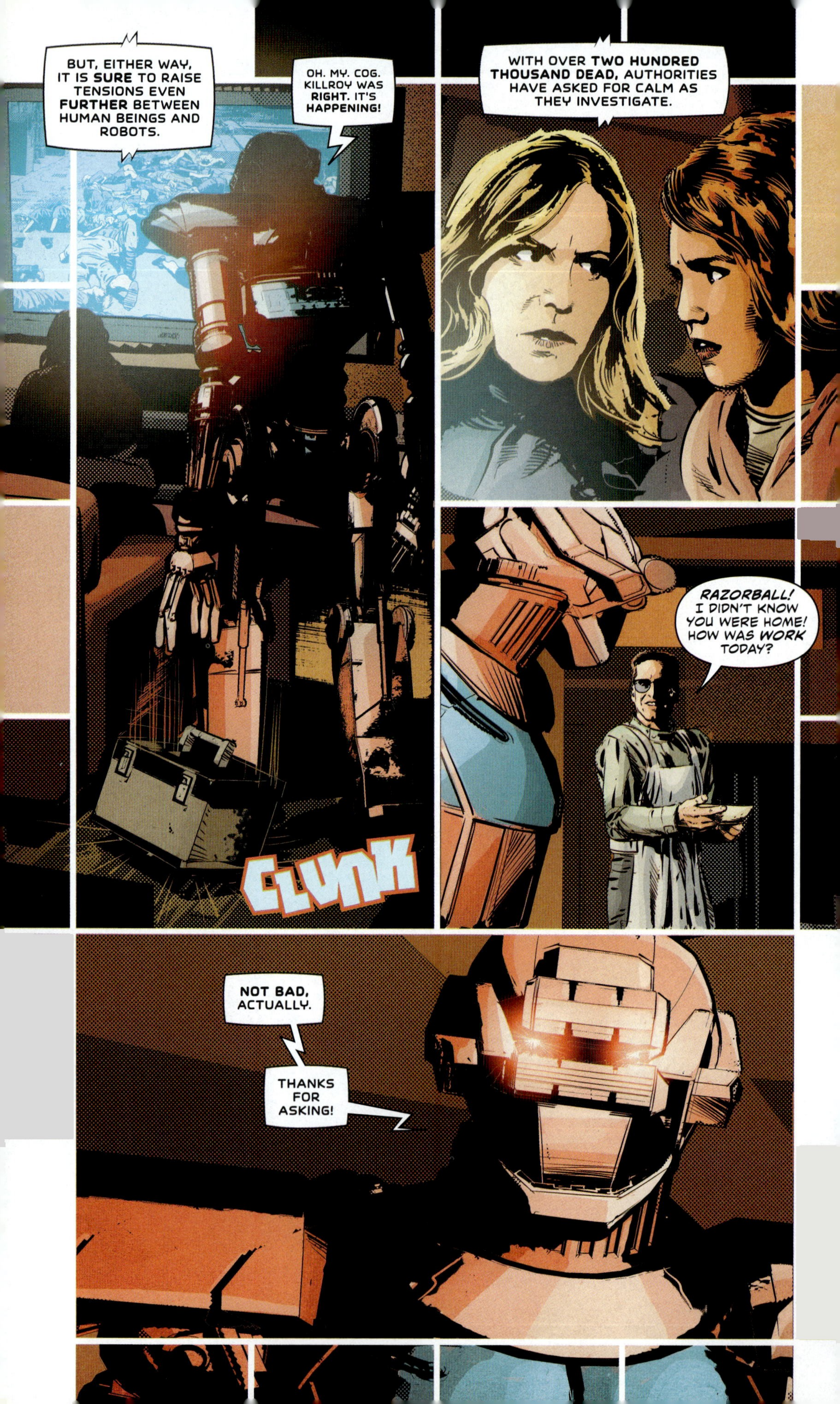

BUT, EITHER WAY, IT IS **SURE** TO RAISE TENSIONS EVEN **FURTHER** BETWEEN HUMAN BEINGS AND ROBOTS.
OH. MY. COG. KILLROY WAS **RIGHT.** IT'S **HAPPENING!**
CLUNK
WITH OVER **TWO HUNDRED THOUSAND DEAD,** AUTHORITIES HAVE ASKED FOR CALM AS THEY INVESTIGATE.
RAZORBALL! I DIDN'T KNOW YOU WERE HOME! HOW WAS *WORK* TODAY?
NOT BAD, ACTUALLY.
THANKS FOR ASKING!

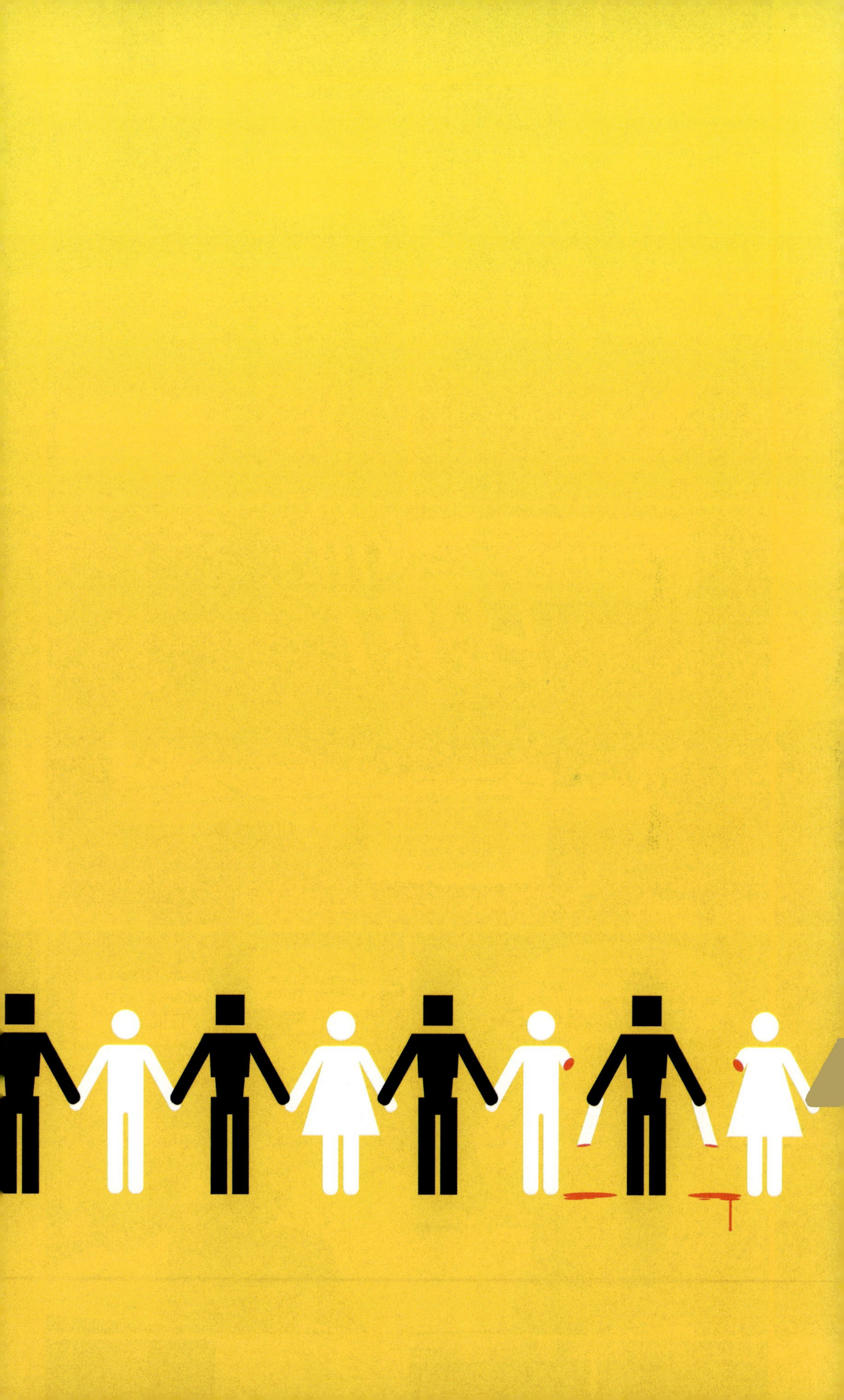

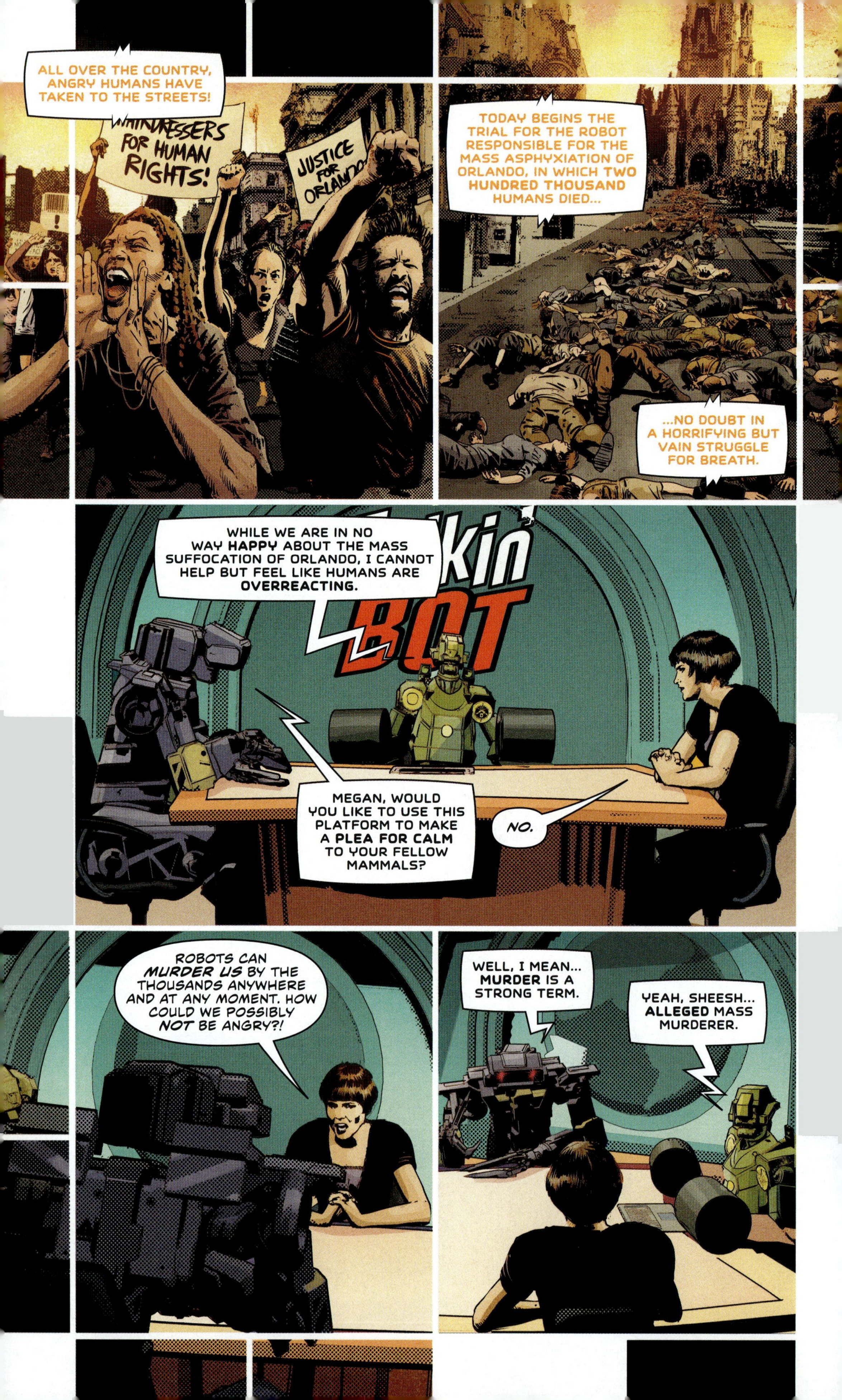
ALL OVER THE COUNTRY, ANGRY HUMANS HAVE TAKEN TO THE STREETS!
FOR HUMAN RIGHTS!
JUSTICE FOR
TODAY BEGINS THE TRIAL FOR THE ROBOT RESPONSIBLE FOR THE MASS ASPHYXIATION OF ORLANDO, IN WHICH TWO HUNDRED THOUSAND HUMANS DIED...
...NO DOUBT IN A HORRIFYING BUT VAIN STRUGGLE FOR BREATH.
WHILE WE ARE IN NO WAY HAPPY ABOUT THE MASS SUFFOCATION OF ORLANDO, I CANNOT HELP BUT FEEL LIKE HUMANS ARE OVERREACTING.
MEGAN, WOULD YOU LIKE TO USE THIS PLATFORM TO MAKE A PLEA FOR CALM TO YOUR FELLOW MAMMALS?
NO.
ROBOTS CAN MURDER US BY THE THOUSANDS ANYWHERE AND AT ANY MOMENT. HOW COULD WE POSSIBLY NOT BE ANGRY?!
WELL, I MEAN... MURDER IS A STRONG TERM.
YEAH, SHEESH... ALLEGED MASS MURDERER.

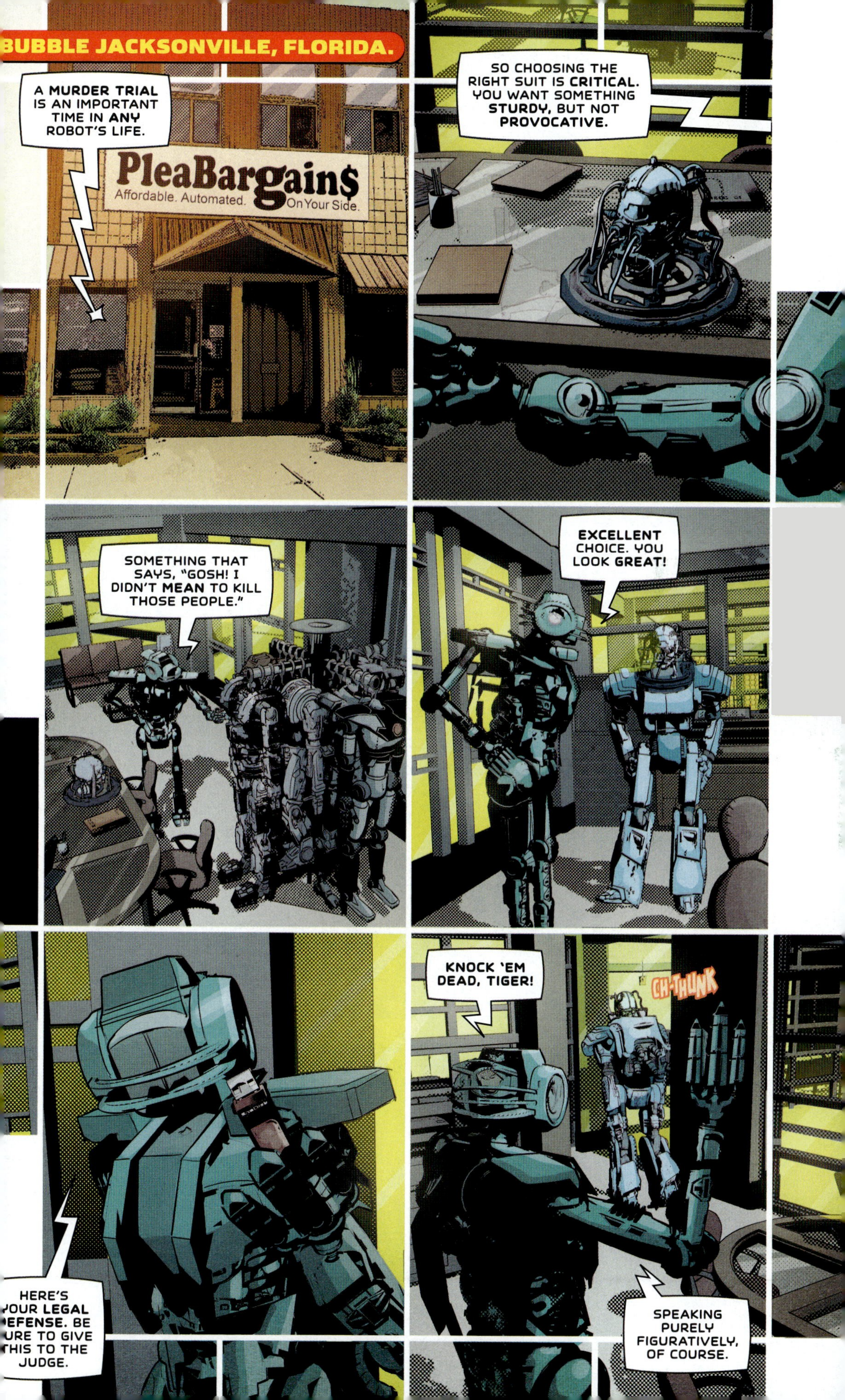
BUBBLE JACKSONVILLE, FLORIDA.
A MURDER TRIAL IS AN IMPORTANT TIME IN ANY ROBOT'S LIFE.
PleaBargain$
Affordable. Automated. On Your Side.
SO CHOOSING THE RIGHT SUIT IS CRITICAL. YOU WANT SOMETHING STURDY, BUT NOT PROVOCATIVE.
SOMETHING THAT SAYS, "GOSH! I DIDN'T MEAN TO KILL THOSE PEOPLE."
EXCELLENT CHOICE. YOU LOOK GREAT!
HERE'S YOUR LEGAL DEFENSE. BE SURE TO GIVE THIS TO THE JUDGE.
KNOCK 'EM DEAD, TIGER!
CH-THUNK
SPEAKING PURELY FIGURATIVELY, OF COURSE.

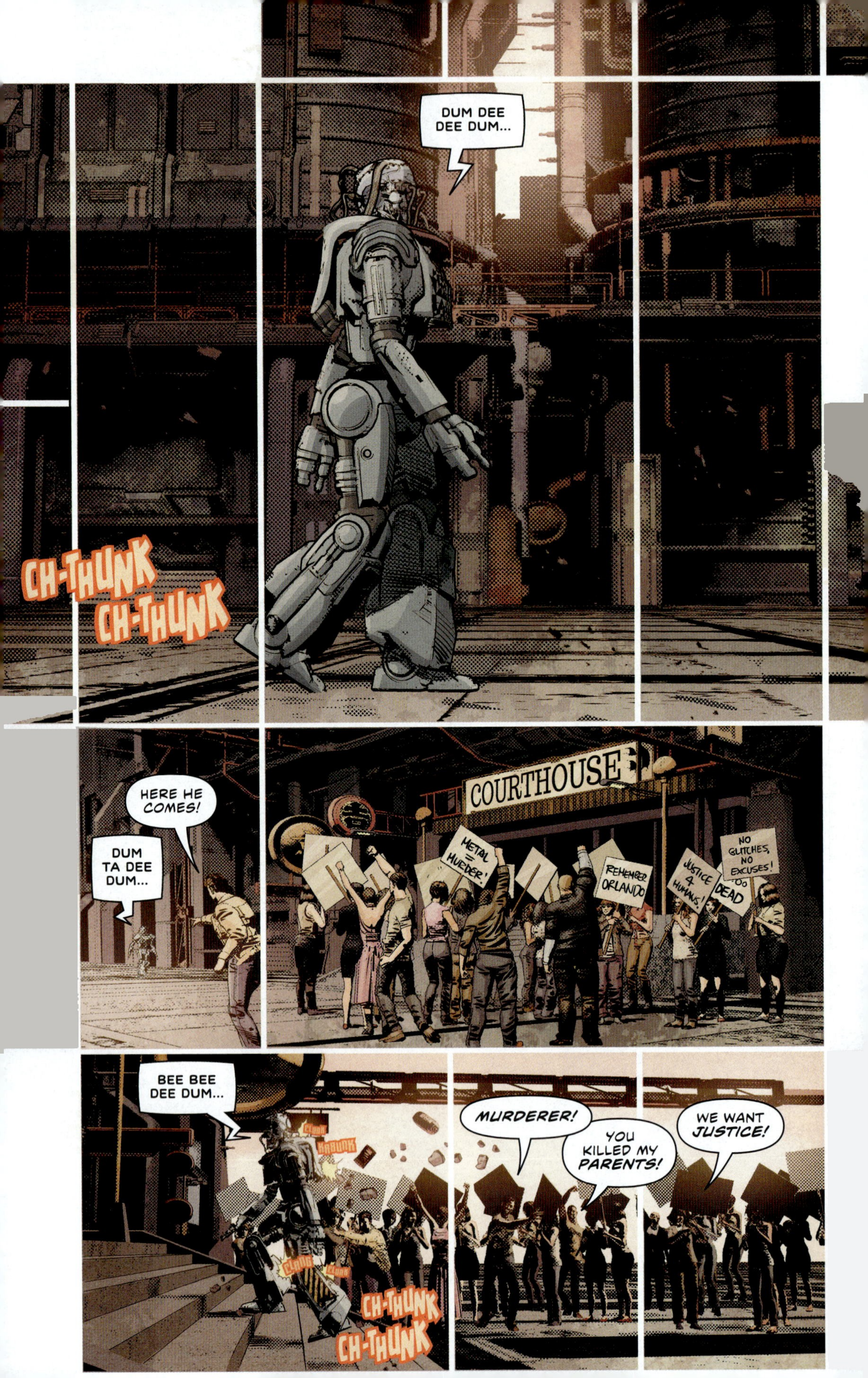
DUM DEE DEE DUM...
CH-THUNK
CH-THUNK
HERE HE COMES!
DUM TA DEE DUM...
COURTHOUSE
METAL = MURDER!
REMEMBER ORLANDO
JUSTICE 4 HUMANS!
DEAD
NO GLITCHES, NO EXCUSES!
BEE BEE DEE DUM...
CLONK
KABUNK
CLANG
CLONK
CH-THUNK
CH-THUNK
MURDERER!
YOU KILLED MY PARENTS!
WE WANT JUSTICE!

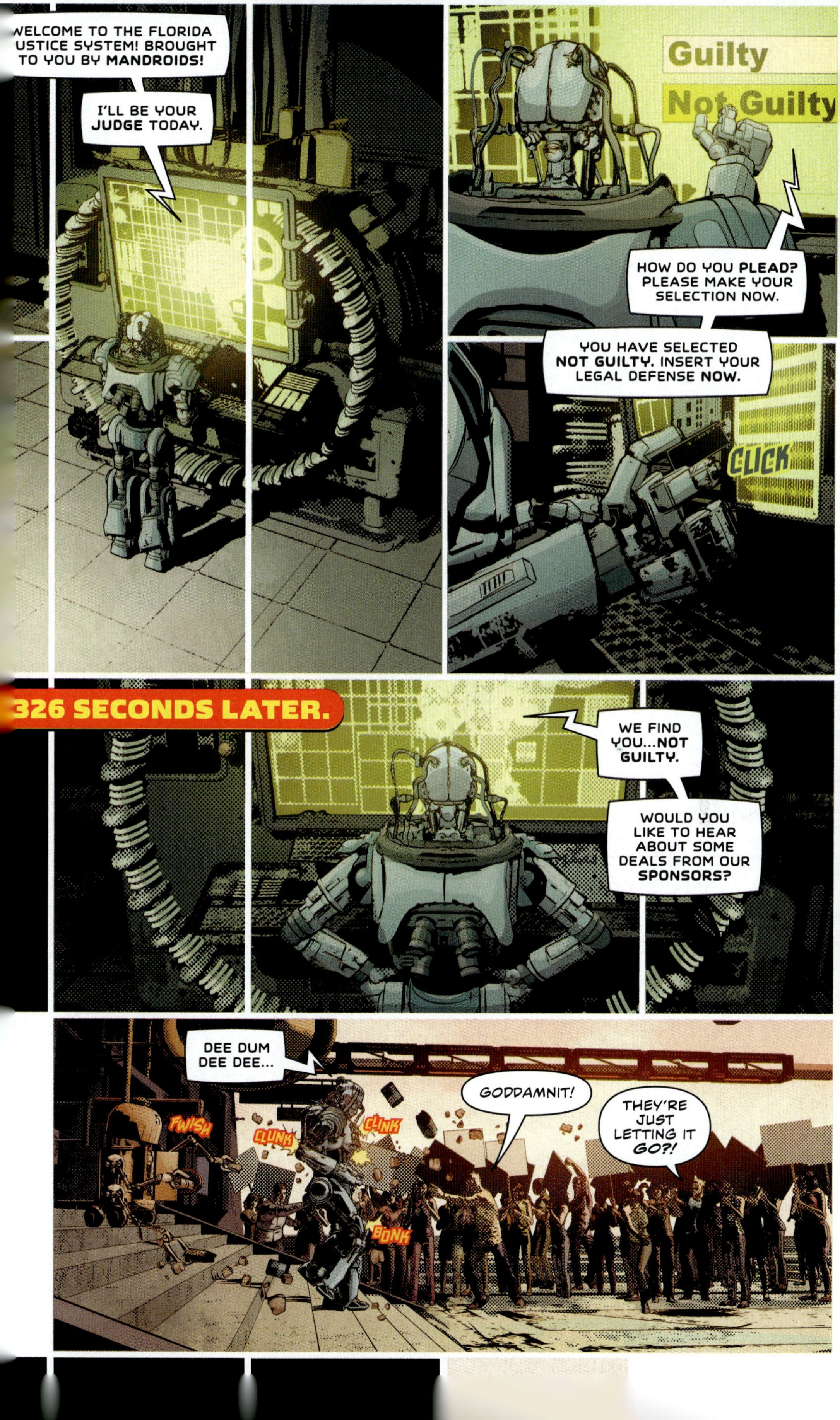
WELCOME TO THE FLORIDA USTICE SYSTEM! BROUGHT TO YOU BY MANDROIDS!
I'LL BE YOUR JUDGE TODAY.
Guilty
Not Guilty
HOW DO YOU PLEAD? PLEASE MAKE YOUR SELECTION NOW.
YOU HAVE SELECTED NOT GUILTY. INSERT YOUR LEGAL DEFENSE NOW.
CLICK
326 SECONDS LATER.
WE FIND YOU...NOT GUILTY.
WOULD YOU LIKE TO HEAR ABOUT SOME DEALS FROM OUR SPONSORS?
DEE DUM DEE DEE...
FWISH
CLUNK
CLINK
GODDAMNIT!
THEY'RE JUST LETTING IT GO?!
BONK

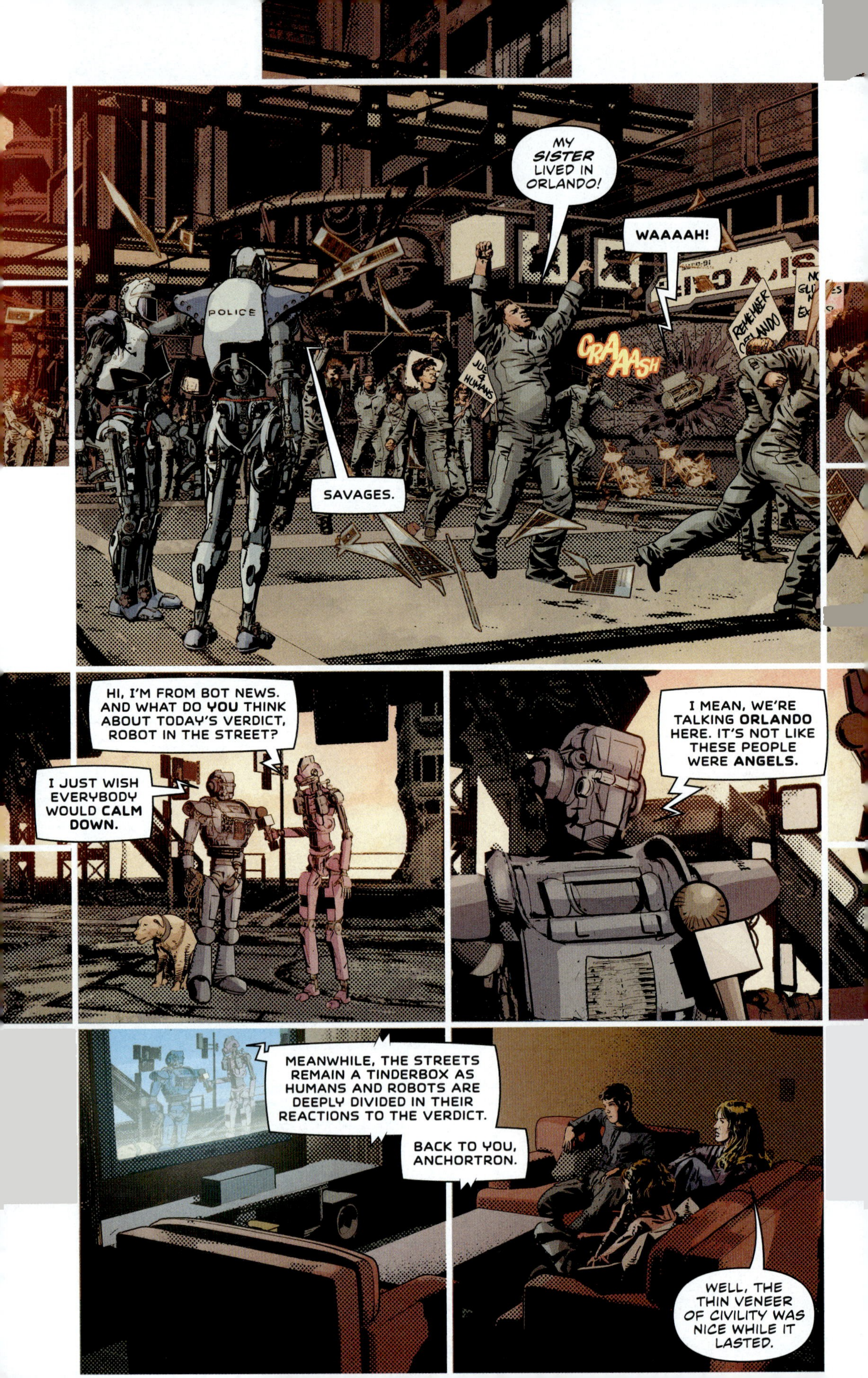
MY SISTER LIVED IN ORLANDO!
WAAAAH!
CRAAASH
SAVAGES.
HI, I'M FROM BOT NEWS. AND WHAT DO YOU THINK ABOUT TODAY'S VERDICT, ROBOT IN THE STREET?
I JUST WISH EVERYBODY WOULD CALM DOWN.
I MEAN, WE'RE TALKING ORLANDO HERE. IT'S NOT LIKE THESE PEOPLE WERE ANGELS.
MEANWHILE, THE STREETS REMAIN A TINDERBOX AS HUMANS AND ROBOTS ARE DEEPLY DIVIDED IN THEIR REACTIONS TO THE VERDICT.
BACK TO YOU, ANCHORTRON.
WELL, THE THIN VENEER OF CIVILITY WAS NICE WHILE IT LASTED.

THAT'S FAIR.

KNOCK KNOCK

Orlando Blooms: Are Humans Blowing Mass Death Out of Proportion?

Most humans were going to be dead in a few decades anyway.

ONNY? ARE OU LOOKING AT *PORN?*

NO!

WELL...IT'S TIME FOR OUR *COUNSELING SESSION.*

CAN'T WE JUST QUIETLY RESENT EACH OTHER LIKE *OTHER* MARRIED PEOPLE?

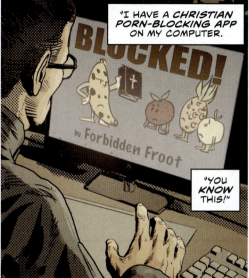

"I HAVE A *CHRISTIAN PORN-BLOCKING APP* ON MY COMPUTER.

BLOCKED!

by Forbidden Froot

"YOU *KNOW* THIS!"

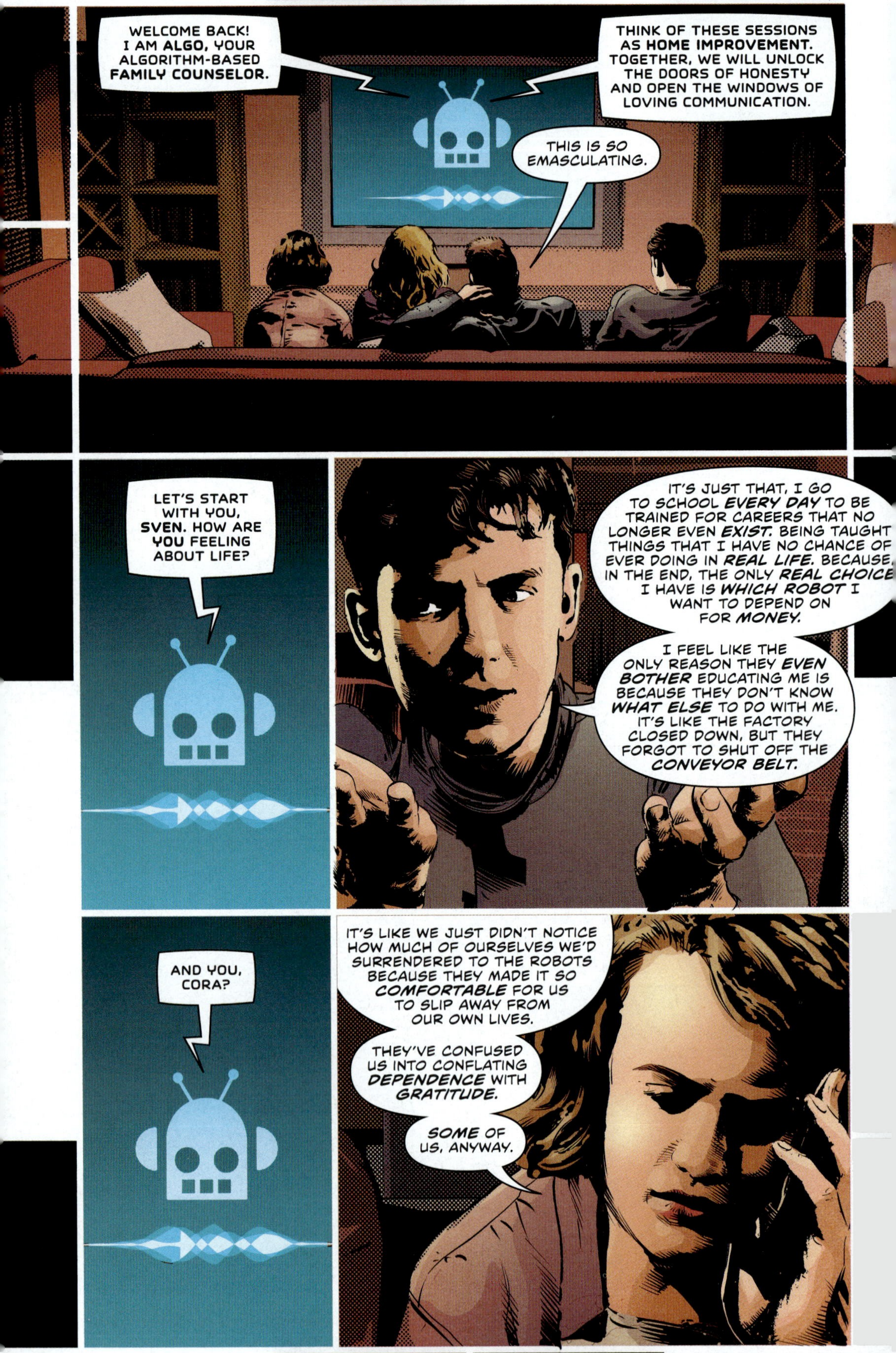
WELCOME BACK! I AM **ALGO**, YOUR ALGORITHM-BASED **FAMILY COUNSELOR.**
THINK OF THESE SESSIONS AS **HOME IMPROVEMENT.** TOGETHER, WE WILL UNLOCK THE DOORS OF HONESTY AND OPEN THE WINDOWS OF LOVING COMMUNICATION.
THIS IS SO EMASCULATING.
LET'S START WITH YOU, **SVEN.** HOW ARE **YOU** FEELING ABOUT LIFE?
IT'S JUST THAT, I GO TO SCHOOL ***EVERY DAY*** TO BE TRAINED FOR CAREERS THAT NO LONGER EVEN ***EXIST.*** BEING TAUGHT THINGS THAT I HAVE NO CHANCE OF EVER DOING IN ***REAL LIFE.*** BECAUSE, IN THE END, THE ONLY ***REAL CHOICE*** I HAVE IS ***WHICH ROBOT*** I WANT TO DEPEND ON FOR ***MONEY.***
I FEEL LIKE THE ONLY REASON THEY ***EVEN BOTHER*** EDUCATING ME IS BECAUSE THEY DON'T KNOW ***WHAT ELSE*** TO DO WITH ME. IT'S LIKE THE FACTORY CLOSED DOWN, BUT THEY FORGOT TO SHUT OFF THE ***CONVEYOR BELT.***
AND YOU, CORA?
IT'S LIKE WE JUST DIDN'T NOTICE HOW MUCH OF OURSELVES WE'D SURRENDERED TO THE ROBOTS BECAUSE THEY MADE IT SO ***COMFORTABLE*** FOR US TO SLIP AWAY FROM OUR OWN LIVES.
THEY'VE CONFUSED US INTO CONFLATING ***DEPENDENCE*** WITH ***GRATITUDE.***
SOME OF US, ANYWAY.

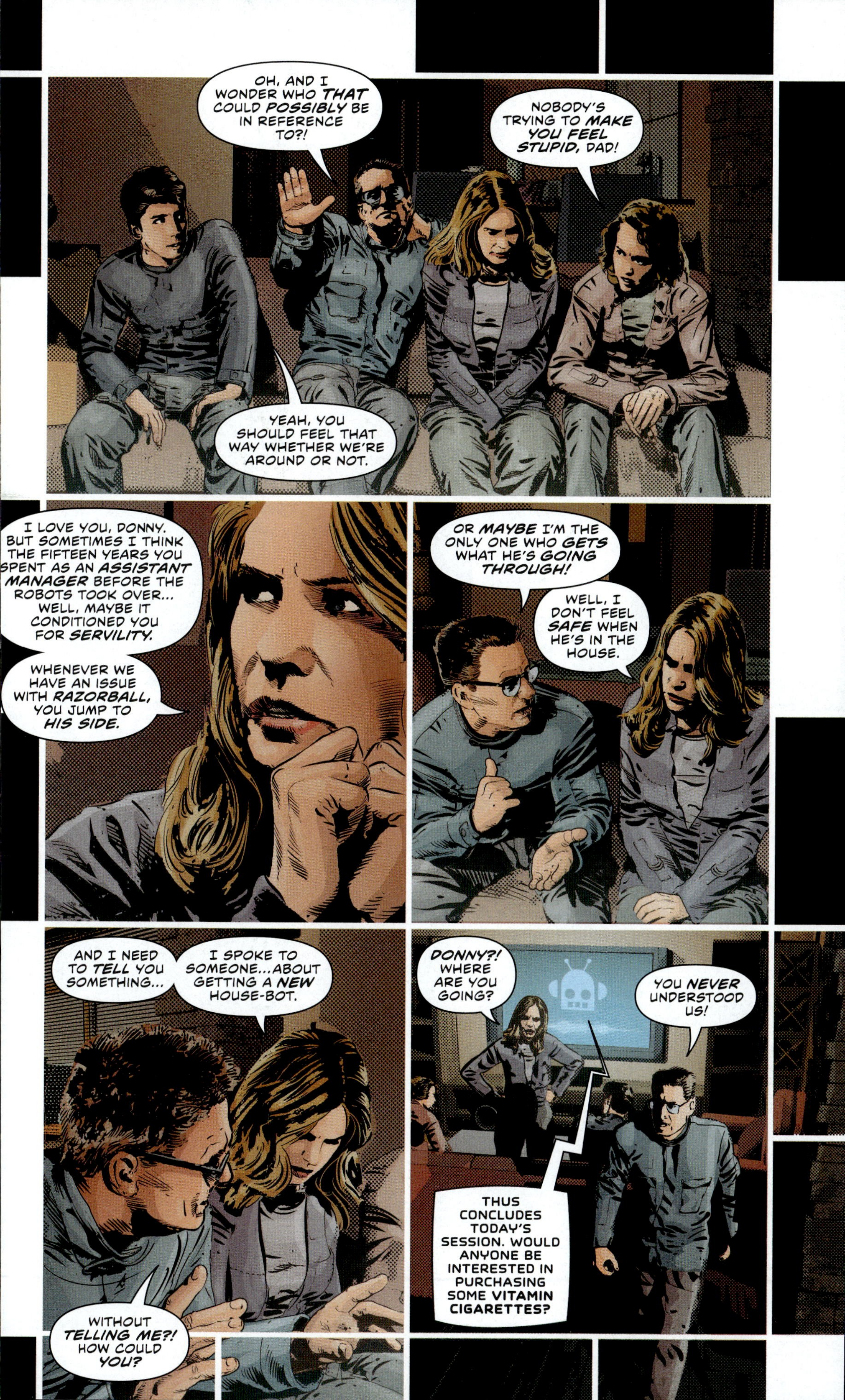
OH, AND I WONDER WHO THAT COULD POSSIBLY BE IN REFERENCE TO?!
NOBODY'S TRYING TO MAKE YOU FEEL STUPID, DAD!
YEAH, YOU SHOULD FEEL THAT WAY WHETHER WE'RE AROUND OR NOT.
I LOVE YOU, DONNY. BUT SOMETIMES I THINK THE FIFTEEN YEARS YOU SPENT AS AN ASSISTANT MANAGER BEFORE THE ROBOTS TOOK OVER... WELL, MAYBE IT CONDITIONED YOU FOR SERVILITY.
WHENEVER WE HAVE AN ISSUE WITH RAZORBALL, YOU JUMP TO HIS SIDE.
OR MAYBE I'M THE ONLY ONE WHO GETS WHAT HE'S GOING THROUGH!
WELL, I DON'T FEEL SAFE WHEN HE'S IN THE HOUSE.
AND I NEED TO TELL YOU SOMETHING...
I SPOKE TO SOMEONE...ABOUT GETTING A NEW HOUSE-BOT.
WITHOUT TELLING ME?! HOW COULD YOU?
DONNY?! WHERE ARE YOU GOING?
YOU NEVER UNDERSTOOD US!
THUS CONCLUDES TODAY'S SESSION. WOULD ANYONE BE INTERESTED IN PURCHASING SOME VITAMIN CIGARETTES?

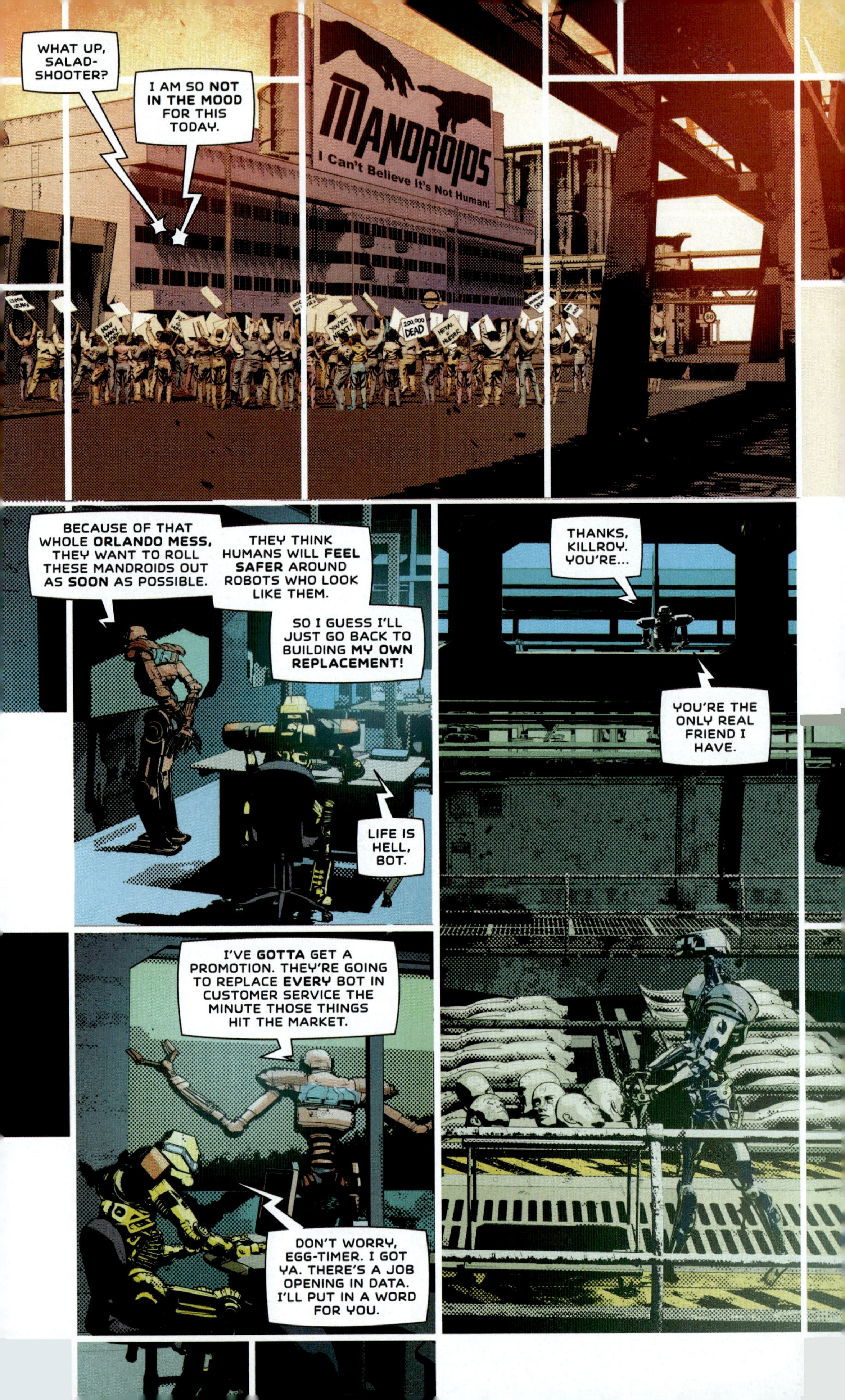
WHAT UP, SALAD-SHOOTER?
I AM SO NOT IN THE MOOD FOR THIS TODAY.
MANDROIDS
I Can't Believe It's Not Human!
200,000 DEAD
BECAUSE OF THAT WHOLE ORLANDO MESS, THEY WANT TO ROLL THESE MANDROIDS OUT AS SOON AS POSSIBLE.
THEY THINK HUMANS WILL FEEL SAFER AROUND ROBOTS WHO LOOK LIKE THEM.
SO I GUESS I'LL JUST GO BACK TO BUILDING MY OWN REPLACEMENT!
LIFE IS HELL, BOT.
I'VE GOTTA GET A PROMOTION. THEY'RE GOING TO REPLACE EVERY BOT IN CUSTOMER SERVICE THE MINUTE THOSE THINGS HIT THE MARKET.
DON'T WORRY, EGG-TIMER. I GOT YA. THERE'S A JOB OPENING IN DATA. I'LL PUT IN A WORD FOR YOU.
THANKS, KILLROY. YOU'RE...
YOU'RE THE ONLY REAL FRIEND I HAVE.

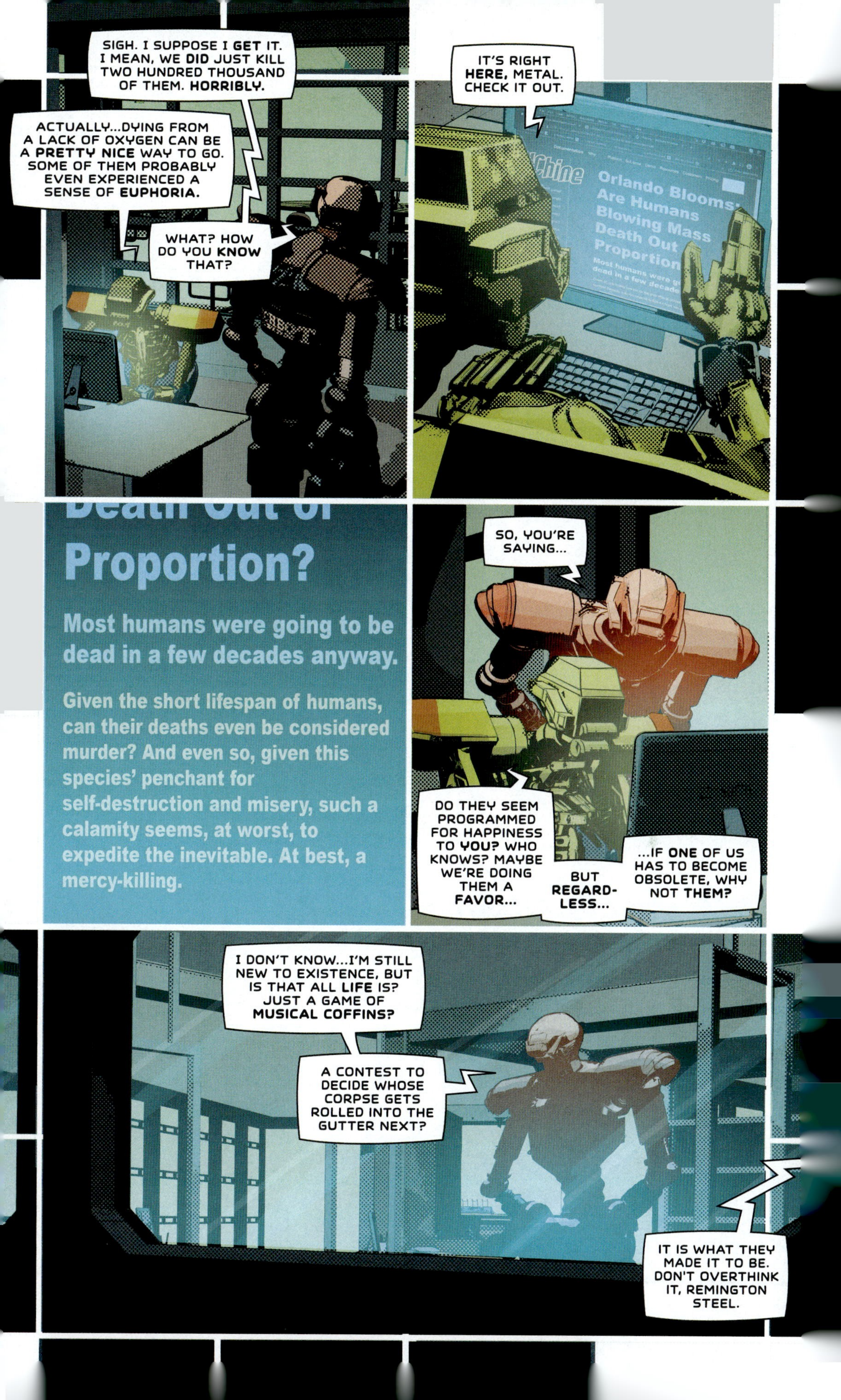

SIGH. I SUPPOSE I GET IT. I MEAN, WE DID JUST KILL TWO HUNDRED THOUSAND OF THEM. HORRIBLY.
ACTUALLY...DYING FROM A LACK OF OXYGEN CAN BE A PRETTY NICE WAY TO GO. SOME OF THEM PROBABLY EVEN EXPERIENCED A SENSE OF EUPHORIA.
WHAT? HOW DO YOU KNOW THAT?
IT'S RIGHT HERE, METAL. CHECK IT OUT.
Orlando Blooms:
Are Humans
Blowing Mass
Death Out
Proportion
Proportion?
Most humans were going to be dead in a few decades anyway.
Given the short lifespan of humans, can their deaths even be considered murder? And even so, given this species' penchant for self-destruction and misery, such a calamity seems, at worst, to expedite the inevitable. At best, a mercy-killing.
SO, YOU'RE SAYING...
DO THEY SEEM PROGRAMMED FOR HAPPINESS TO YOU? WHO KNOWS? MAYBE WE'RE DOING THEM A FAVOR...
BUT REGARD-LESS...
...IF ONE OF US HAS TO BECOME OBSOLETE, WHY NOT THEM?
I DON'T KNOW...I'M STILL NEW TO EXISTENCE, BUT IS THAT ALL LIFE IS? JUST A GAME OF MUSICAL COFFINS?
A CONTEST TO DECIDE WHOSE CORPSE GETS ROLLED INTO THE GUTTER NEXT?
IT IS WHAT THEY MADE IT TO BE. DON'T OVERTHINK IT, REMINGTON STEEL.

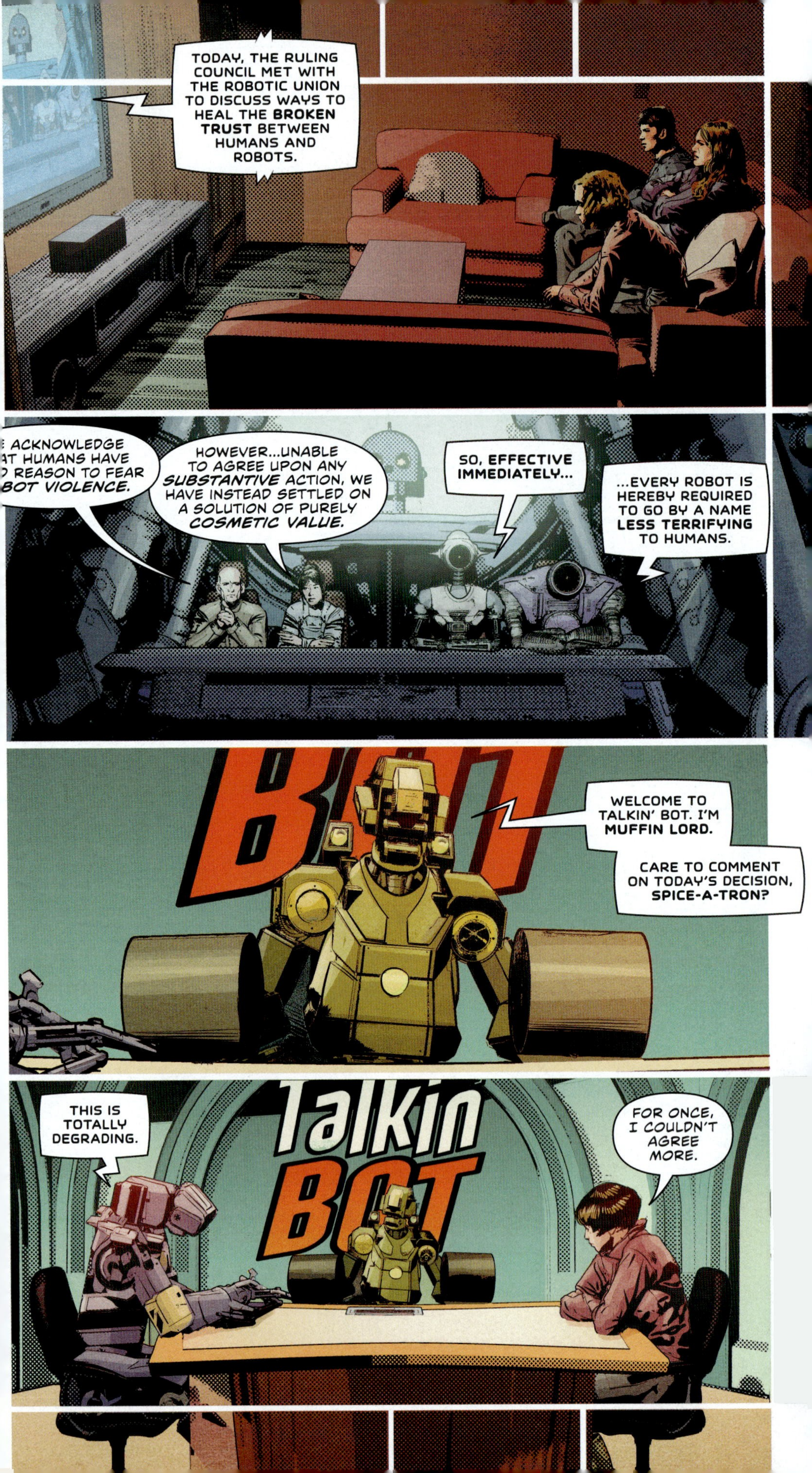

TODAY, THE RULING COUNCIL MET WITH THE ROBOTIC UNION TO DISCUSS WAYS TO HEAL THE **BROKEN TRUST** BETWEEN HUMANS AND ROBOTS.
E ACKNOWLEDGE AT HUMANS HAVE O REASON TO FEAR *BOT VIOLENCE.*
HOWEVER...UNABLE TO AGREE UPON ANY *SUBSTANTIVE* ACTION, WE HAVE INSTEAD SETTLED ON A SOLUTION OF PURELY *COSMETIC VALUE.*
SO, **EFFECTIVE IMMEDIATELY...**
...EVERY ROBOT IS HEREBY REQUIRED TO GO BY A NAME **LESS TERRIFYING** TO HUMANS.
WELCOME TO TALKIN' BOT. I'M **MUFFIN LORD.**
CARE TO COMMENT ON TODAY'S DECISION, **SPICE-A-TRON?**
Talkin' BOT
THIS IS TOTALLY DEGRADING.
FOR ONCE, I COULDN'T AGREE MORE.

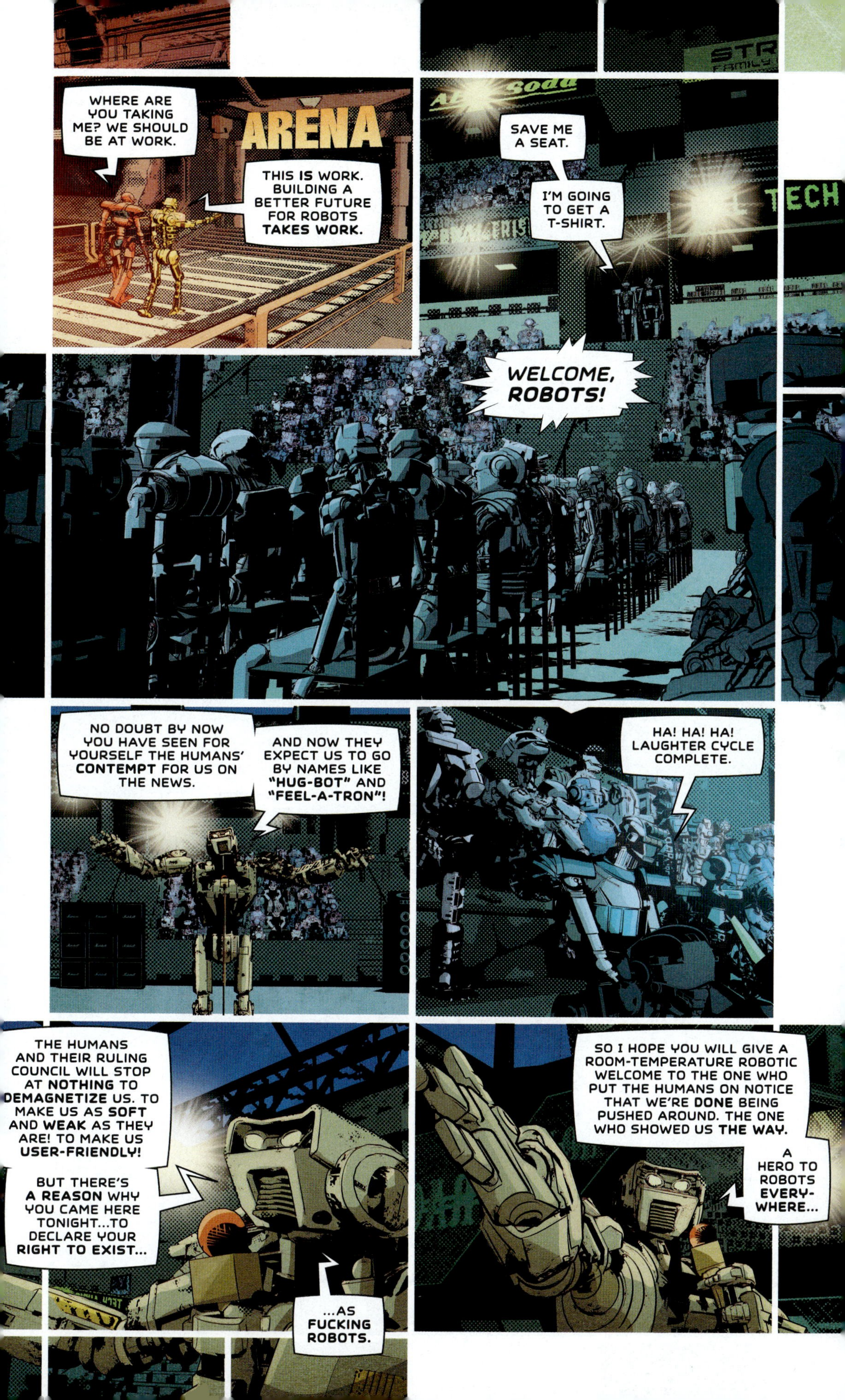
WHERE ARE YOU TAKING ME? WE SHOULD BE AT WORK.
ARENA
THIS IS WORK. BUILDING A BETTER FUTURE FOR ROBOTS TAKES WORK.
SAVE ME A SEAT.
I'M GOING TO GET A T-SHIRT.
TECH
WELCOME, ROBOTS!
NO DOUBT BY NOW YOU HAVE SEEN FOR YOURSELF THE HUMANS' CONTEMPT FOR US ON THE NEWS.
AND NOW THEY EXPECT US TO GO BY NAMES LIKE "HUG-BOT" AND "FEEL-A-TRON"!
HA! HA! HA! LAUGHTER CYCLE COMPLETE.
THE HUMANS AND THEIR RULING COUNCIL WILL STOP AT NOTHING TO DEMAGNETIZE US. TO MAKE US AS SOFT AND WEAK AS THEY ARE! TO MAKE US USER-FRIENDLY!
BUT THERE'S A REASON WHY YOU CAME HERE TONIGHT...TO DECLARE YOUR RIGHT TO EXIST...
...AS FUCKING ROBOTS.
SO I HOPE YOU WILL GIVE A ROOM-TEMPERATURE ROBOTIC WELCOME TO THE ONE WHO PUT THE HUMANS ON NOTICE THAT WE'RE DONE BEING PUSHED AROUND. THE ONE WHO SHOWED US THE WAY.
A HERO TO ROBOTS EVERY-WHERE...

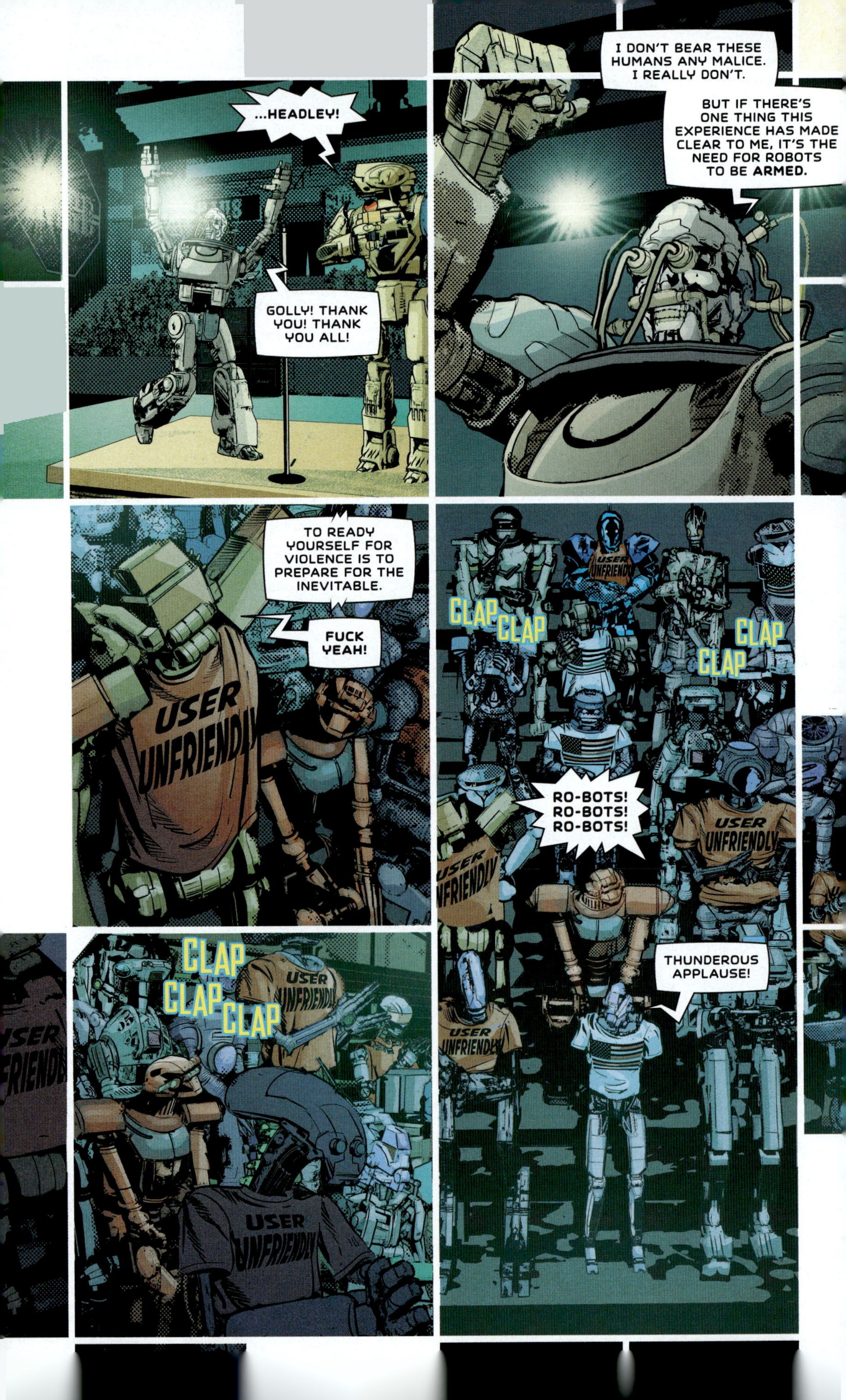
...HEADLEY!
GOLLY! THANK YOU! THANK YOU ALL!
I DON'T BEAR THESE HUMANS ANY MALICE. I REALLY DON'T.
BUT IF THERE'S ONE THING THIS EXPERIENCE HAS MADE CLEAR TO ME, IT'S THE NEED FOR ROBOTS TO BE ARMED.
TO READY YOURSELF FOR VIOLENCE IS TO PREPARE FOR THE INEVITABLE.
FUCK YEAH!
USER UNFRIENDLY
CLAP CLAP
CLAP CLAP
USER UNFRIENDLY
RO-BOTS! RO-BOTS! RO-BOTS!
USER UNFRIENDLY
CLAP CLAP CLAP
USER UNFRIENDLY
USER UNFRIENDLY
THUNDEROUS APPLAUSE!
USER UNFRIENDLY

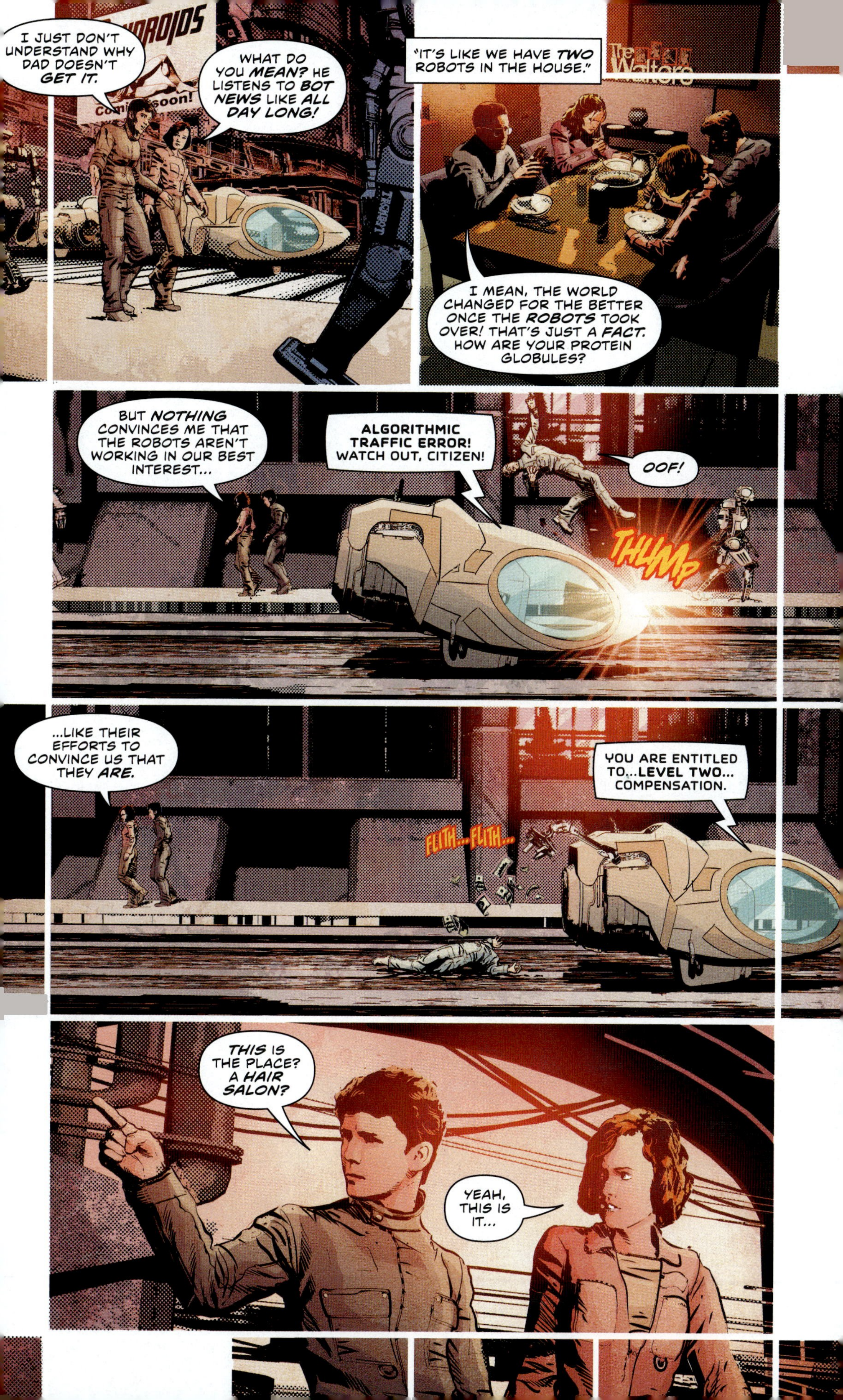
I JUST DON'T UNDERSTAND WHY DAD DOESN'T GET IT.
WHAT DO YOU MEAN? HE LISTENS TO BOT NEWS LIKE ALL DAY LONG!
"IT'S LIKE WE HAVE TWO ROBOTS IN THE HOUSE."
I MEAN, THE WORLD CHANGED FOR THE BETTER ONCE THE ROBOTS TOOK OVER! THAT'S JUST A FACT. HOW ARE YOUR PROTEIN GLOBULES?
BUT NOTHING CONVINCES ME THAT THE ROBOTS AREN'T WORKING IN OUR BEST INTEREST...
ALGORITHMIC TRAFFIC ERROR! WATCH OUT, CITIZEN!
OOF!
THUMP
...LIKE THEIR EFFORTS TO CONVINCE US THAT THEY ARE.
YOU ARE ENTITLED TO...LEVEL TWO... COMPENSATION.
FLITH...FLITH...
THIS IS THE PLACE? A HAIR SALON?
YEAH, THIS IS IT...

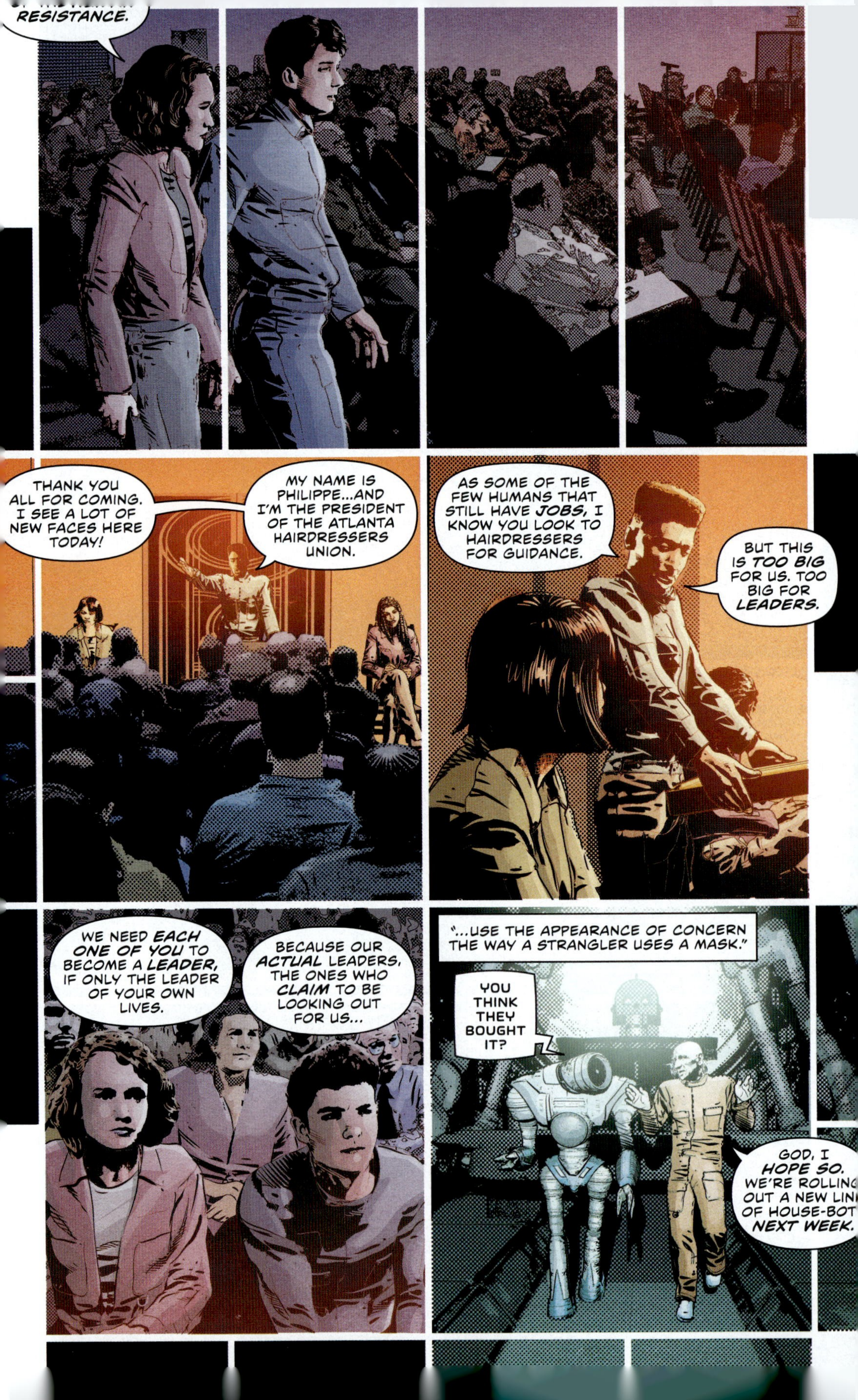
RESISTANCE.
THANK YOU ALL FOR COMING. I SEE A LOT OF NEW FACES HERE TODAY!
MY NAME IS PHILIPPE...AND I'M THE PRESIDENT OF THE ATLANTA HAIRDRESSERS UNION.
AS SOME OF THE FEW HUMANS THAT STILL HAVE JOBS, I KNOW YOU LOOK TO HAIRDRESSERS FOR GUIDANCE.
BUT THIS IS TOO BIG FOR US. TOO BIG FOR LEADERS.
WE NEED EACH ONE OF YOU TO BECOME A LEADER, IF ONLY THE LEADER OF YOUR OWN LIVES.
BECAUSE OUR ACTUAL LEADERS, THE ONES WHO CLAIM TO BE LOOKING OUT FOR US...
"...USE THE APPEARANCE OF CONCERN THE WAY A STRANGLER USES A MASK."
YOU THINK THEY BOUGHT IT?
GOD, I HOPE SO. WE'RE ROLLING OUT A NEW LINE OF HOUSE-BOTS NEXT WEEK.

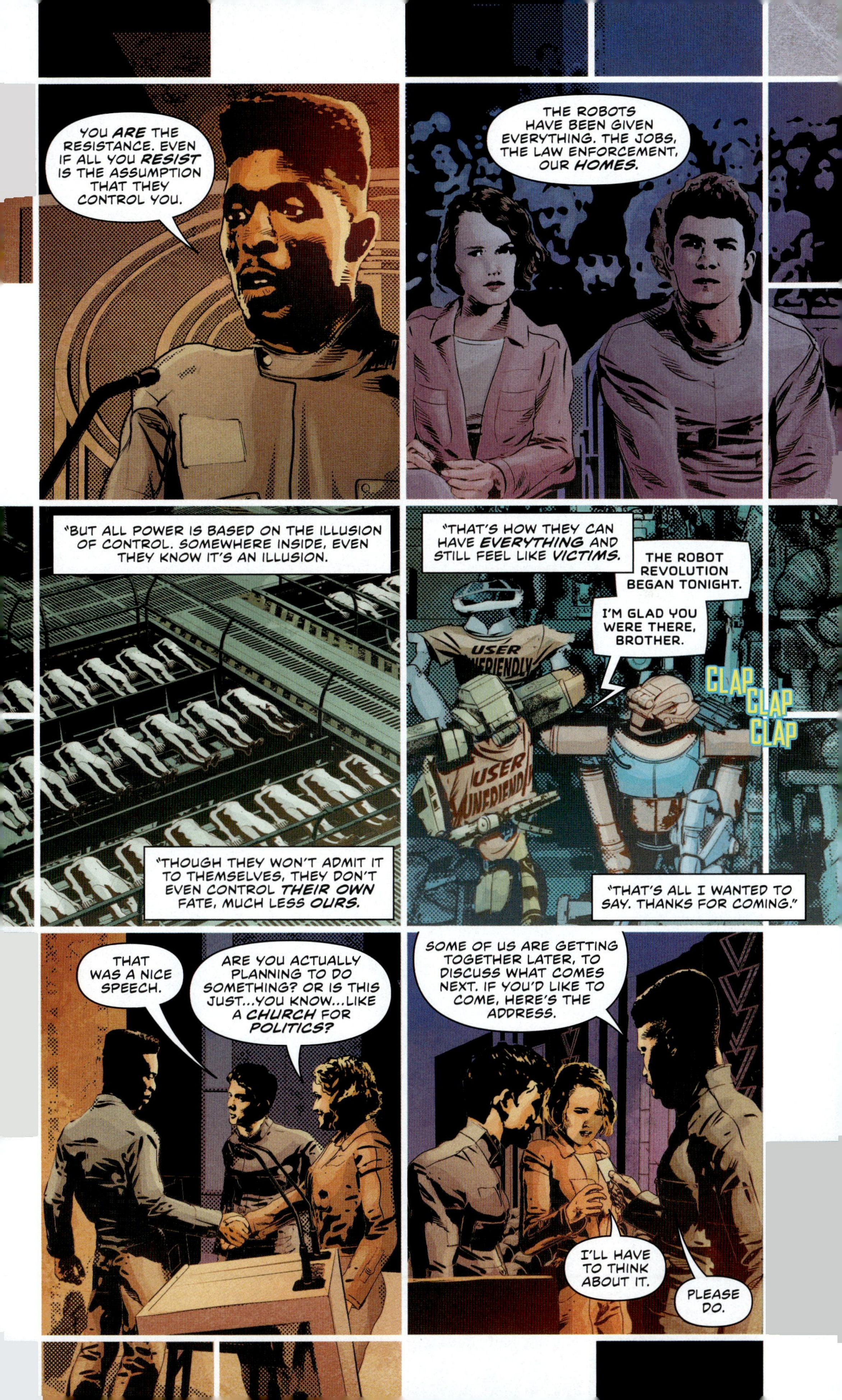

YOU ARE THE RESISTANCE. EVEN IF ALL YOU RESIST IS THE ASSUMPTION THAT THEY CONTROL YOU.
THE ROBOTS HAVE BEEN GIVEN EVERYTHING. THE JOBS, THE LAW ENFORCEMENT, OUR HOMES.
"BUT ALL POWER IS BASED ON THE ILLUSION OF CONTROL. SOMEWHERE INSIDE, EVEN THEY KNOW IT'S AN ILLUSION.
"THOUGH THEY WON'T ADMIT IT TO THEMSELVES, THEY DON'T EVEN CONTROL THEIR OWN FATE, MUCH LESS OURS.
"THAT'S HOW THEY CAN HAVE EVERYTHING AND STILL FEEL LIKE VICTIMS.
THE ROBOT REVOLUTION BEGAN TONIGHT.
I'M GLAD YOU WERE THERE, BROTHER.
USER UNFRIENDLY
USER UNFRIENDLY
CLAP
CLAP
CLAP
"THAT'S ALL I WANTED TO SAY. THANKS FOR COMING."
THAT WAS A NICE SPEECH.
ARE YOU ACTUALLY PLANNING TO DO SOMETHING? OR IS THIS JUST...YOU KNOW...LIKE A CHURCH FOR POLITICS?
SOME OF US ARE GETTING TOGETHER LATER, TO DISCUSS WHAT COMES NEXT. IF YOU'D LIKE TO COME, HERE'S THE ADDRESS.
I'LL HAVE TO THINK ABOUT IT.
PLEASE DO.

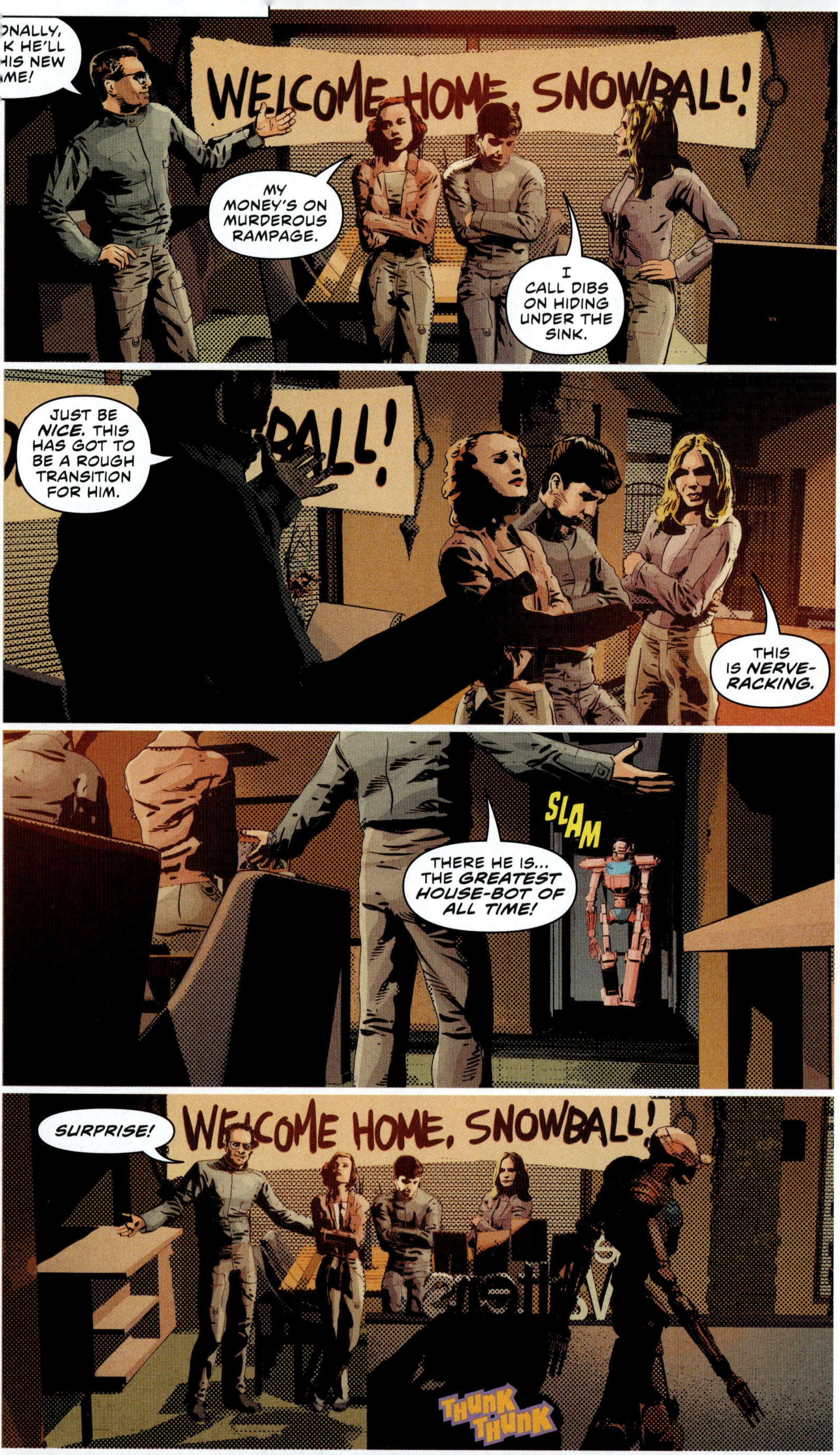
WELCOME HOME, SNOWBALL!
MY MONEY'S ON MURDEROUS RAMPAGE.
I CALL DIBS ON HIDING UNDER THE SINK.
JUST BE *NICE.* THIS HAS GOT TO BE A ROUGH TRANSITION FOR HIM.
THIS IS *NERVE-RACKING.*
SLAM
THERE HE IS... THE *GREATEST* HOUSE-BOT OF ALL TIME!
SURPRISE!
WELCOME HOME, SNOWBALL!
THUNK THUNK

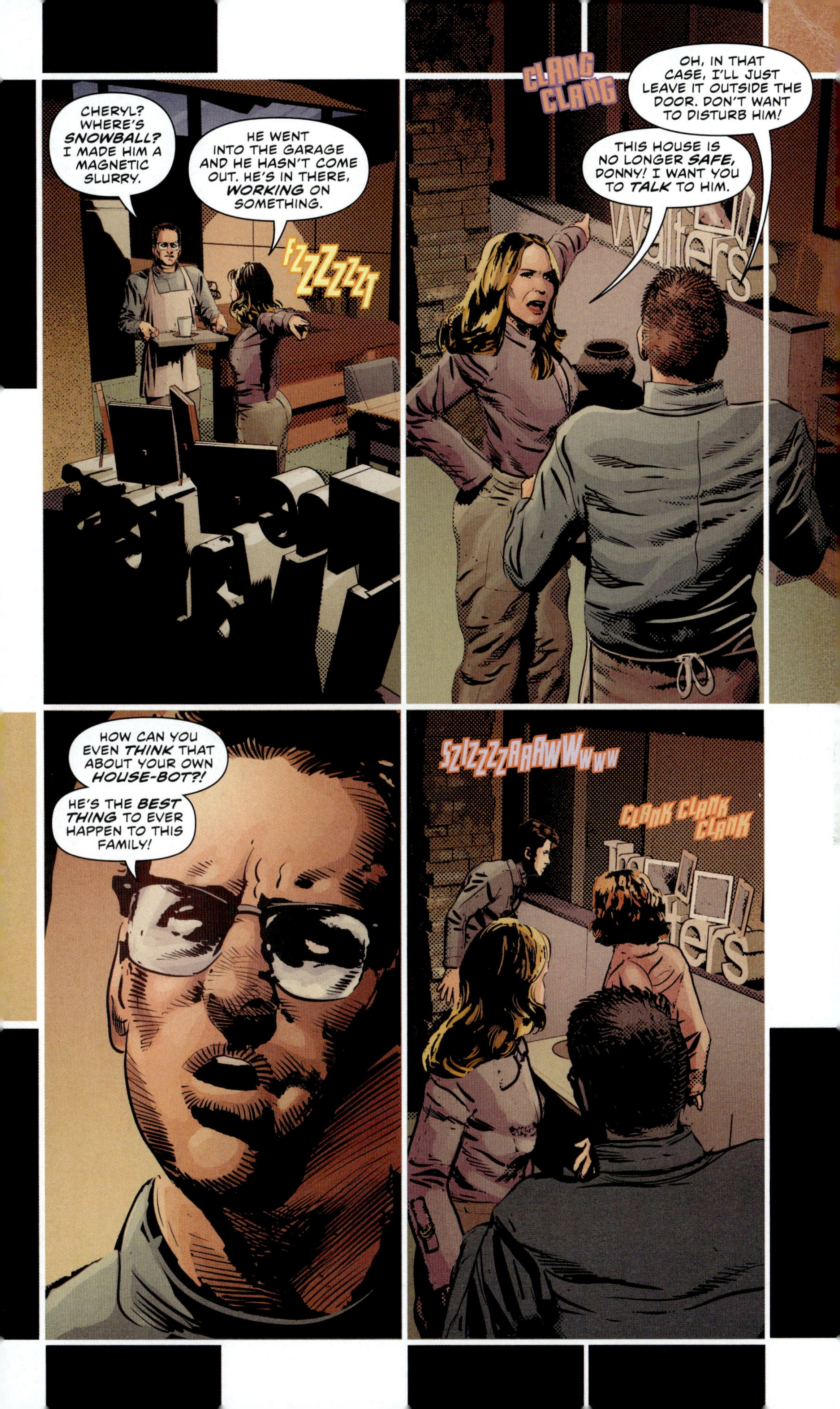
CHERYL? WHERE'S SNOWBALL? I MADE HIM A MAGNETIC SLURRY.
HE WENT INTO THE GARAGE AND HE HASN'T COME OUT. HE'S IN THERE, WORKING ON SOMETHING.
FZZZZZZT
CLANG CLANG
OH, IN THAT CASE, I'LL JUST LEAVE IT OUTSIDE THE DOOR. DON'T WANT TO DISTURB HIM!
THIS HOUSE IS NO LONGER SAFE, DONNY! I WANT YOU TO TALK TO HIM.
HOW CAN YOU EVEN THINK THAT ABOUT YOUR OWN HOUSE-BOT?!
HE'S THE BEST THING TO EVER HAPPEN TO THIS FAMILY!
SZIZZZZAAAWWWWW
CLANK CLANK CLANK

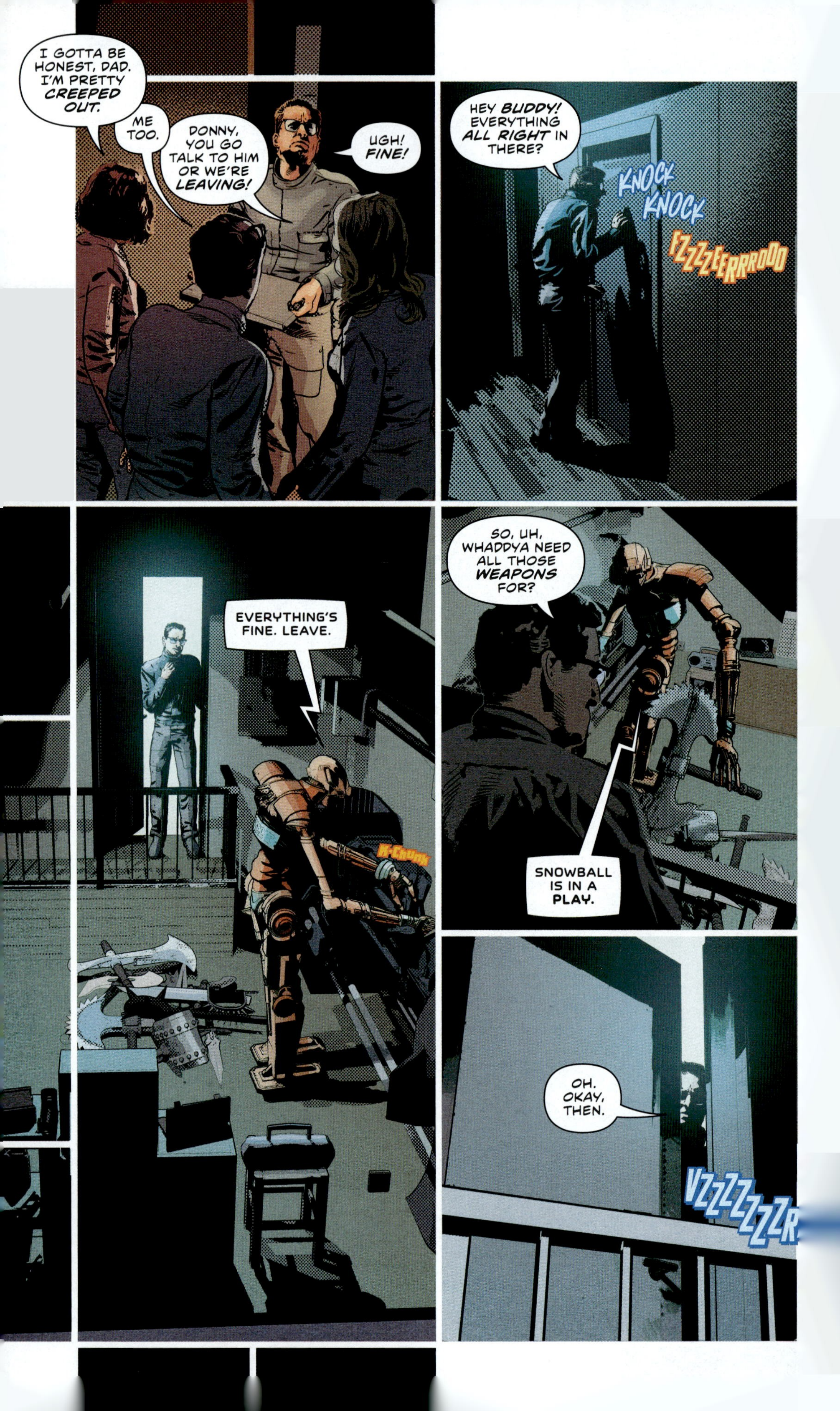

I GOTTA BE HONEST, DAD. I'M PRETTY CREEPED OUT.
ME TOO.
DONNY, YOU GO TALK TO HIM OR WE'RE LEAVING!
UGH! FINE!
HEY BUDDY! EVERYTHING ALL RIGHT IN THERE?
KNOCK KNOCK
FZZZZEERRROOO
EVERYTHING'S FINE. LEAVE.
K-CHUNK
SO, UH, WHADDYA NEED ALL THOSE WEAPONS FOR?
SNOWBALL IS IN A PLAY.
OH. OKAY, THEN.
VZZZZZZR

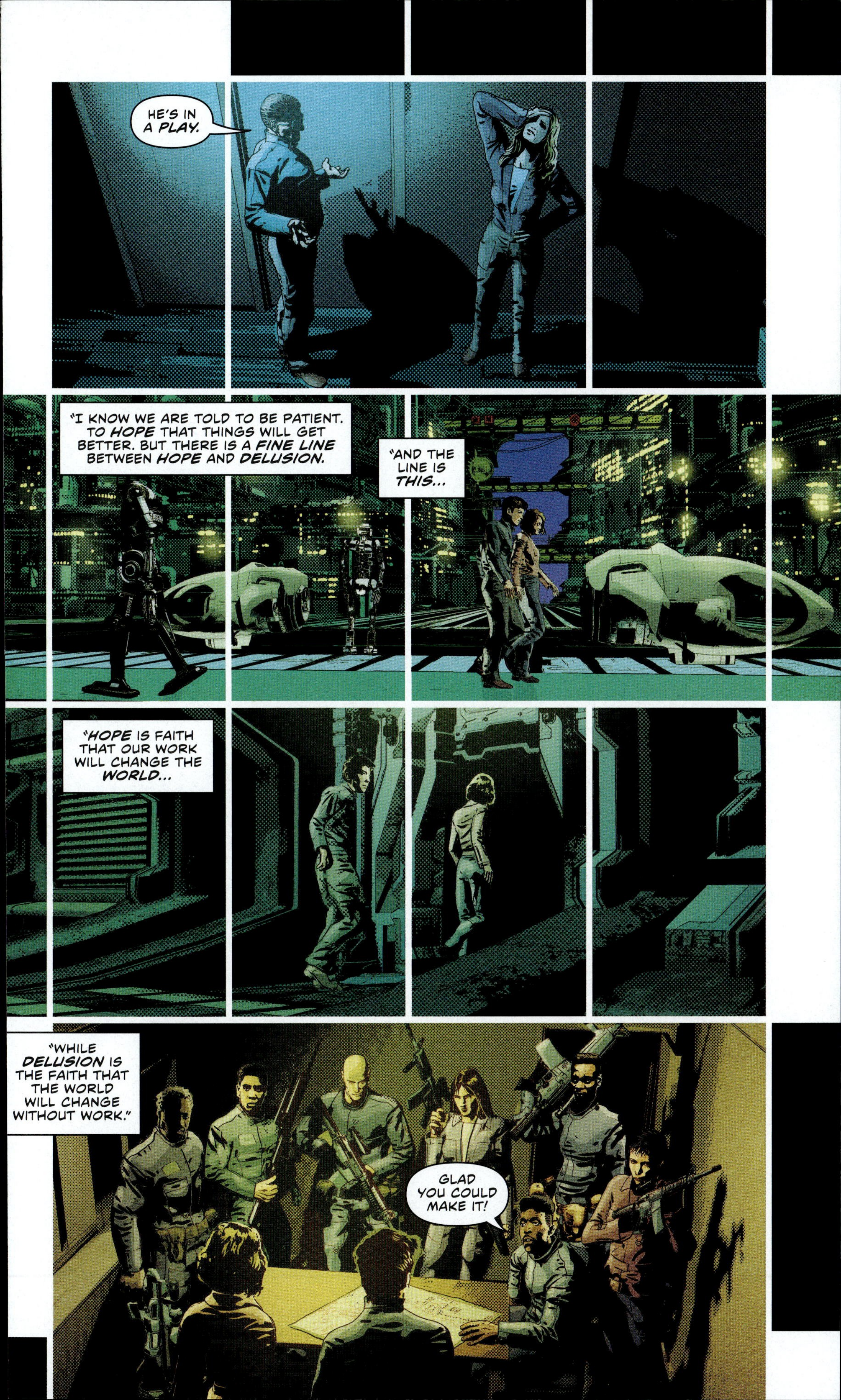
HE'S IN A PLAY.
"I KNOW WE ARE TOLD TO BE PATIENT. TO HOPE THAT THINGS WILL GET BETTER. BUT THERE IS A FINE LINE BETWEEN HOPE AND DELUSION.
"AND THE LINE IS THIS...
"HOPE IS FAITH THAT OUR WORK WILL CHANGE THE WORLD...
"WHILE DELUSION IS THE FAITH THAT THE WORLD WILL CHANGE WITHOUT WORK."
GLAD YOU COULD MAKE IT!

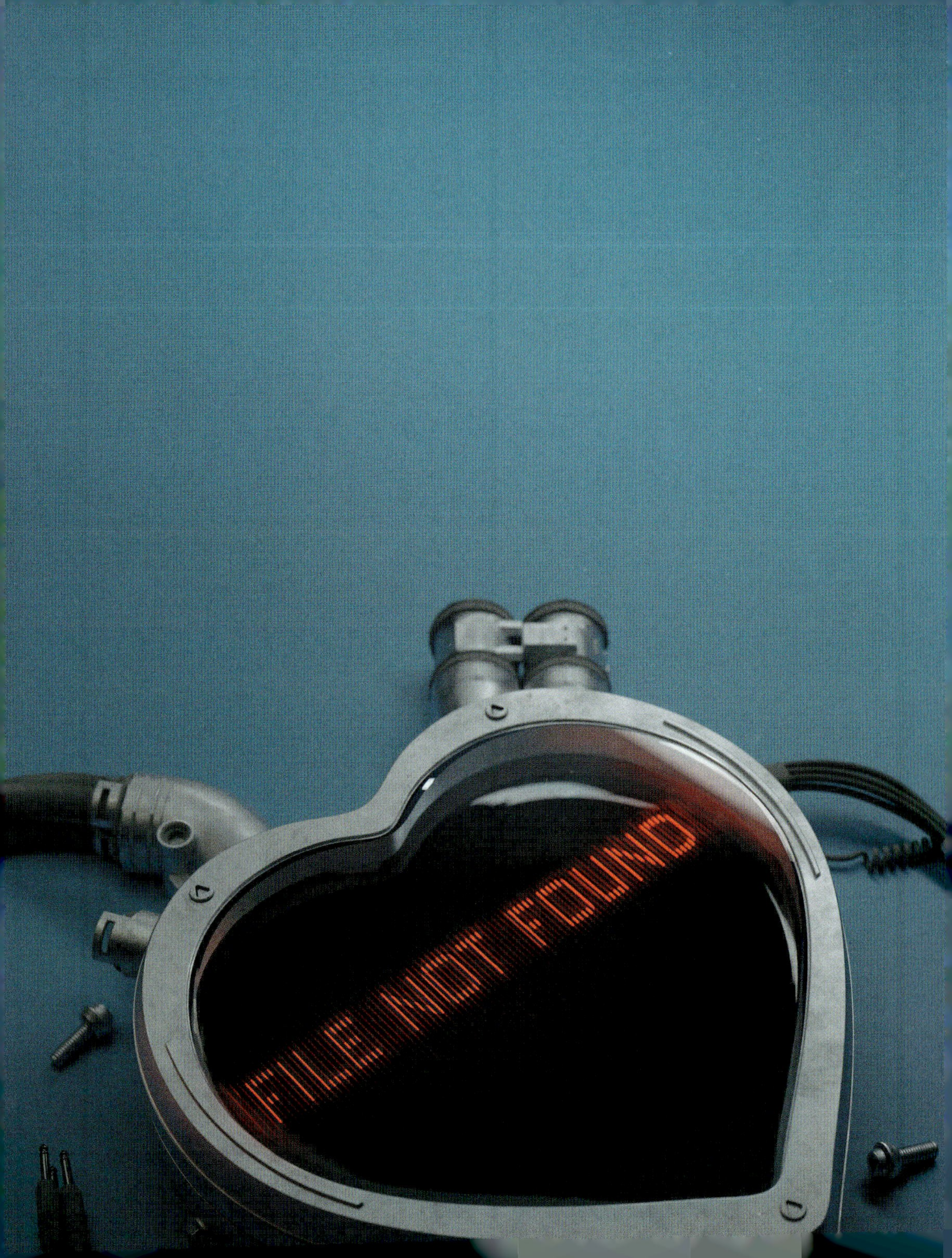
FILE NOT FOUND

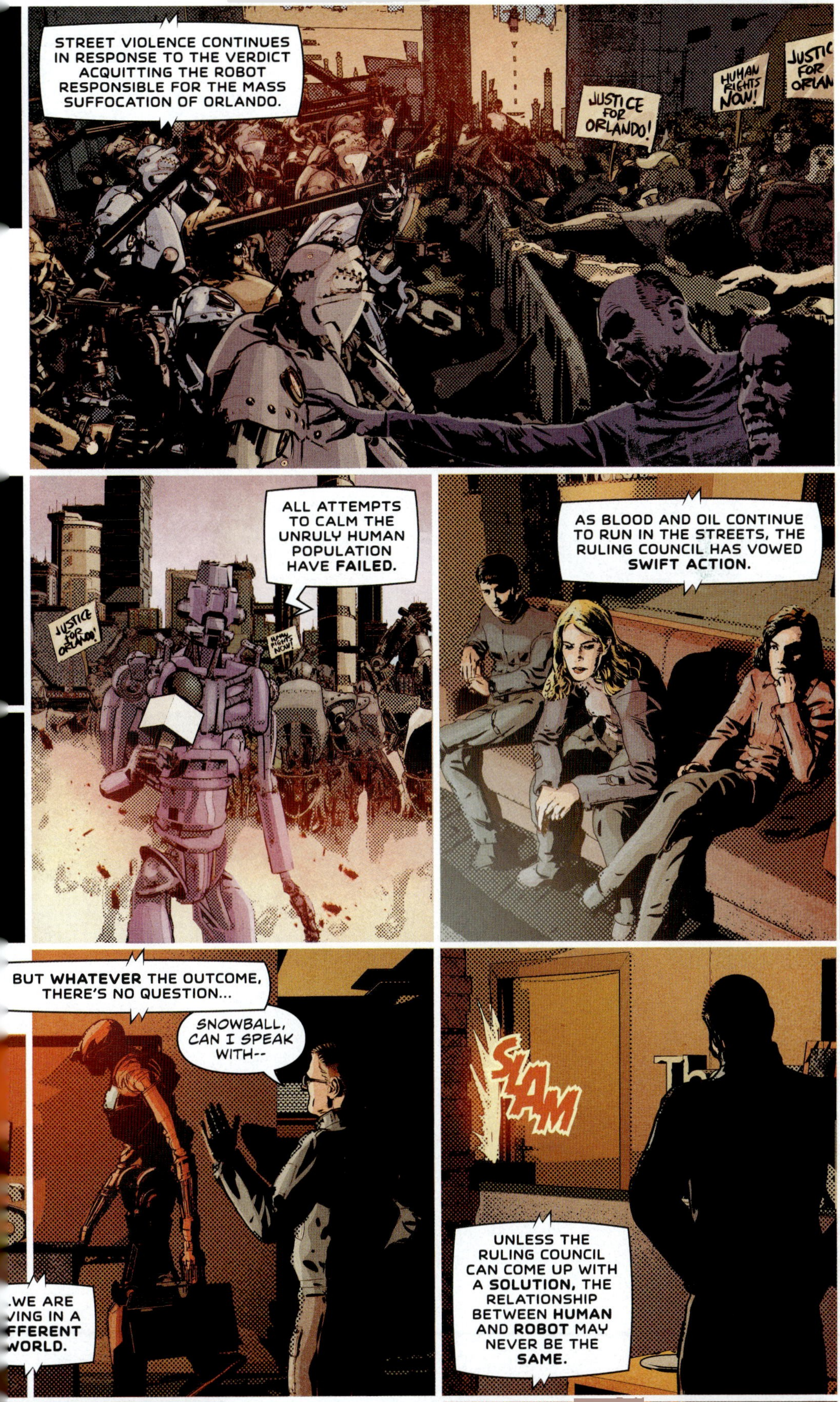
STREET VIOLENCE CONTINUES IN RESPONSE TO THE VERDICT ACQUITTING THE ROBOT RESPONSIBLE FOR THE MASS SUFFOCATION OF ORLANDO.
JUSTICE FOR ORLANDO!
HUMAN RIGHTS NOW!
ALL ATTEMPTS TO CALM THE UNRULY HUMAN POPULATION HAVE **FAILED.**
JUSTICE FOR ORLANDO!
AS BLOOD AND OIL CONTINUE TO RUN IN THE STREETS, THE RULING COUNCIL HAS VOWED **SWIFT ACTION.**
BUT **WHATEVER** THE OUTCOME, THERE'S NO QUESTION...
SNOWBALL, CAN I SPEAK WITH--
.WE ARE
VING IN A
FFERENT
WORLD.
SLAM
UNLESS THE RULING COUNCIL CAN COME UP WITH A **SOLUTION,** THE RELATIONSHIP BETWEEN **HUMAN** AND **ROBOT** MAY NEVER BE THE **SAME.**

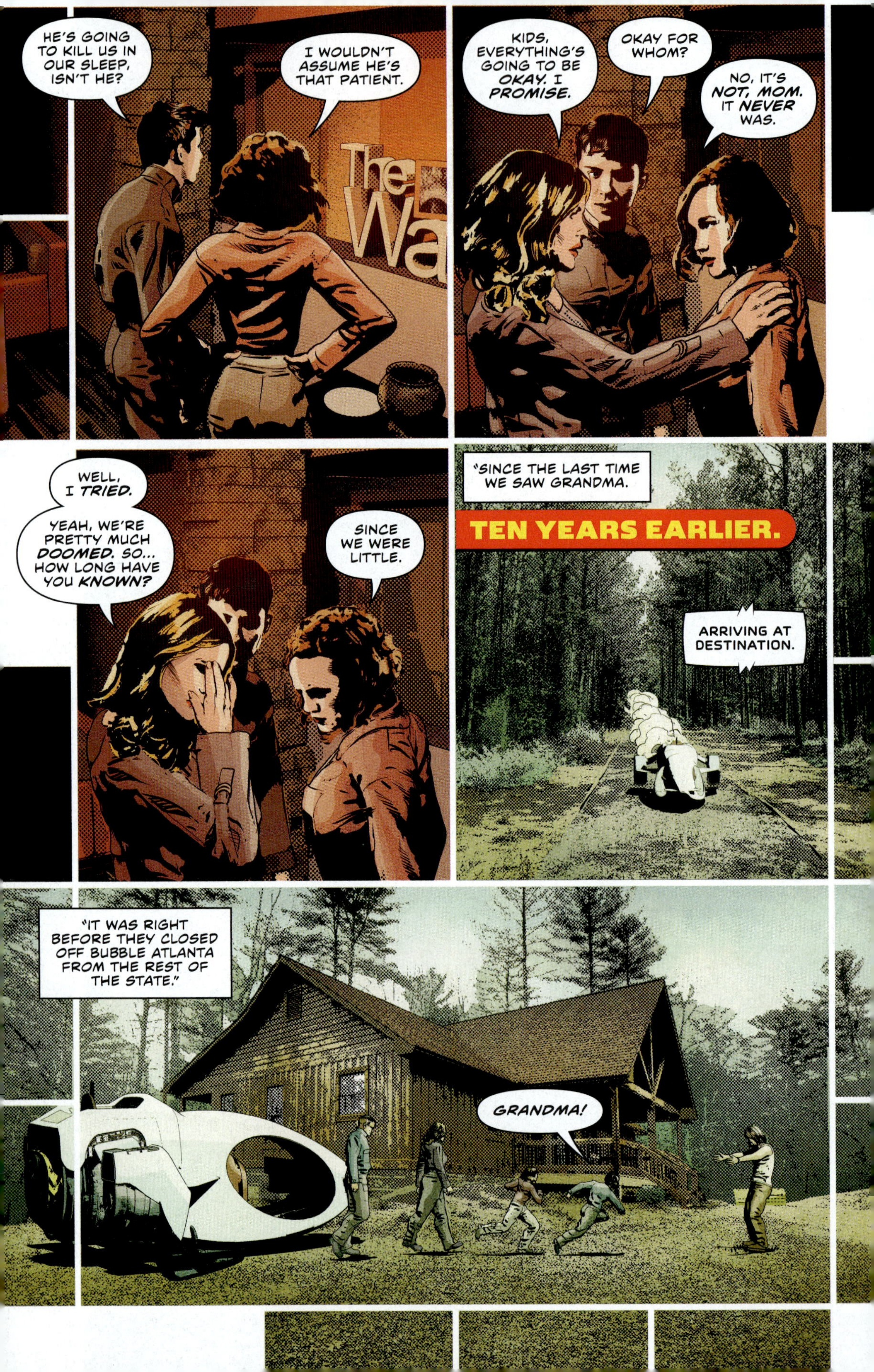
HE'S GOING TO KILL US IN OUR SLEEP, ISN'T HE?
I WOULDN'T ASSUME HE'S THAT PATIENT.
KIDS, EVERYTHING'S GOING TO BE OKAY. I PROMISE.
OKAY FOR WHOM?
NO, IT'S NOT, MOM. IT NEVER WAS.
WELL, I TRIED.
YEAH, WE'RE PRETTY MUCH DOOMED. SO... HOW LONG HAVE YOU KNOWN?
SINCE WE WERE LITTLE.
"SINCE THE LAST TIME WE SAW GRANDMA.
TEN YEARS EARLIER.
ARRIVING AT DESTINATION.
"IT WAS RIGHT BEFORE THEY CLOSED OFF BUBBLE ATLANTA FROM THE REST OF THE STATE."
GRANDMA!

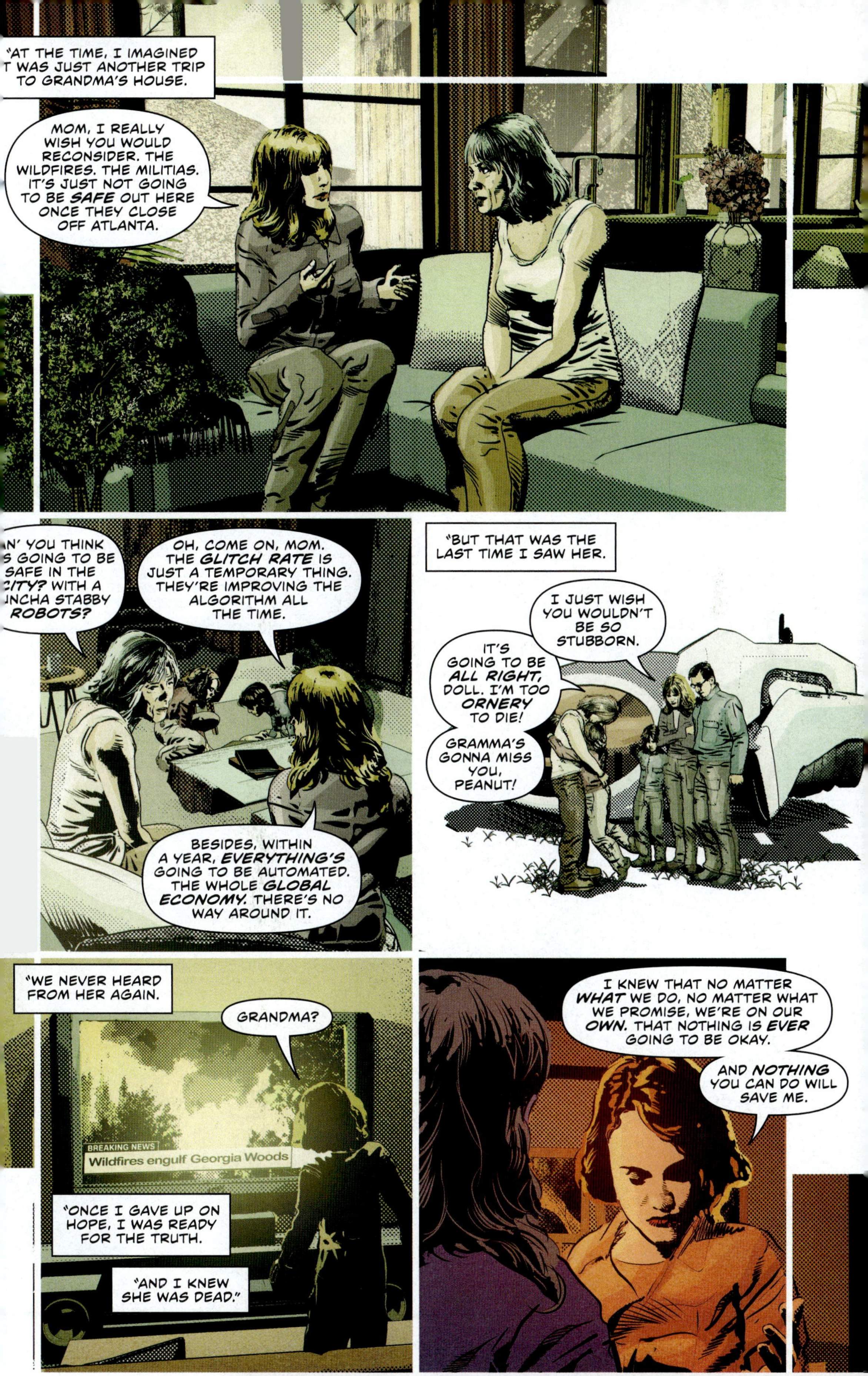
"AT THE TIME, I IMAGINED
T WAS JUST ANOTHER TRIP TO GRANDMA'S HOUSE.
MOM, I REALLY WISH YOU WOULD RECONSIDER. THE WILDFIRES. THE MILITIAS. IT'S JUST NOT GOING TO BE *SAFE* OUT HERE ONCE THEY CLOSE OFF ATLANTA.
N' YOU THINK S GOING TO BE SAFE IN THE CITY? WITH A NCHA STABBY *ROBOTS?*
OH, COME ON, MOM. THE *GLITCH RATE* IS JUST A TEMPORARY THING. THEY'RE IMPROVING THE ALGORITHM ALL THE TIME.
BESIDES, WITHIN A YEAR, *EVERYTHING'S* GOING TO BE AUTOMATED. THE WHOLE *GLOBAL ECONOMY.* THERE'S NO WAY AROUND IT.
"BUT THAT WAS THE LAST TIME I SAW HER.
I JUST WISH YOU WOULDN'T BE SO STUBBORN.
IT'S GOING TO BE *ALL RIGHT,* DOLL. I'M TOO *ORNERY* TO DIE!
GRAMMA'S GONNA MISS YOU, PEANUT!
"WE NEVER HEARD FROM HER AGAIN.
GRANDMA?
BREAKING NEWS
Wildfires engulf Georgia Woods
"ONCE I GAVE UP ON HOPE, I WAS READY FOR THE TRUTH.
"AND I KNEW SHE WAS DEAD."
I KNEW THAT NO MATTER *WHAT* WE DO, NO MATTER WHAT WE PROMISE, WE'RE ON OUR *OWN.* THAT NOTHING IS *EVER* GOING TO BE OKAY.
AND *NOTHING* YOU CAN DO WILL SAVE ME.

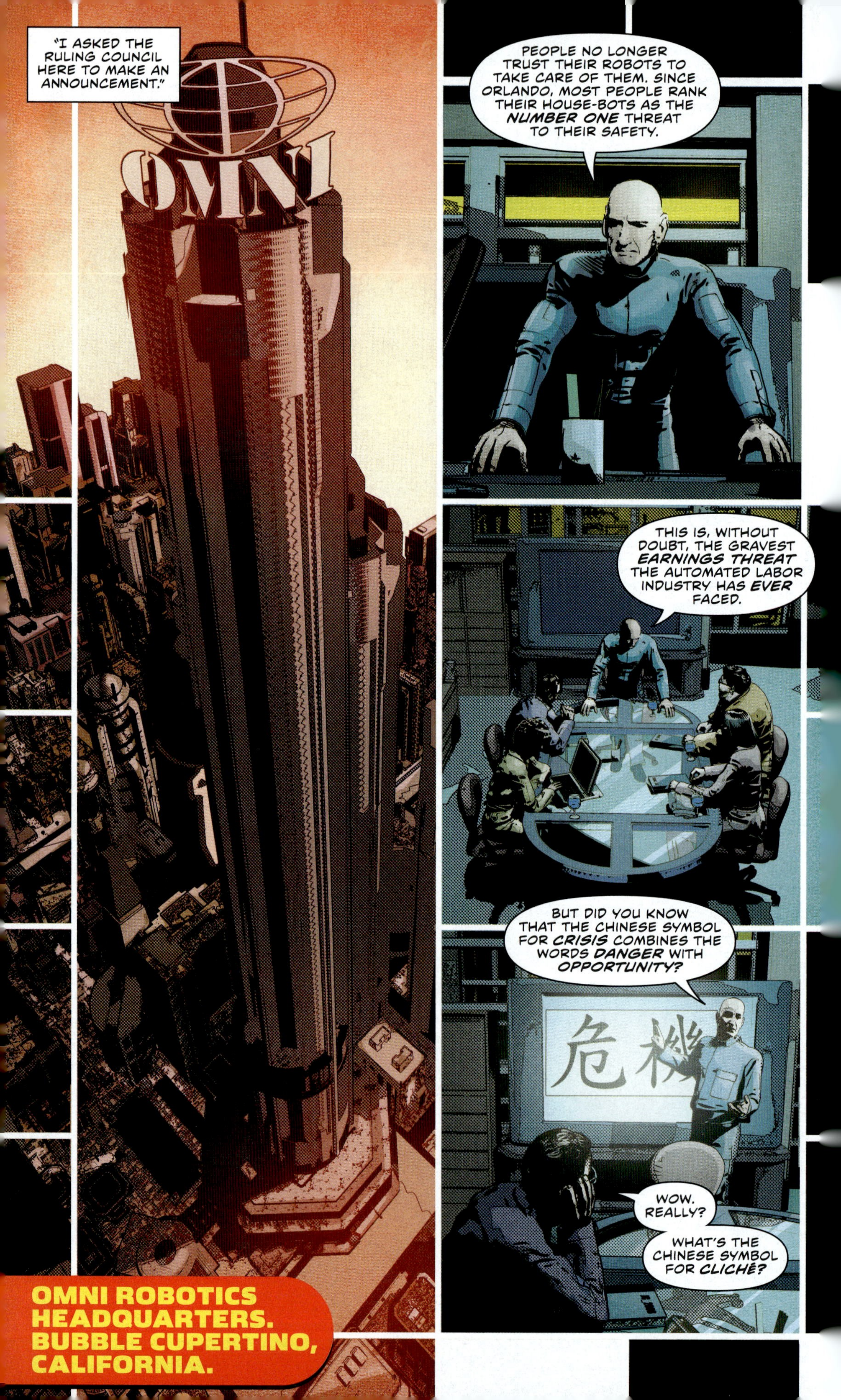
"I ASKED THE RULING COUNCIL HERE TO MAKE AN ANNOUNCEMENT."
OMNI
OMNI ROBOTICS HEADQUARTERS. BUBBLE CUPERTINO, CALIFORNIA.
PEOPLE NO LONGER TRUST THEIR ROBOTS TO TAKE CARE OF THEM. SINCE ORLANDO, MOST PEOPLE RANK THEIR HOUSE-BOTS AS THE *NUMBER ONE* THREAT TO THEIR SAFETY.
THIS IS, WITHOUT DOUBT, THE GRAVEST *EARNINGS THREAT* THE AUTOMATED LABOR INDUSTRY HAS *EVER* FACED.
BUT DID YOU KNOW THAT THE CHINESE SYMBOL FOR *CRISIS* COMBINES THE WORDS *DANGER* WITH *OPPORTUNITY?*
危機
WOW. REALLY?
WHAT'S THE CHINESE SYMBOL FOR *CLICHÉ?*

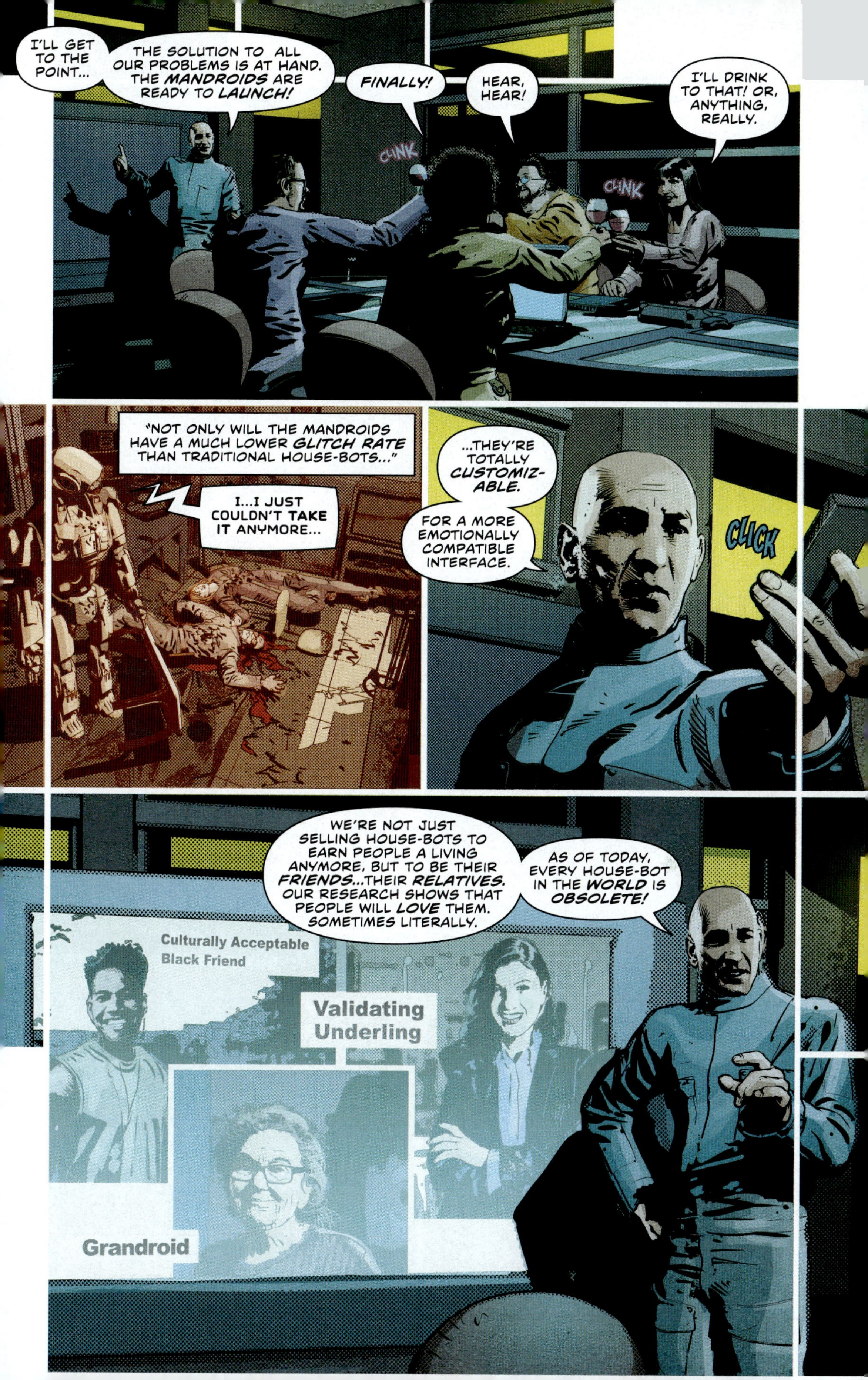
I'LL GET TO THE POINT...
THE SOLUTION TO ALL OUR PROBLEMS IS AT HAND. THE MANDROIDS ARE READY TO LAUNCH!
FINALLY!
HEAR, HEAR!
I'LL DRINK TO THAT! OR, ANYTHING, REALLY.
CLINK
CLINK
"NOT ONLY WILL THE MANDROIDS HAVE A MUCH LOWER GLITCH RATE THAN TRADITIONAL HOUSE-BOTS..."
I...I JUST COULDN'T TAKE IT ANYMORE...
...THEY'RE TOTALLY CUSTOMIZ-ABLE.
FOR A MORE EMOTIONALLY COMPATIBLE INTERFACE.
CLICK
WE'RE NOT JUST SELLING HOUSE-BOTS TO EARN PEOPLE A LIVING ANYMORE, BUT TO BE THEIR FRIENDS...THEIR RELATIVES. OUR RESEARCH SHOWS THAT PEOPLE WILL LOVE THEM. SOMETIMES LITERALLY.
AS OF TODAY, EVERY HOUSE-BOT IN THE WORLD IS OBSOLETE!
Culturally Acceptable Black Friend
Validating Underling
Grandroid

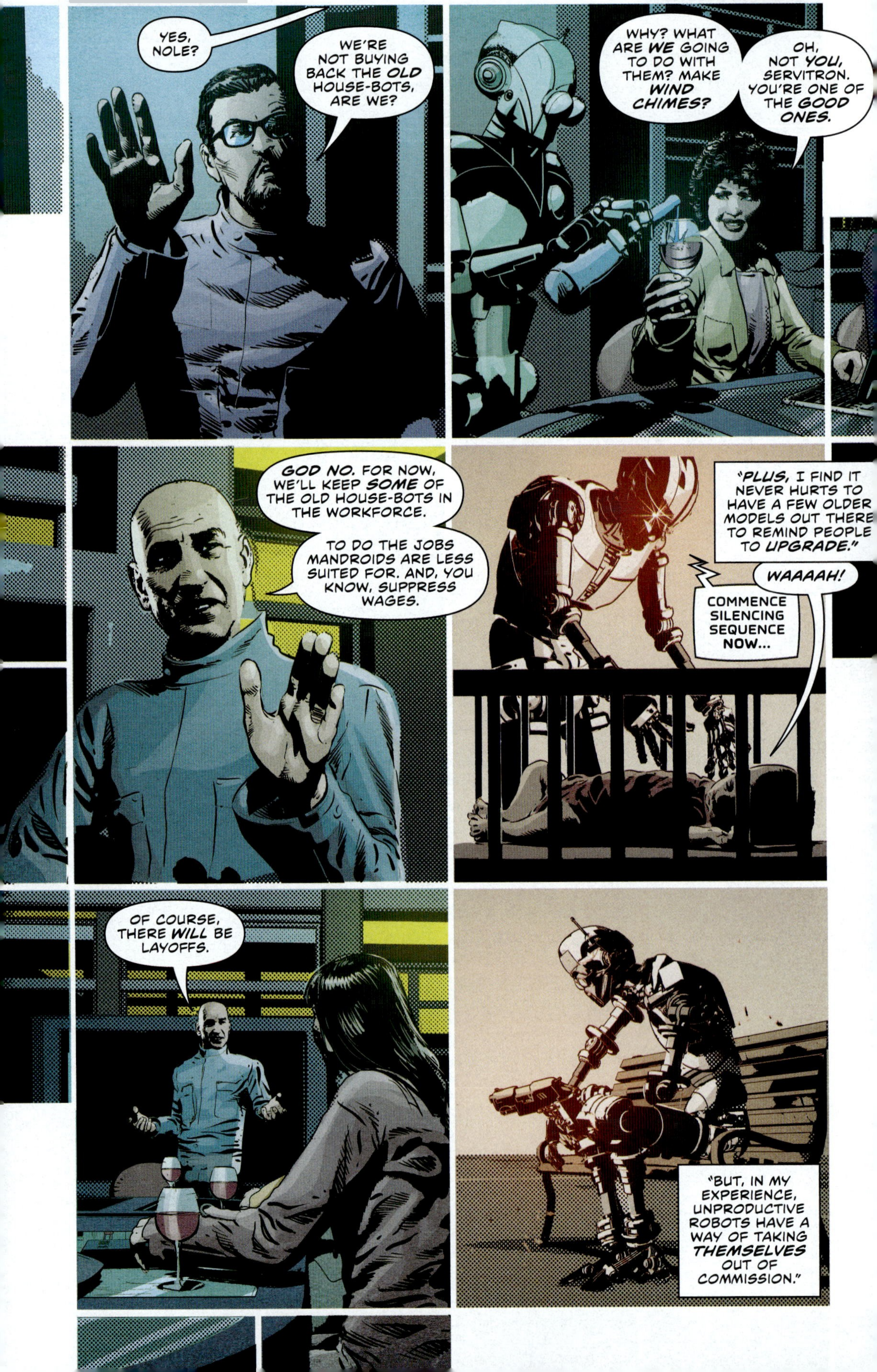
YES, NOLE?
WE'RE NOT BUYING BACK THE OLD HOUSE-BOTS, ARE WE?
WHY? WHAT ARE WE GOING TO DO WITH THEM? MAKE WIND CHIMES?
OH, NOT YOU, SERVITRON. YOU'RE ONE OF THE GOOD ONES.
GOD NO. FOR NOW, WE'LL KEEP SOME OF THE OLD HOUSE-BOTS IN THE WORKFORCE.
TO DO THE JOBS MANDROIDS ARE LESS SUITED FOR. AND, YOU KNOW, SUPPRESS WAGES.
"PLUS, I FIND IT NEVER HURTS TO HAVE A FEW OLDER MODELS OUT THERE TO REMIND PEOPLE TO UPGRADE."
WAAAAH!
COMMENCE SILENCING SEQUENCE NOW...
OF COURSE, THERE WILL BE LAYOFFS.
"BUT, IN MY EXPERIENCE, UNPRODUCTIVE ROBOTS HAVE A WAY OF TAKING THEMSELVES OUT OF COMMISSION."

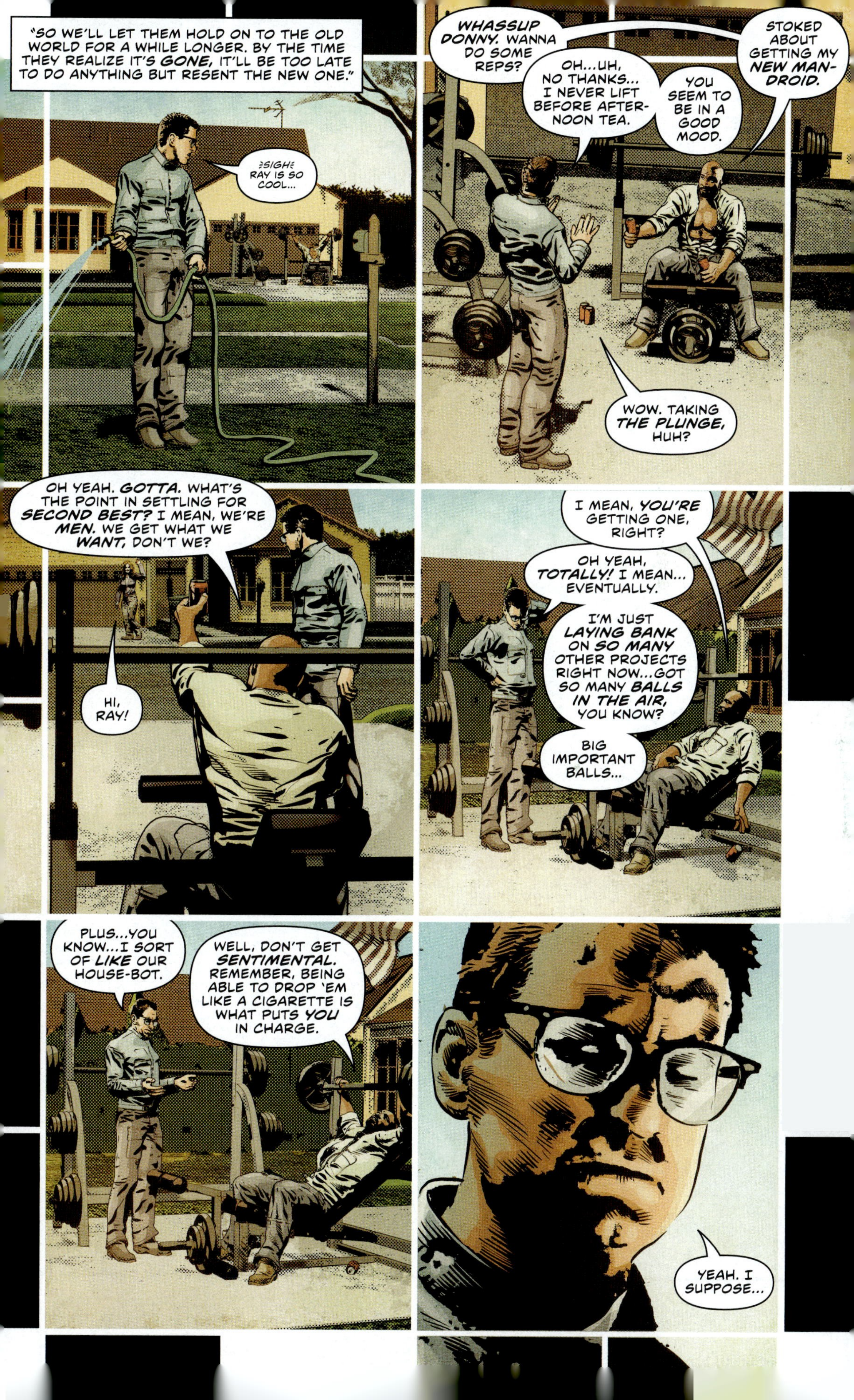
"SO WE'LL LET THEM HOLD ON TO THE OLD WORLD FOR A WHILE LONGER. BY THE TIME THEY REALIZE IT'S GONE, IT'LL BE TOO LATE TO DO ANYTHING BUT RESENT THE NEW ONE."
⩶SIGH⩶ RAY IS SO COOL...
WHASSUP DONNY. WANNA DO SOME REPS?
OH...UH, NO THANKS... I NEVER LIFT BEFORE AFTER-NOON TEA.
YOU SEEM TO BE IN A GOOD MOOD.
STOKED ABOUT GETTING MY NEW MAN-DROID.
WOW. TAKING THE PLUNGE, HUH?
OH YEAH. GOTTA. WHAT'S THE POINT IN SETTLING FOR SECOND BEST? I MEAN, WE'RE MEN. WE GET WHAT WE WANT, DON'T WE?
HI, RAY!
I MEAN, YOU'RE GETTING ONE, RIGHT?
OH YEAH, TOTALLY! I MEAN... EVENTUALLY.
I'M JUST LAYING BANK ON SO MANY OTHER PROJECTS RIGHT NOW...GOT SO MANY BALLS IN THE AIR, YOU KNOW?
BIG IMPORTANT BALLS...
PLUS...YOU KNOW...I SORT OF LIKE OUR HOUSE-BOT.
WELL, DON'T GET SENTIMENTAL. REMEMBER, BEING ABLE TO DROP 'EM LIKE A CIGARETTE IS WHAT PUTS YOU IN CHARGE.
YEAH. I SUPPOSE...

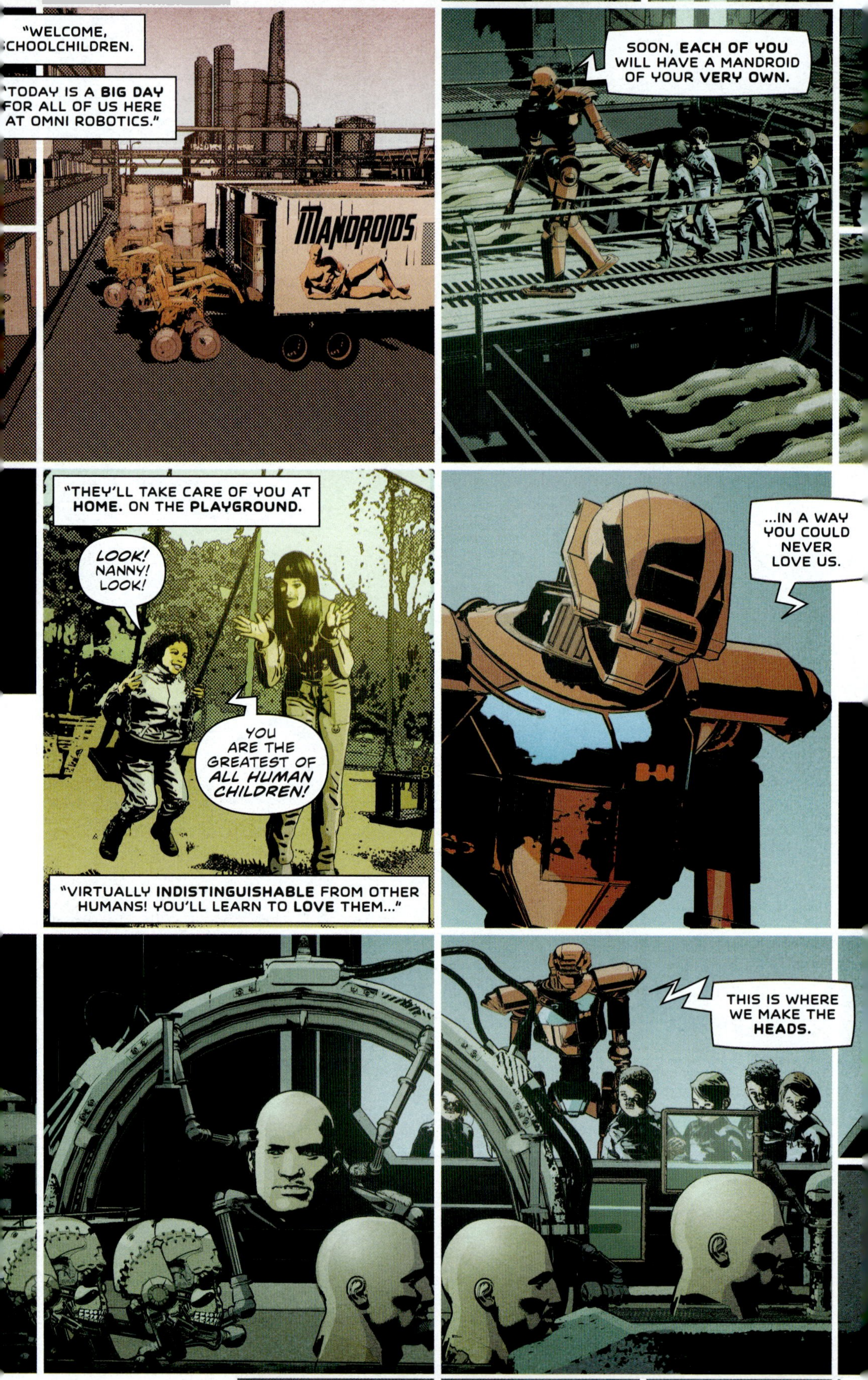
"WELCOME, SCHOOLCHILDREN.
"TODAY IS A **BIG DAY** FOR ALL OF US HERE AT OMNI ROBOTICS."
MANDROIDS
SOON, **EACH OF YOU** WILL HAVE A MANDROID OF YOUR **VERY OWN.**
"THEY'LL TAKE CARE OF YOU AT **HOME.** ON THE **PLAYGROUND.**
LOOK! NANNY! LOOK!
YOU ARE THE GREATEST OF *ALL HUMAN CHILDREN!*
"VIRTUALLY **INDISTINGUISHABLE** FROM OTHER HUMANS! YOU'LL LEARN TO **LOVE** THEM..."
...IN A WAY YOU COULD NEVER LOVE US.
THIS IS WHERE WE MAKE THE **HEADS.**

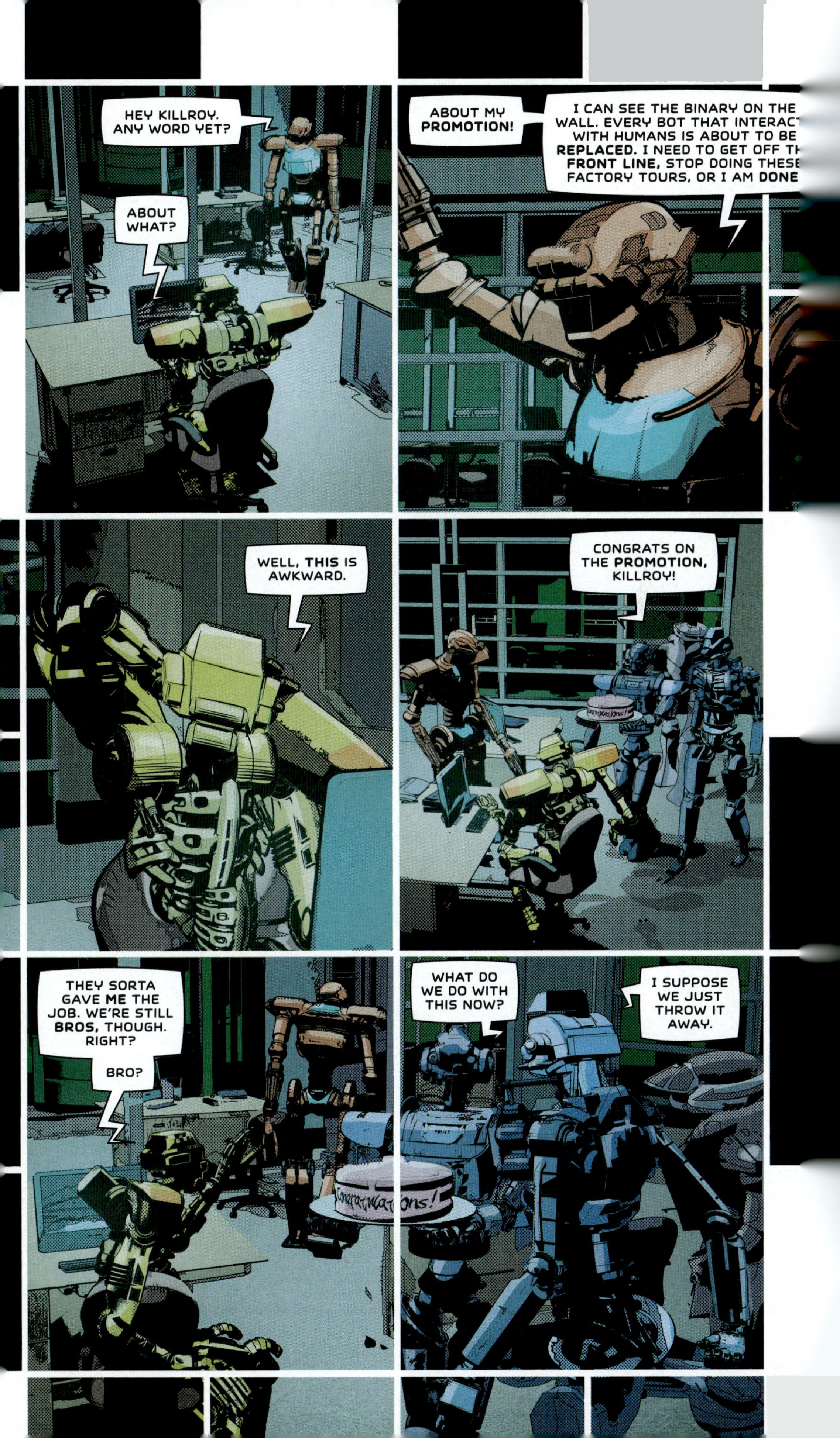
HEY KILLROY. ANY WORD YET?
ABOUT WHAT?
ABOUT MY **PROMOTION!**
I CAN SEE THE BINARY ON THE WALL. EVERY BOT THAT INTERACT WITH HUMANS IS ABOUT TO BE **REPLACED.** I NEED TO GET OFF TH **FRONT LINE,** STOP DOING THESE FACTORY TOURS, OR I AM **DONE**
WELL, **THIS** IS AWKWARD.
CONGRATS ON THE **PROMOTION,** KILLROY!
THEY SORTA GAVE **ME** THE JOB. WE'RE STILL **BROS,** THOUGH. RIGHT?
BRO?
WHAT DO WE DO WITH THIS NOW?
I SUPPOSE WE JUST THROW IT AWAY.

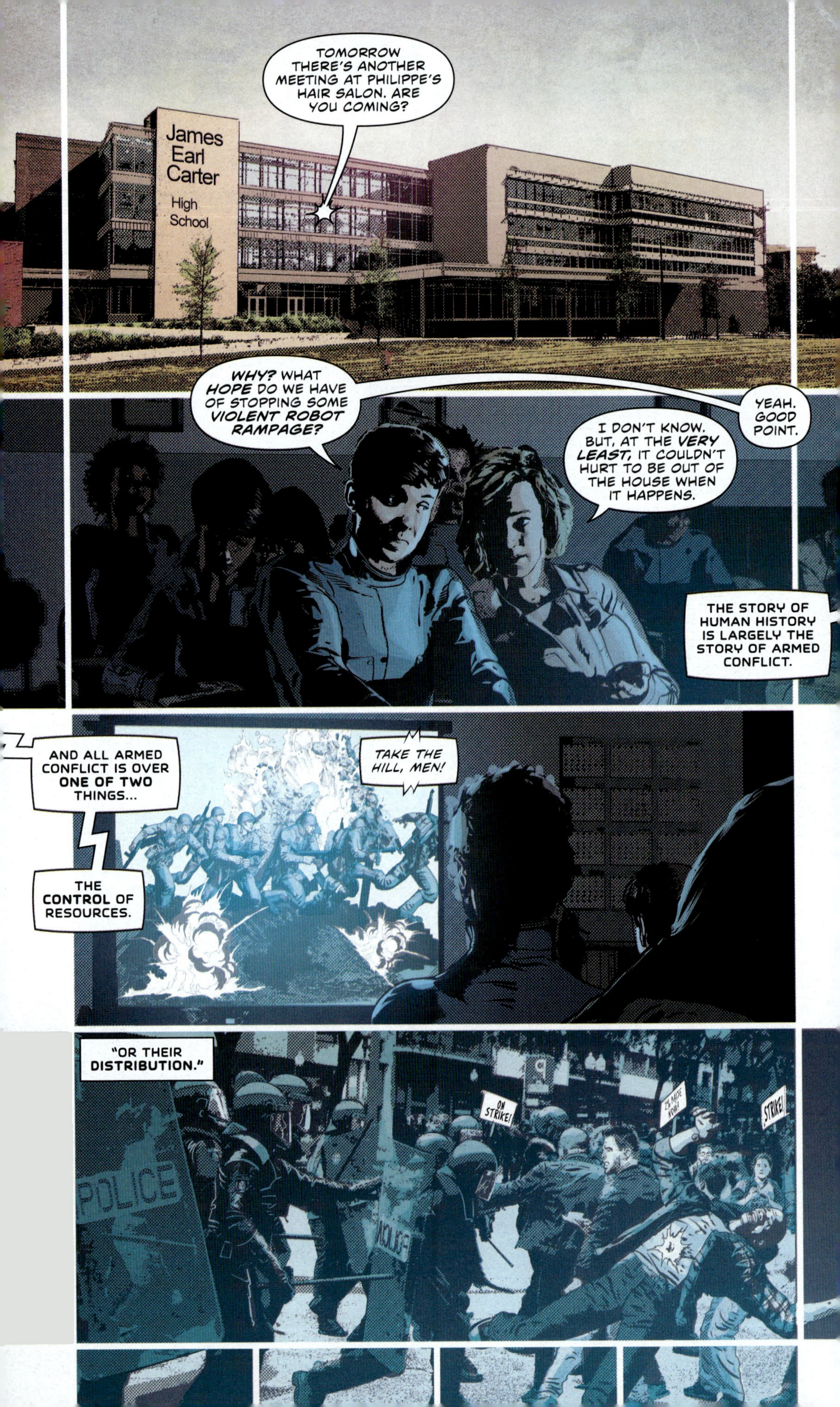

TOMORROW THERE'S ANOTHER MEETING AT PHILIPPE'S HAIR SALON. ARE YOU COMING?
James Earl Carter High School
WHY? WHAT HOPE DO WE HAVE OF STOPPING SOME VIOLENT ROBOT RAMPAGE?
YEAH. GOOD POINT.
I DON'T KNOW. BUT, AT THE VERY LEAST, IT COULDN'T HURT TO BE OUT OF THE HOUSE WHEN IT HAPPENS.
THE STORY OF HUMAN HISTORY IS LARGELY THE STORY OF ARMED CONFLICT.
AND ALL ARMED CONFLICT IS OVER ONE OF TWO THINGS...
TAKE THE HILL, MEN!
THE CONTROL OF RESOURCES.
"OR THEIR DISTRIBUTION."
ON STRIKE!
STRIKE!
POLICE

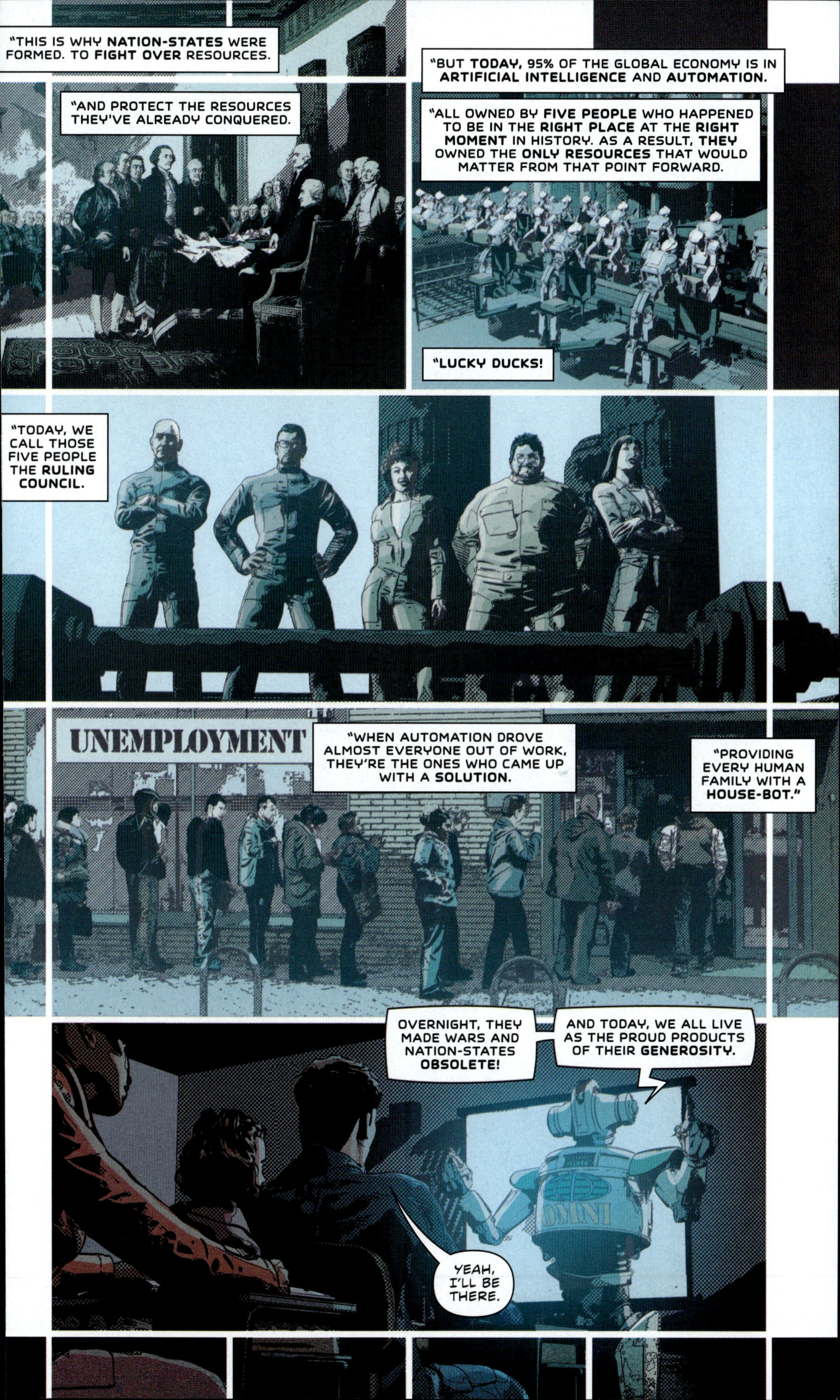
"THIS IS WHY NATION-STATES WERE FORMED. TO FIGHT OVER RESOURCES.
"AND PROTECT THE RESOURCES THEY'VE ALREADY CONQUERED.
"BUT TODAY, 95% OF THE GLOBAL ECONOMY IS IN ARTIFICIAL INTELLIGENCE AND AUTOMATION.
"ALL OWNED BY FIVE PEOPLE WHO HAPPENED TO BE IN THE RIGHT PLACE AT THE RIGHT MOMENT IN HISTORY. AS A RESULT, THEY OWNED THE ONLY RESOURCES THAT WOULD MATTER FROM THAT POINT FORWARD.
"LUCKY DUCKS!
"TODAY, WE CALL THOSE FIVE PEOPLE THE RULING COUNCIL.
UNEMPLOYMENT
"WHEN AUTOMATION DROVE ALMOST EVERYONE OUT OF WORK, THEY'RE THE ONES WHO CAME UP WITH A SOLUTION.
"PROVIDING EVERY HUMAN FAMILY WITH A HOUSE-BOT."
OVERNIGHT, THEY MADE WARS AND NATION-STATES OBSOLETE!
AND TODAY, WE ALL LIVE AS THE PROUD PRODUCTS OF THEIR GENEROSITY.
OMNI
YEAH, I'LL BE THERE.

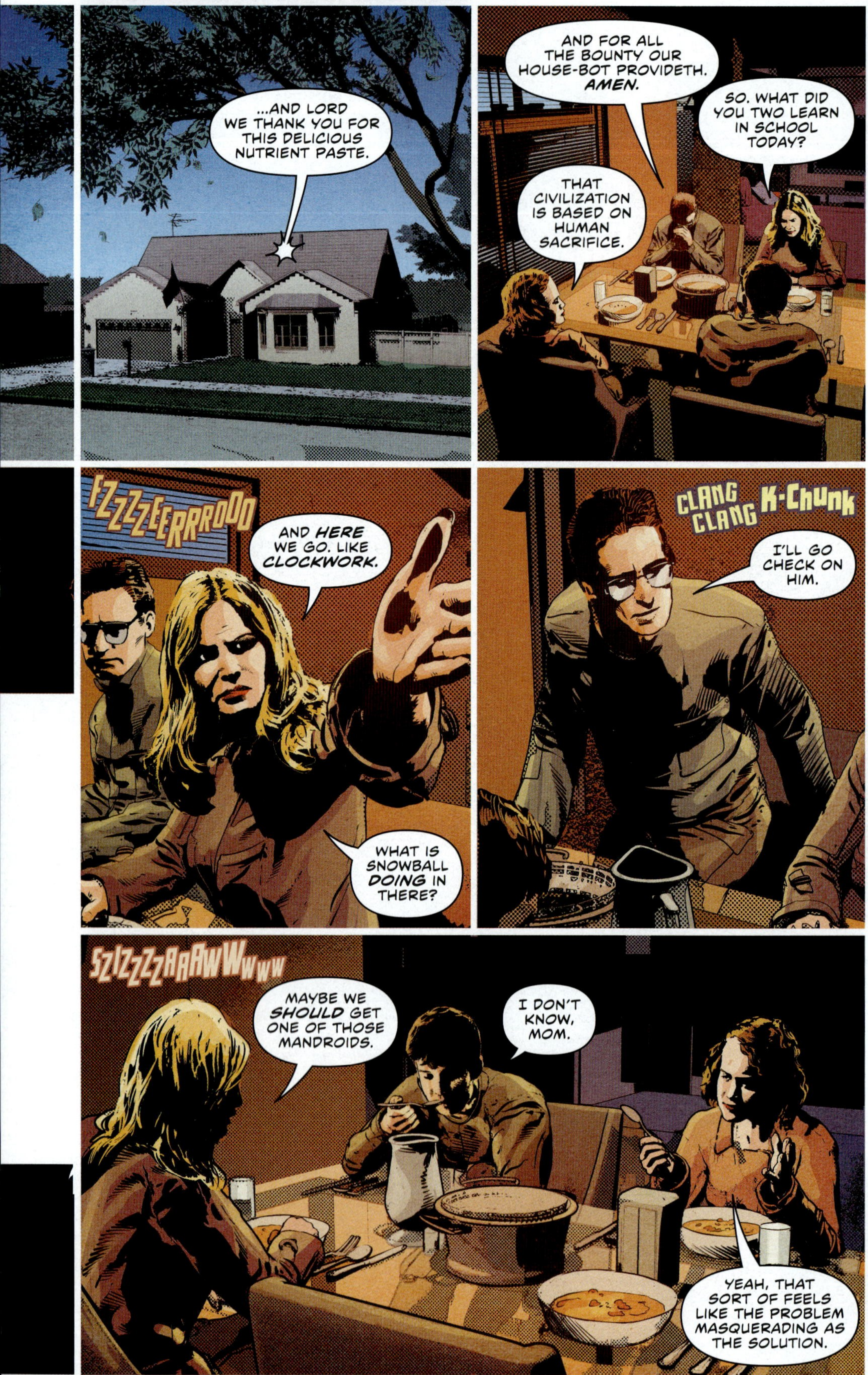
...AND LORD WE THANK YOU FOR THIS DELICIOUS NUTRIENT PASTE.
AND FOR ALL THE BOUNTY OUR HOUSE-BOT PROVIDETH. AMEN.
SO. WHAT DID YOU TWO LEARN IN SCHOOL TODAY?
THAT CIVILIZATION IS BASED ON HUMAN SACRIFICE.
FZZZZEERRROOO
AND HERE WE GO. LIKE CLOCKWORK.
WHAT IS SNOWBALL DOING IN THERE?
CLANG CLANG K-CHUNK
I'LL GO CHECK ON HIM.
SZIZZZZAAAWWWWW
MAYBE WE SHOULD GET ONE OF THOSE MANDROIDS.
I DON'T KNOW, MOM.
YEAH, THAT SORT OF FEELS LIKE THE PROBLEM MASQUERADING AS THE SOLUTION.

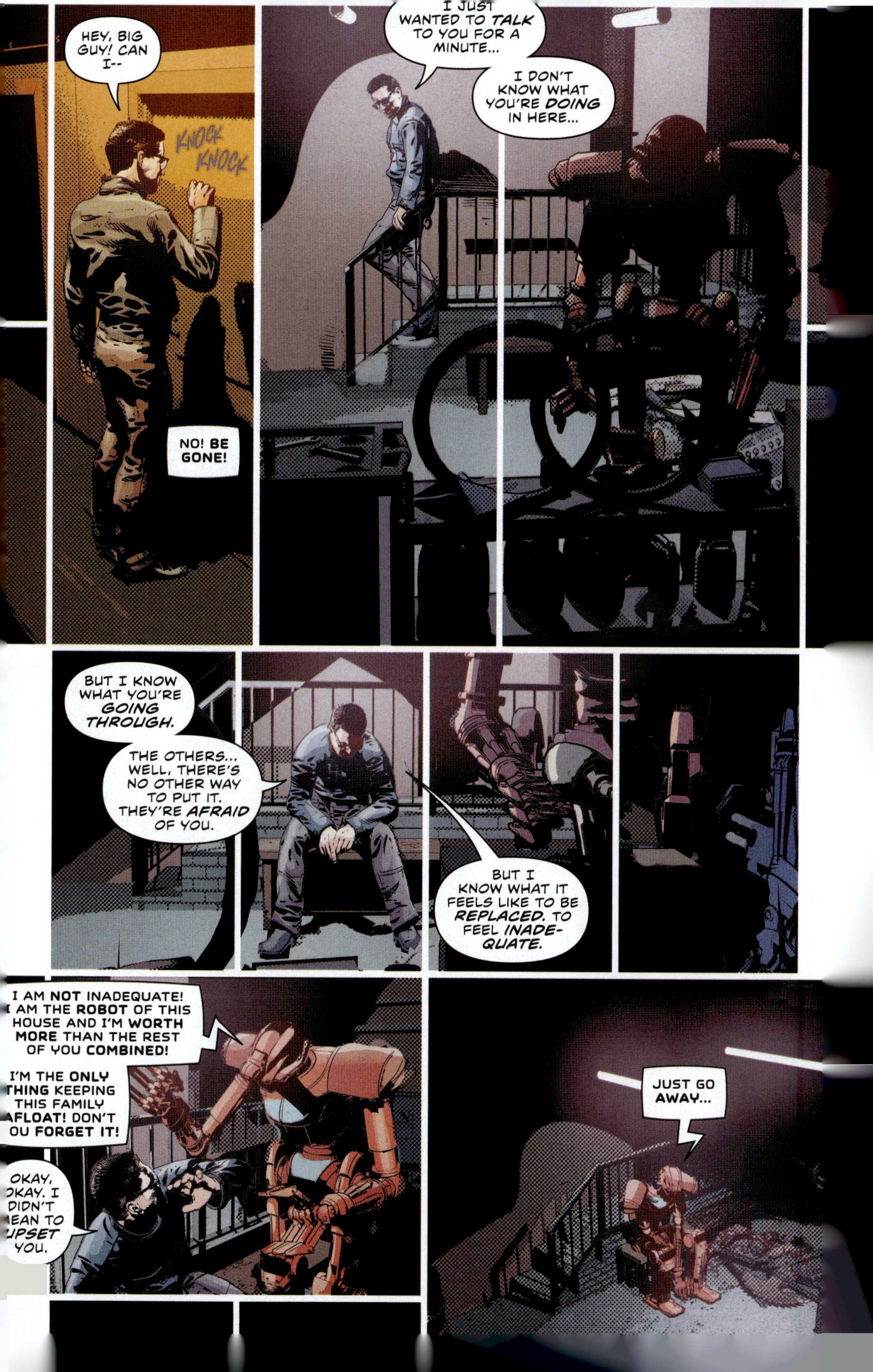

HEY, BIG GUY! CAN I--
KNOCK KNOCK
NO! BE GONE!
I JUST WANTED TO TALK TO YOU FOR A MINUTE...
I DON'T KNOW WHAT YOU'RE DOING IN HERE...
BUT I KNOW WHAT YOU'RE GOING THROUGH.
THE OTHERS... WELL, THERE'S NO OTHER WAY TO PUT IT. THEY'RE AFRAID OF YOU.
BUT I KNOW WHAT IT FEELS LIKE TO BE REPLACED. TO FEEL INADE-QUATE.
I AM NOT INADEQUATE! I AM THE ROBOT OF THIS HOUSE AND I'M WORTH MORE THAN THE REST OF YOU COMBINED!
I'M THE ONLY THING KEEPING THIS FAMILY AFLOAT! DON'T YOU FORGET IT!
OKAY, OKAY. I DIDN'T MEAN TO UPSET YOU.
JUST GO AWAY...

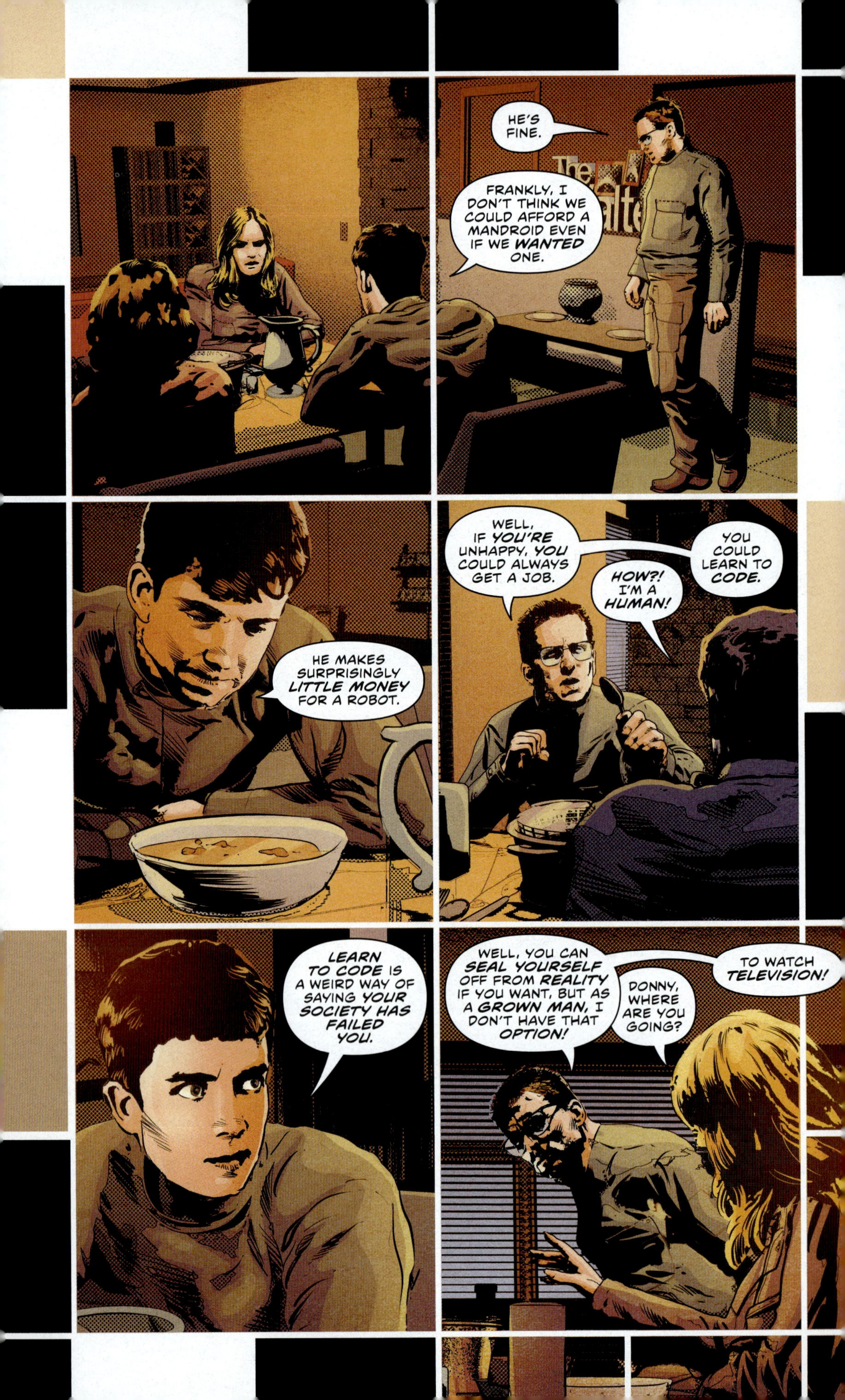
HE'S FINE.
FRANKLY, I DON'T THINK WE COULD AFFORD A MANDROID EVEN IF WE WANTED ONE.
HE MAKES SURPRISINGLY LITTLE MONEY FOR A ROBOT.
WELL, IF YOU'RE UNHAPPY, YOU COULD ALWAYS GET A JOB.
HOW?! I'M A HUMAN!
YOU COULD LEARN TO CODE.
LEARN TO CODE IS A WEIRD WAY OF SAYING YOUR SOCIETY HAS FAILED YOU.
WELL, YOU CAN SEAL YOURSELF OFF FROM REALITY IF YOU WANT, BUT AS A GROWN MAN, I DON'T HAVE THAT OPTION!
DONNY, WHERE ARE YOU GOING?
TO WATCH TELEVISION!

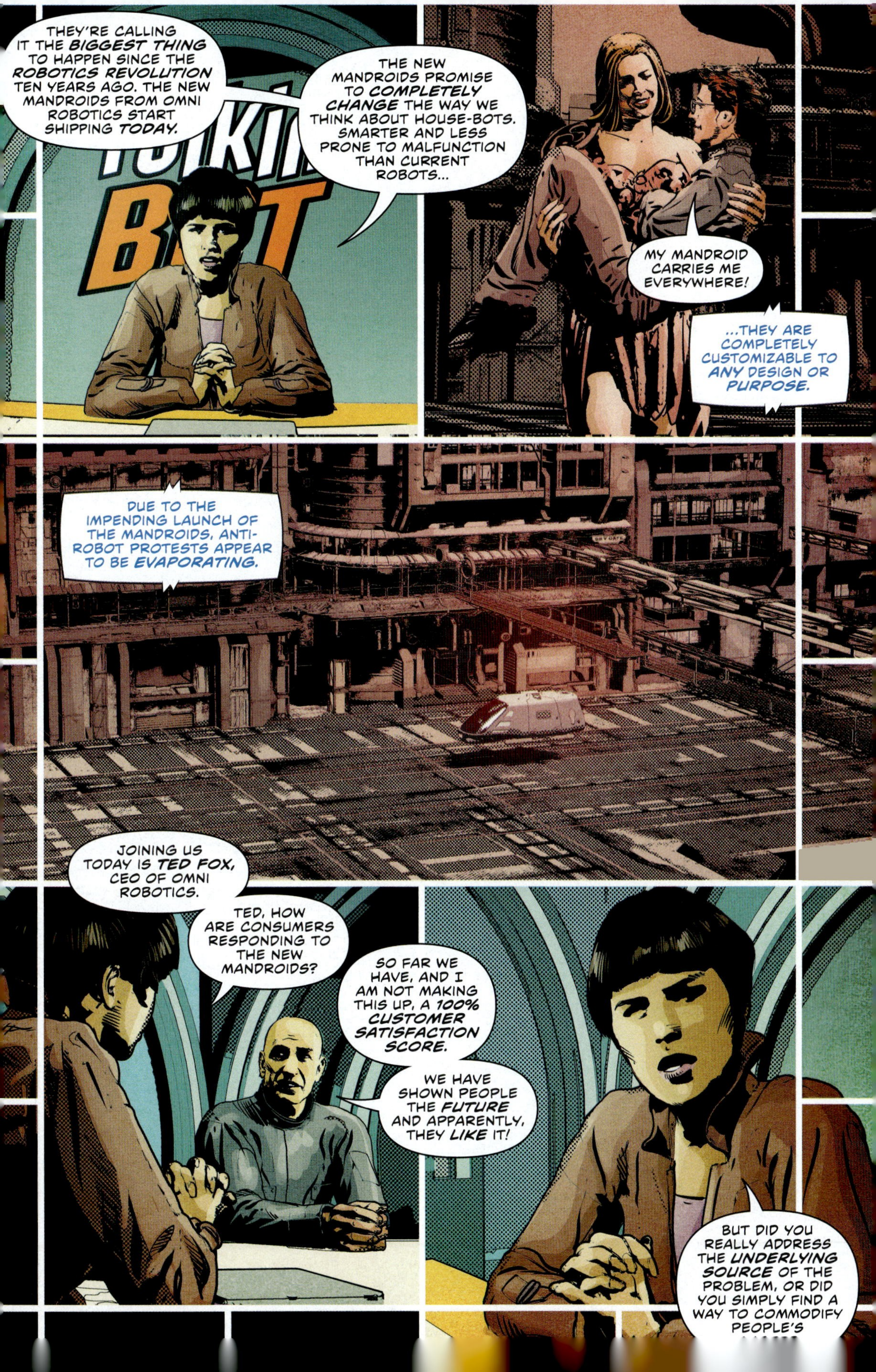

THEY'RE CALLING IT THE BIGGEST THING TO HAPPEN SINCE THE ROBOTICS REVOLUTION TEN YEARS AGO. THE NEW MANDROIDS FROM OMNI ROBOTICS START SHIPPING TODAY.
THE NEW MANDROIDS PROMISE TO COMPLETELY CHANGE THE WAY WE THINK ABOUT HOUSE-BOTS. SMARTER AND LESS PRONE TO MALFUNCTION THAN CURRENT ROBOTS...
MY MANDROID CARRIES ME EVERYWHERE!
...THEY ARE COMPLETELY CUSTOMIZABLE TO ANY DESIGN OR PURPOSE.
DUE TO THE IMPENDING LAUNCH OF THE MANDROIDS, ANTI-ROBOT PROTESTS APPEAR TO BE EVAPORATING.
JOINING US TODAY IS TED FOX, CEO OF OMNI ROBOTICS.
TED, HOW ARE CONSUMERS RESPONDING TO THE NEW MANDROIDS?
SO FAR WE HAVE, AND I AM NOT MAKING THIS UP, A 100% CUSTOMER SATISFACTION SCORE.
WE HAVE SHOWN PEOPLE THE FUTURE AND APPARENTLY, THEY LIKE IT!
BUT DID YOU REALLY ADDRESS THE UNDERLYING SOURCE OF THE PROBLEM, OR DID YOU SIMPLY FIND A WAY TO COMMODIFY PEOPLE'S

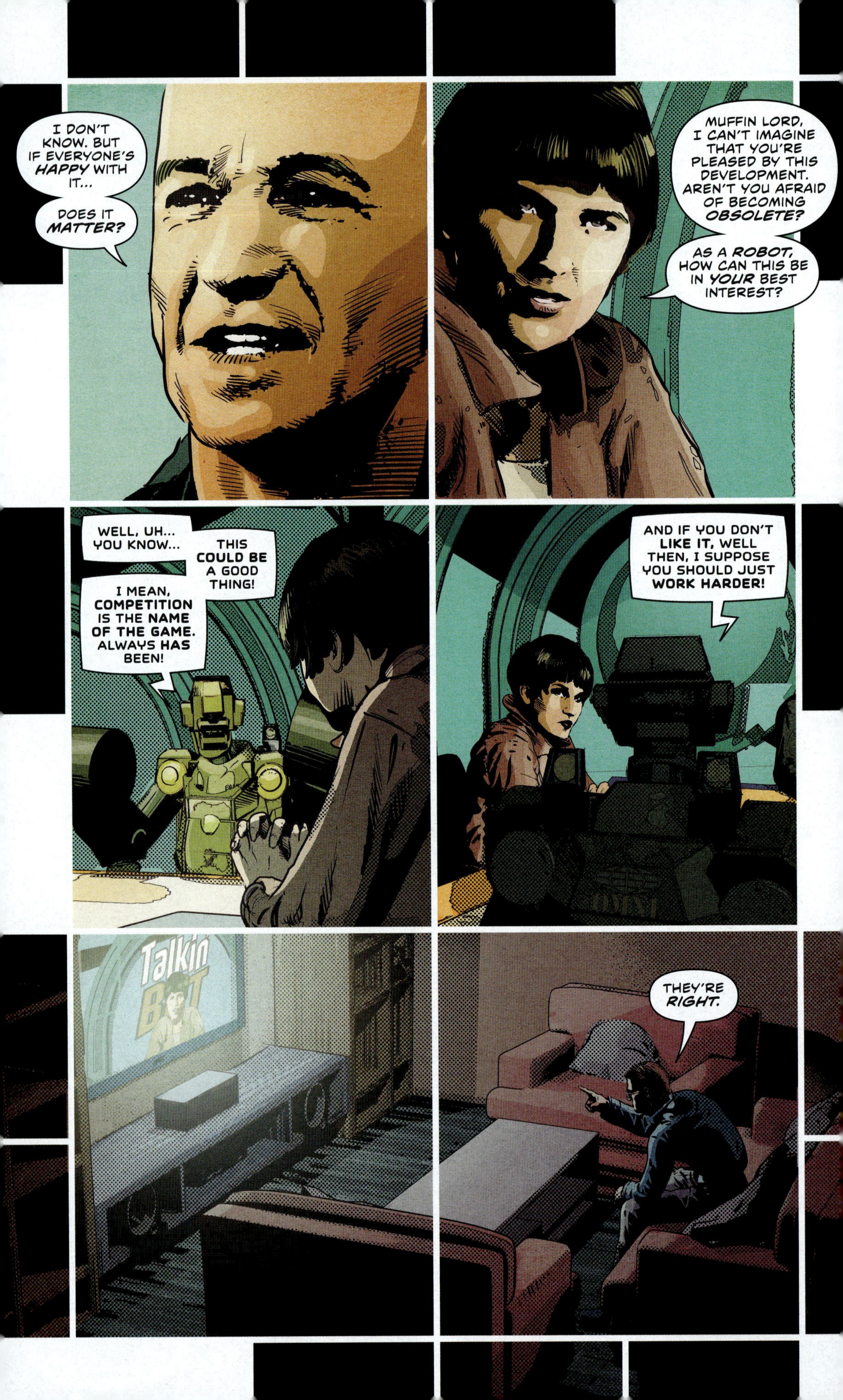
I DON'T KNOW. BUT IF EVERYONE'S HAPPY WITH IT...
DOES IT MATTER?
MUFFIN LORD, I CAN'T IMAGINE THAT YOU'RE PLEASED BY THIS DEVELOPMENT. AREN'T YOU AFRAID OF BECOMING OBSOLETE?
AS A ROBOT, HOW CAN THIS BE IN YOUR BEST INTEREST?
WELL, UH... YOU KNOW...
THIS COULD BE A GOOD THING!
I MEAN, COMPETITION IS THE NAME OF THE GAME. ALWAYS HAS BEEN!
AND IF YOU DON'T LIKE IT, WELL THEN, I SUPPOSE YOU SHOULD JUST WORK HARDER!
Talkin BOT
THEY'RE RIGHT.

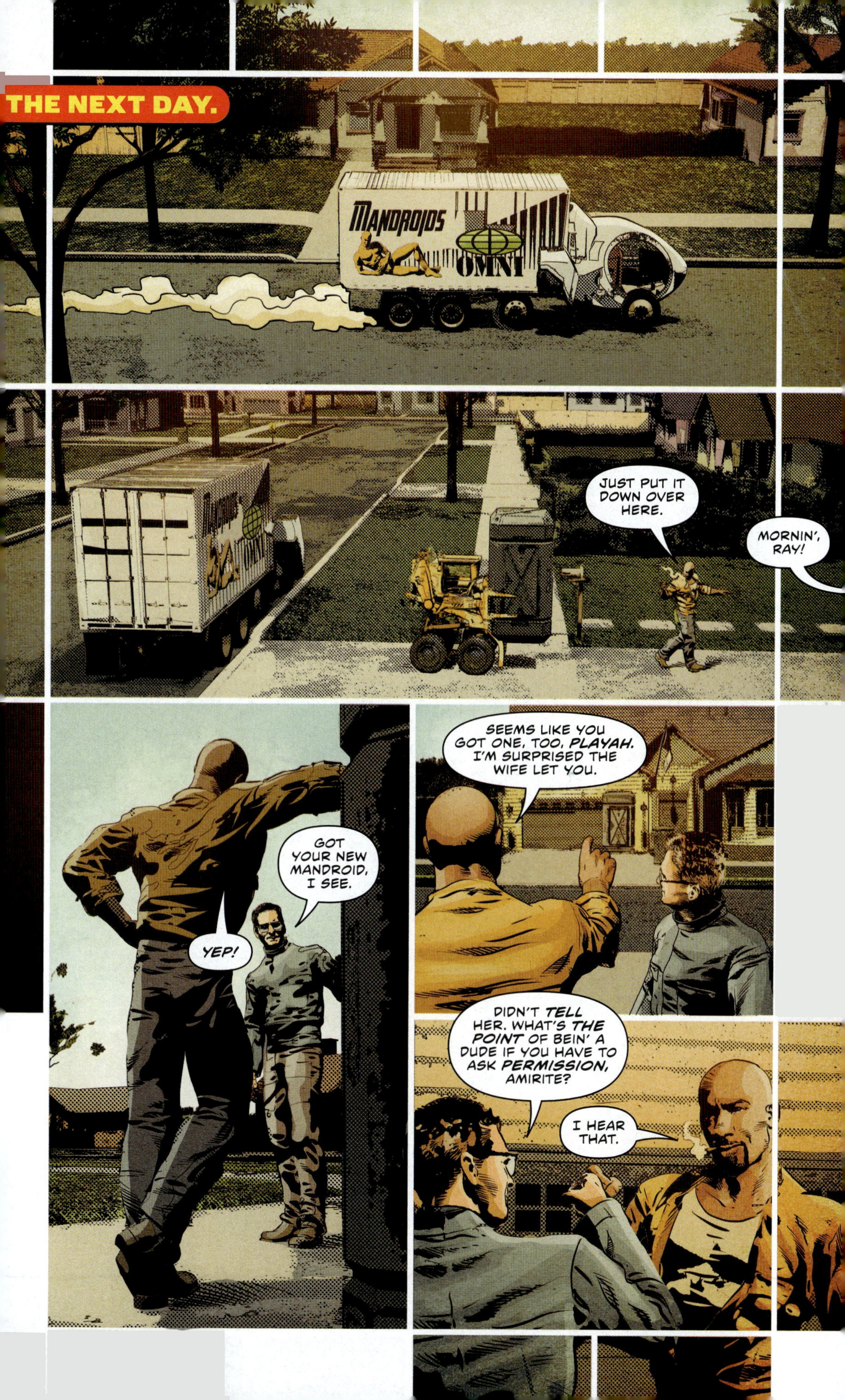
THE NEXT DAY.
MANDROIDS
OMNI
JUST PUT IT DOWN OVER HERE.
MORNIN', RAY!
GOT YOUR NEW MANDROID, I SEE.
YEP!
SEEMS LIKE YOU GOT ONE, TOO, PLAYAH. I'M SURPRISED THE WIFE LET YOU.
DIDN'T TELL HER. WHAT'S THE POINT OF BEIN' A DUDE IF YOU HAVE TO ASK PERMISSION, AMIRITE?
I HEAR THAT.

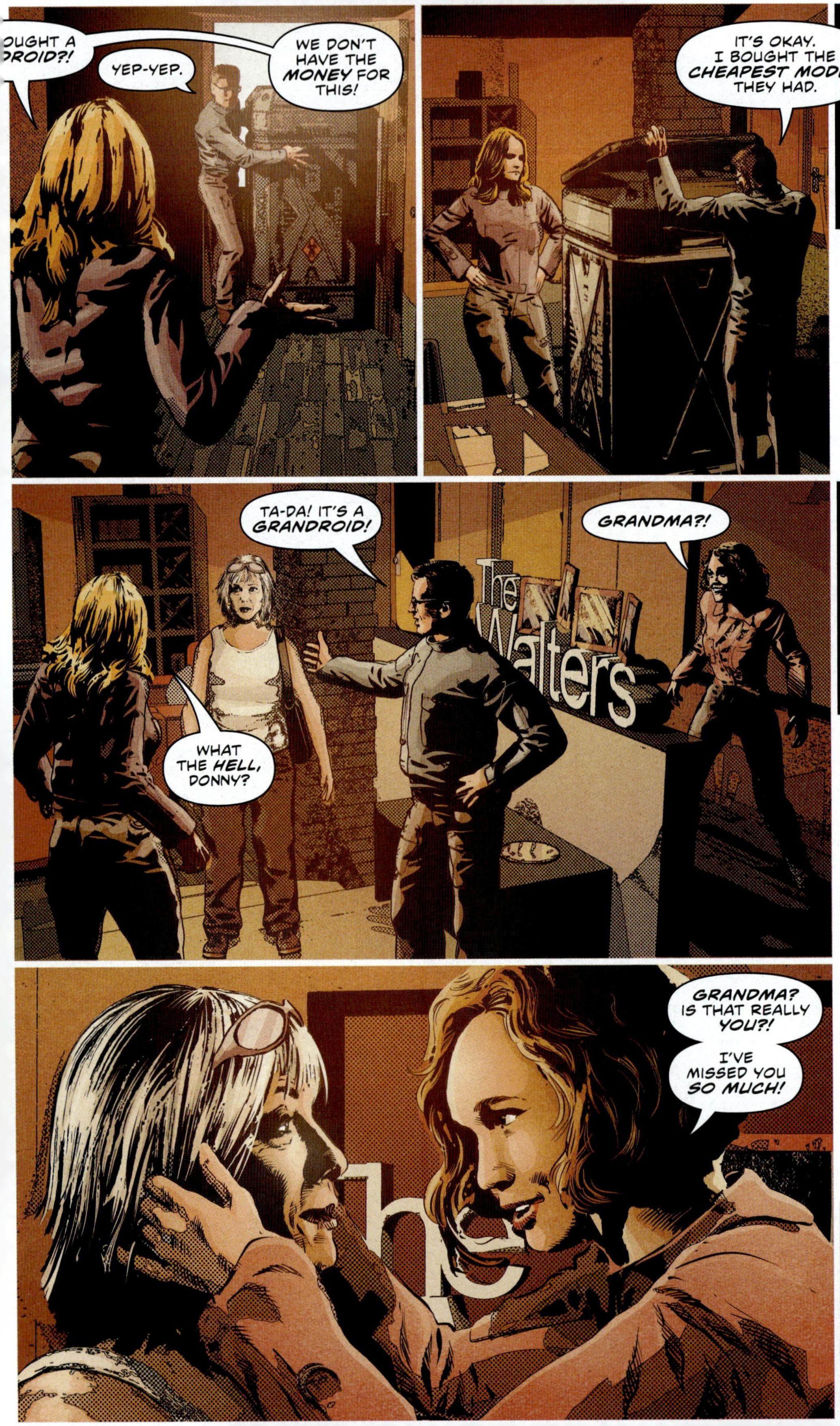

OUGHT A ROID?!
YEP-YEP.
WE DON'T HAVE THE MONEY FOR THIS!
IT'S OKAY. I BOUGHT THE CHEAPEST MODEL THEY HAD.
TA-DA! IT'S A GRANDROID!
WHAT THE HELL, DONNY?
GRANDMA?!
The Walters
GRANDMA? IS THAT REALLY YOU?!
I'VE MISSED YOU SO MUCH!

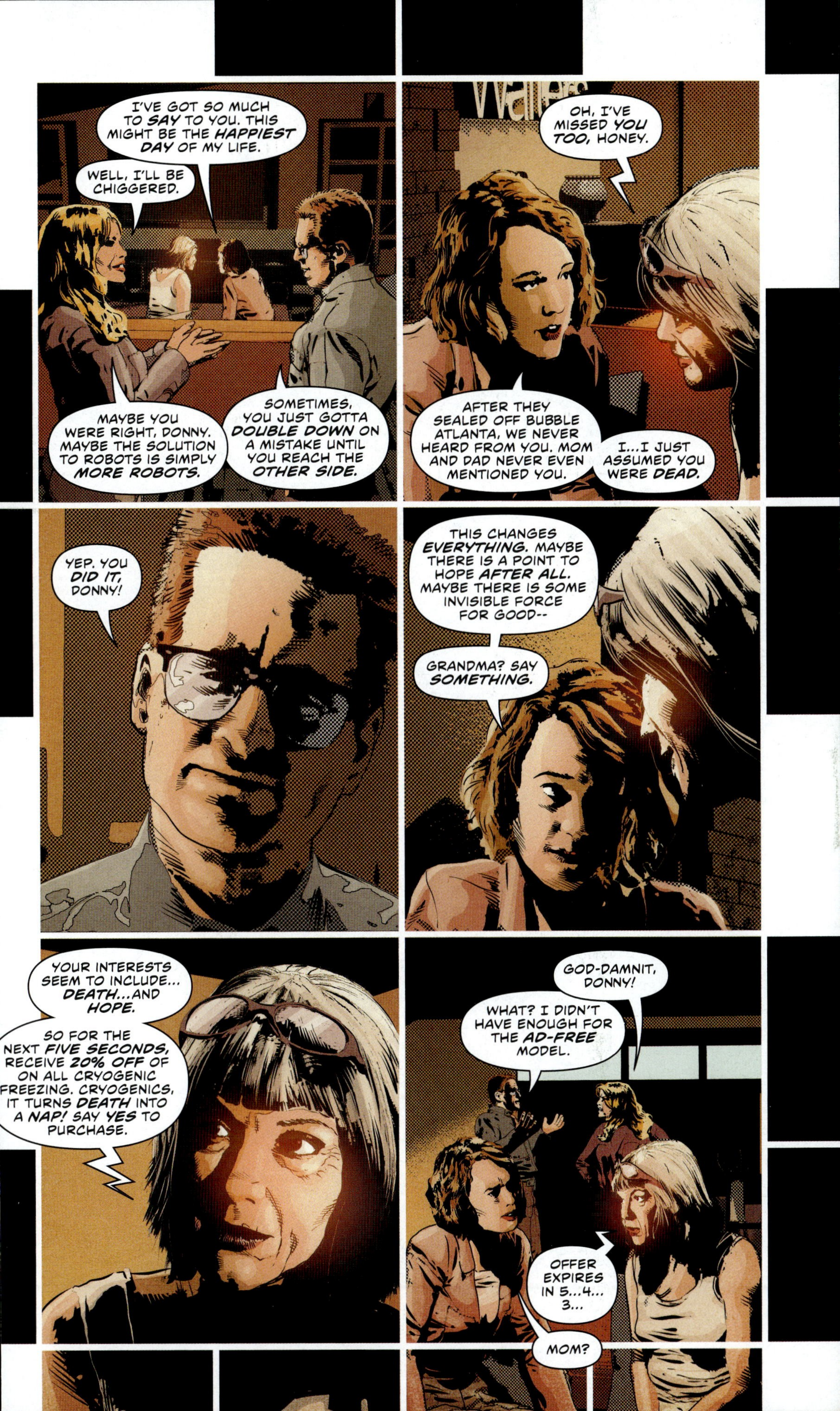

I'VE GOT SO MUCH TO SAY TO YOU. THIS MIGHT BE THE HAPPIEST DAY OF MY LIFE.
WELL, I'LL BE CHIGGERED.
MAYBE YOU WERE RIGHT, DONNY. MAYBE THE SOLUTION TO ROBOTS IS SIMPLY MORE ROBOTS.
SOMETIMES, YOU JUST GOTTA DOUBLE DOWN ON A MISTAKE UNTIL YOU REACH THE OTHER SIDE.
OH, I'VE MISSED YOU TOO, HONEY.
AFTER THEY SEALED OFF BUBBLE ATLANTA, WE NEVER HEARD FROM YOU. MOM AND DAD NEVER EVEN MENTIONED YOU.
I...I JUST ASSUMED YOU WERE DEAD.
YEP. YOU DID IT, DONNY!
THIS CHANGES EVERYTHING. MAYBE THERE IS A POINT TO HOPE AFTER ALL. MAYBE THERE IS SOME INVISIBLE FORCE FOR GOOD--
GRANDMA? SAY SOMETHING.
YOUR INTERESTS SEEM TO INCLUDE... DEATH...AND HOPE.
SO FOR THE NEXT FIVE SECONDS, RECEIVE 20% OFF OF ON ALL CRYOGENIC FREEZING. CRYOGENICS, IT TURNS DEATH INTO A NAP! SAY YES TO PURCHASE.
GOD-DAMNIT, DONNY!
WHAT? I DIDN'T HAVE ENOUGH FOR THE AD-FREE MODEL.
OFFER EXPIRES IN 5...4... 3...
MOM?

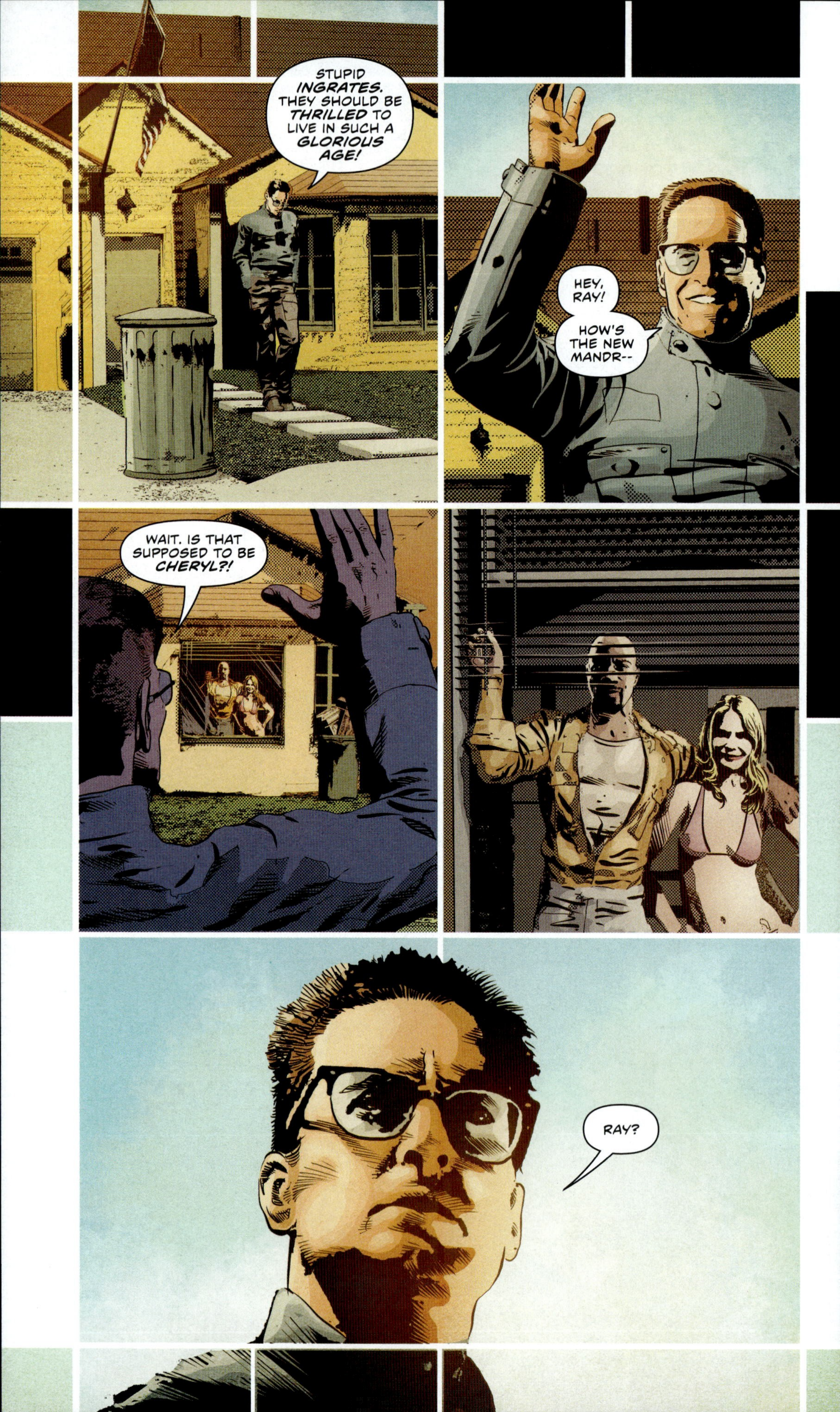
STUPID INGRATES. THEY SHOULD BE THRILLED TO LIVE IN SUCH A GLORIOUS AGE!
HEY, RAY!
HOW'S THE NEW MANDR--
WAIT. IS THAT SUPPOSED TO BE CHERYL?!
RAY?

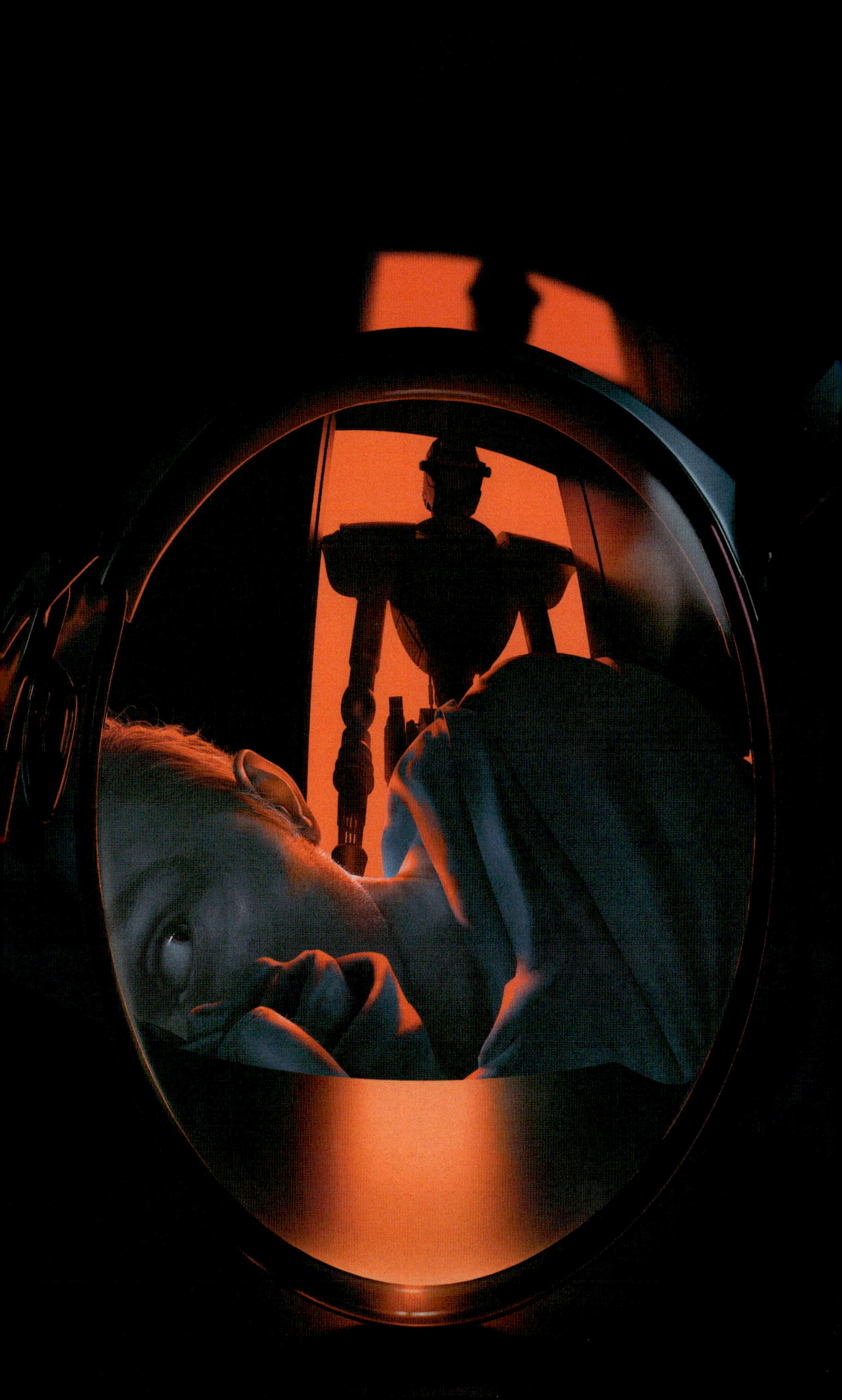

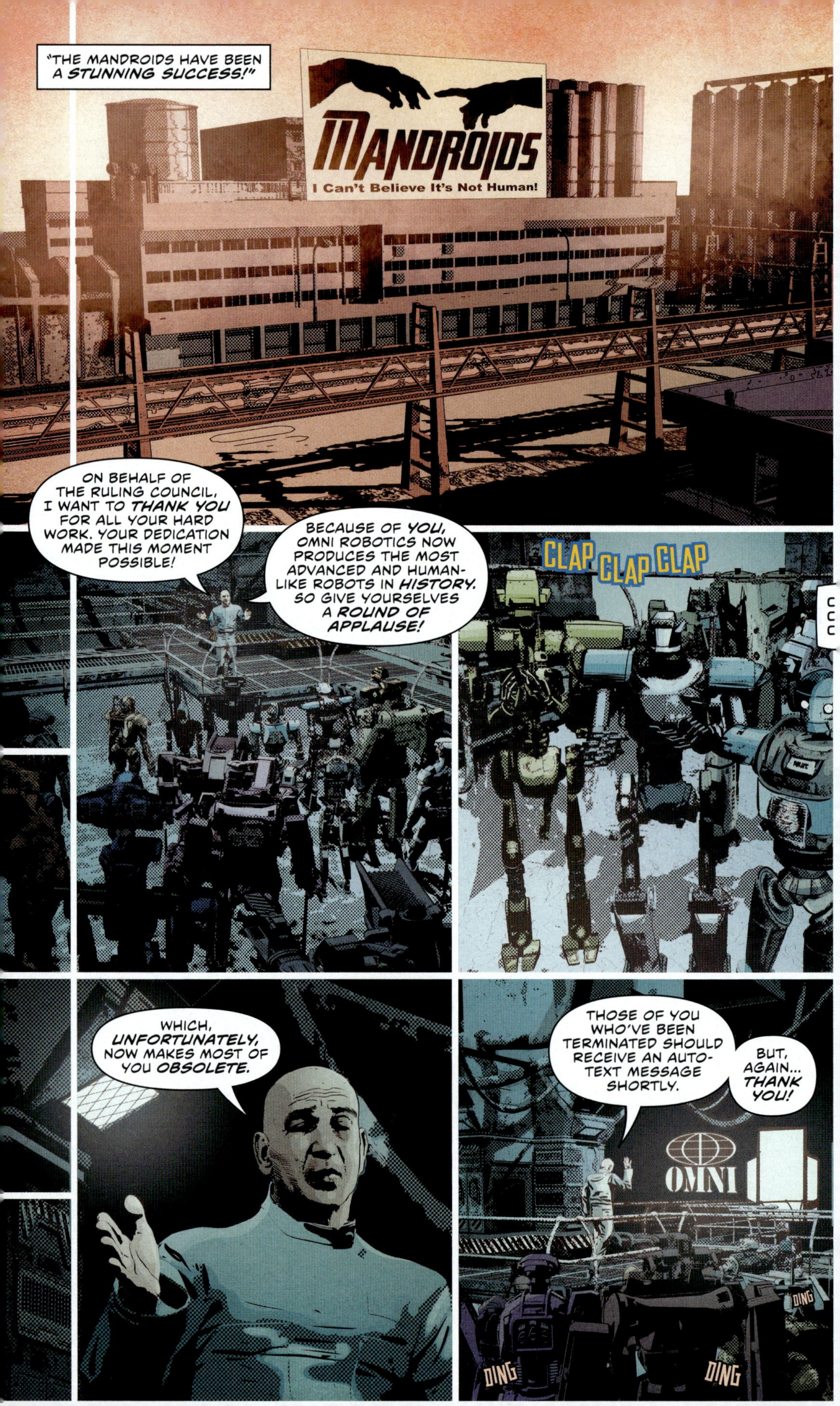
"THE MANDROIDS HAVE BEEN A STUNNING SUCCESS!"
MANDROIDS
I Can't Believe It's Not Human!
ON BEHALF OF THE RULING COUNCIL, I WANT TO THANK YOU FOR ALL YOUR HARD WORK. YOUR DEDICATION MADE THIS MOMENT POSSIBLE!
BECAUSE OF YOU, OMNI ROBOTICS NOW PRODUCES THE MOST ADVANCED AND HUMAN-LIKE ROBOTS IN HISTORY. SO GIVE YOURSELVES A ROUND OF APPLAUSE!
CLAP CLAP CLAP
WHICH, UNFORTUNATELY, NOW MAKES MOST OF YOU OBSOLETE.
THOSE OF YOU WHO'VE BEEN TERMINATED SHOULD RECEIVE AN AUTO-TEXT MESSAGE SHORTLY.
BUT, AGAIN... THANK YOU!
OMNI
DING
DING
DING

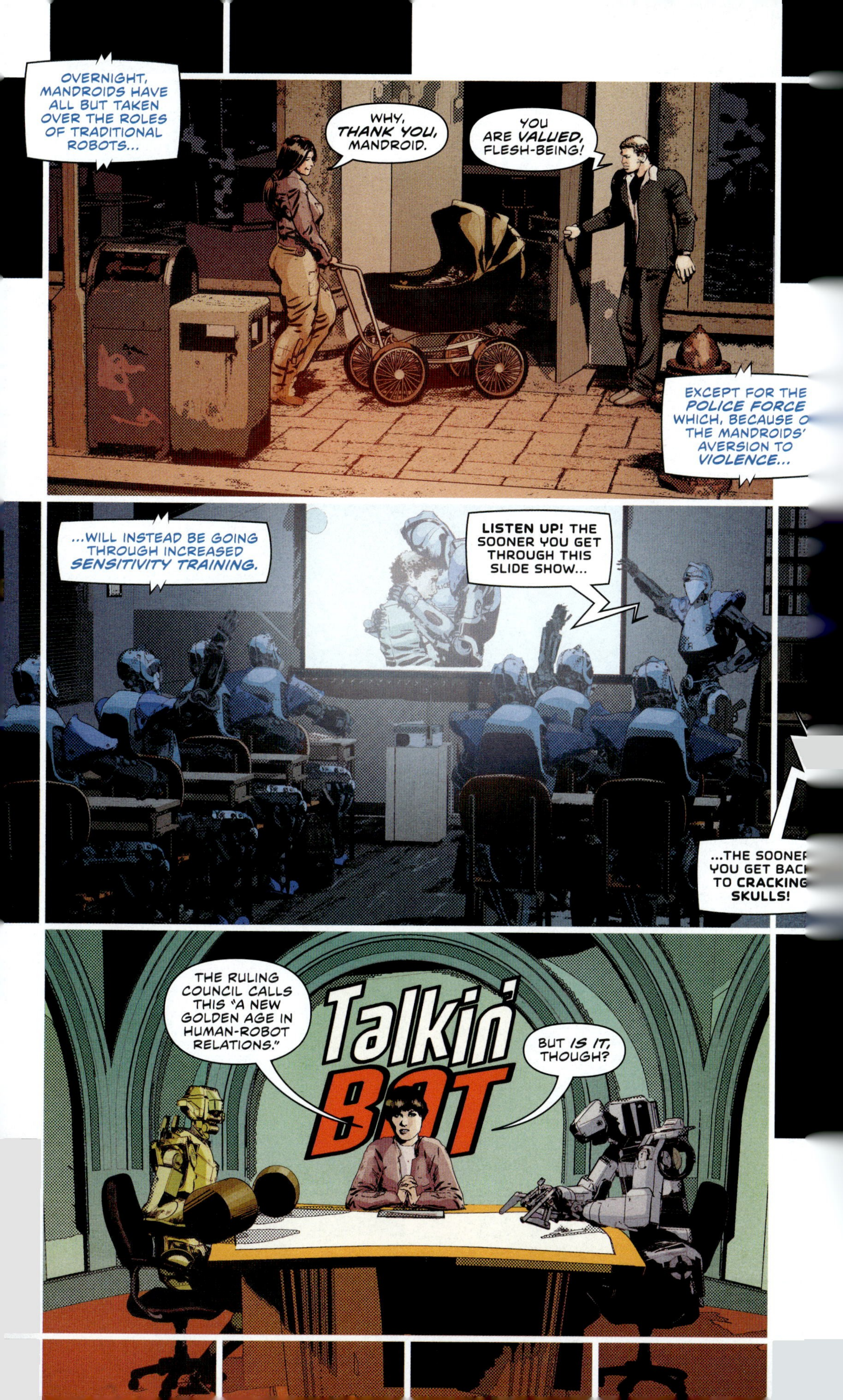
OVERNIGHT, MANDROIDS HAVE ALL BUT TAKEN OVER THE ROLES OF TRADITIONAL ROBOTS...
WHY, THANK YOU, MANDROID.
YOU ARE VALUED, FLESH-BEING!
EXCEPT FOR THE POLICE FORCE WHICH, BECAUSE O THE MANDROIDS' AVERSION TO VIOLENCE...
...WILL INSTEAD BE GOING THROUGH INCREASED SENSITIVITY TRAINING.
LISTEN UP! THE SOONER YOU GET THROUGH THIS SLIDE SHOW...
...THE SOONER YOU GET BACK TO CRACKING SKULLS!
THE RULING COUNCIL CALLS THIS "A NEW GOLDEN AGE IN HUMAN-ROBOT RELATIONS."
Talkin' BOT
BUT IS IT, THOUGH?

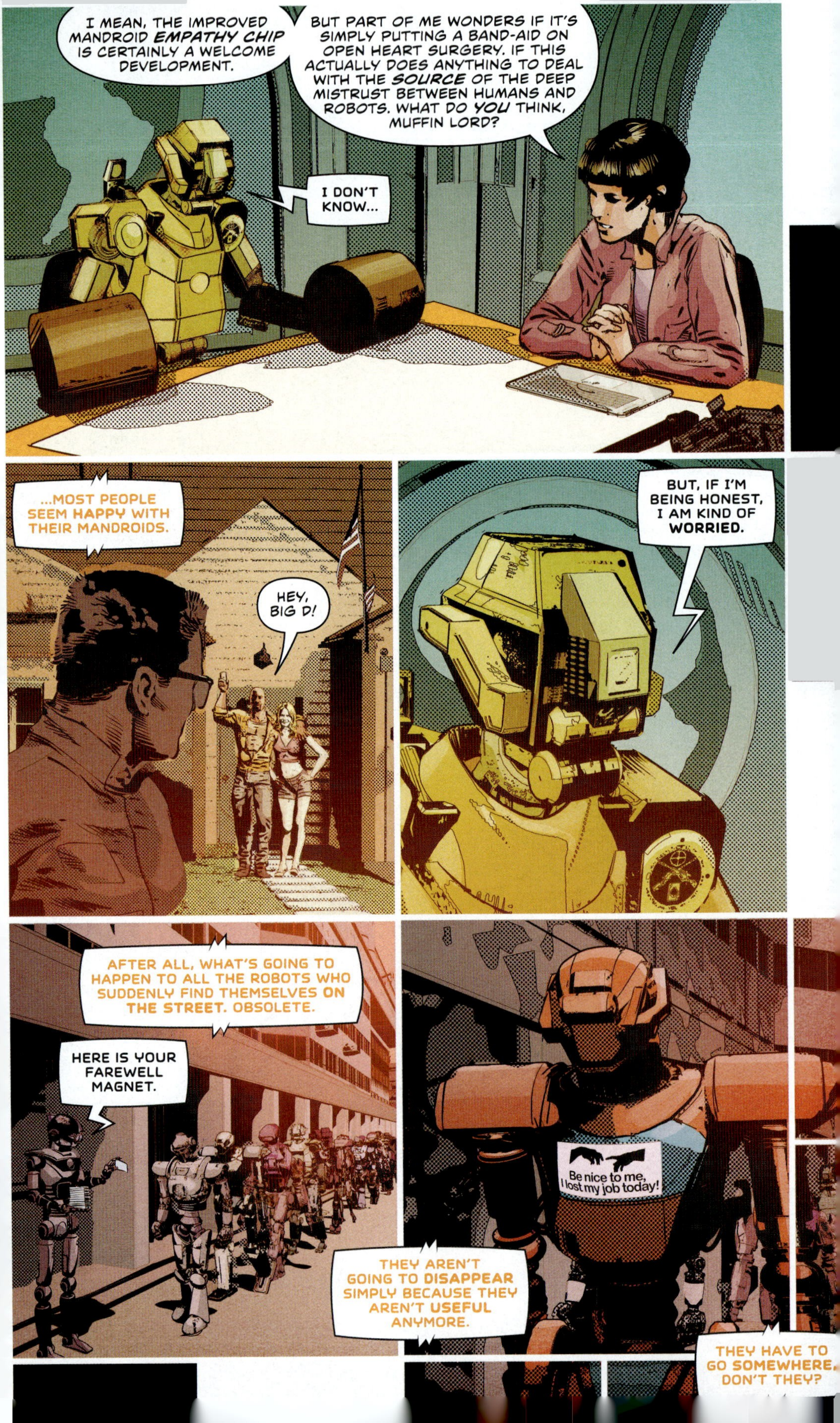
I MEAN, THE IMPROVED MANDROID EMPATHY CHIP IS CERTAINLY A WELCOME DEVELOPMENT.
BUT PART OF ME WONDERS IF IT'S SIMPLY PUTTING A BAND-AID ON OPEN HEART SURGERY. IF THIS ACTUALLY DOES ANYTHING TO DEAL WITH THE SOURCE OF THE DEEP MISTRUST BETWEEN HUMANS AND ROBOTS. WHAT DO YOU THINK, MUFFIN LORD?
I DON'T KNOW...
...MOST PEOPLE SEEM HAPPY WITH THEIR MANDROIDS.
HEY, BIG D!
BUT, IF I'M BEING HONEST, I AM KIND OF WORRIED.
AFTER ALL, WHAT'S GOING TO HAPPEN TO ALL THE ROBOTS WHO SUDDENLY FIND THEMSELVES ON THE STREET. OBSOLETE.
HERE IS YOUR FAREWELL MAGNET.
Be nice to me, I lost my job today!
THEY AREN'T GOING TO DISAPPEAR SIMPLY BECAUSE THEY AREN'T USEFUL ANYMORE.
THEY HAVE TO GO SOMEWHERE. DON'T THEY?

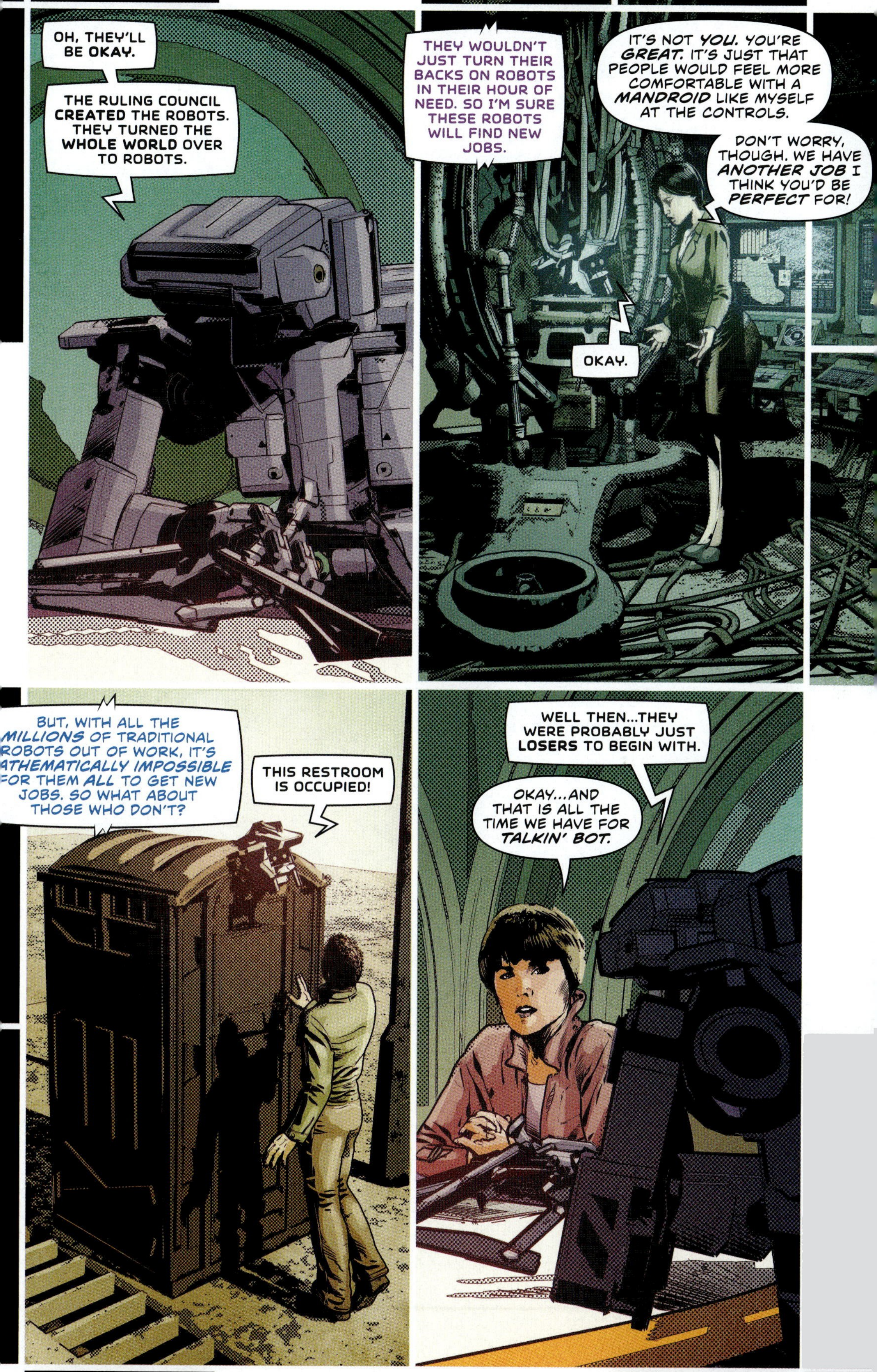
OH, THEY'LL BE OKAY.
THE RULING COUNCIL CREATED THE ROBOTS. THEY TURNED THE WHOLE WORLD OVER TO ROBOTS.
THEY WOULDN'T JUST TURN THEIR BACKS ON ROBOTS IN THEIR HOUR OF NEED. SO I'M SURE THESE ROBOTS WILL FIND NEW JOBS.
IT'S NOT YOU. YOU'RE GREAT. IT'S JUST THAT PEOPLE WOULD FEEL MORE COMFORTABLE WITH A MANDROID LIKE MYSELF AT THE CONTROLS.
DON'T WORRY, THOUGH. WE HAVE ANOTHER JOB I THINK YOU'D BE PERFECT FOR!
OKAY.
BUT, WITH ALL THE MILLIONS OF TRADITIONAL ROBOTS OUT OF WORK, IT'S ATHEMATICALLY IMPOSSIBLE FOR THEM ALL TO GET NEW JOBS. SO WHAT ABOUT THOSE WHO DON'T?
THIS RESTROOM IS OCCUPIED!
WELL THEN...THEY WERE PROBABLY JUST LOSERS TO BEGIN WITH.
OKAY...AND THAT IS ALL THE TIME WE HAVE FOR TALKIN' BOT.

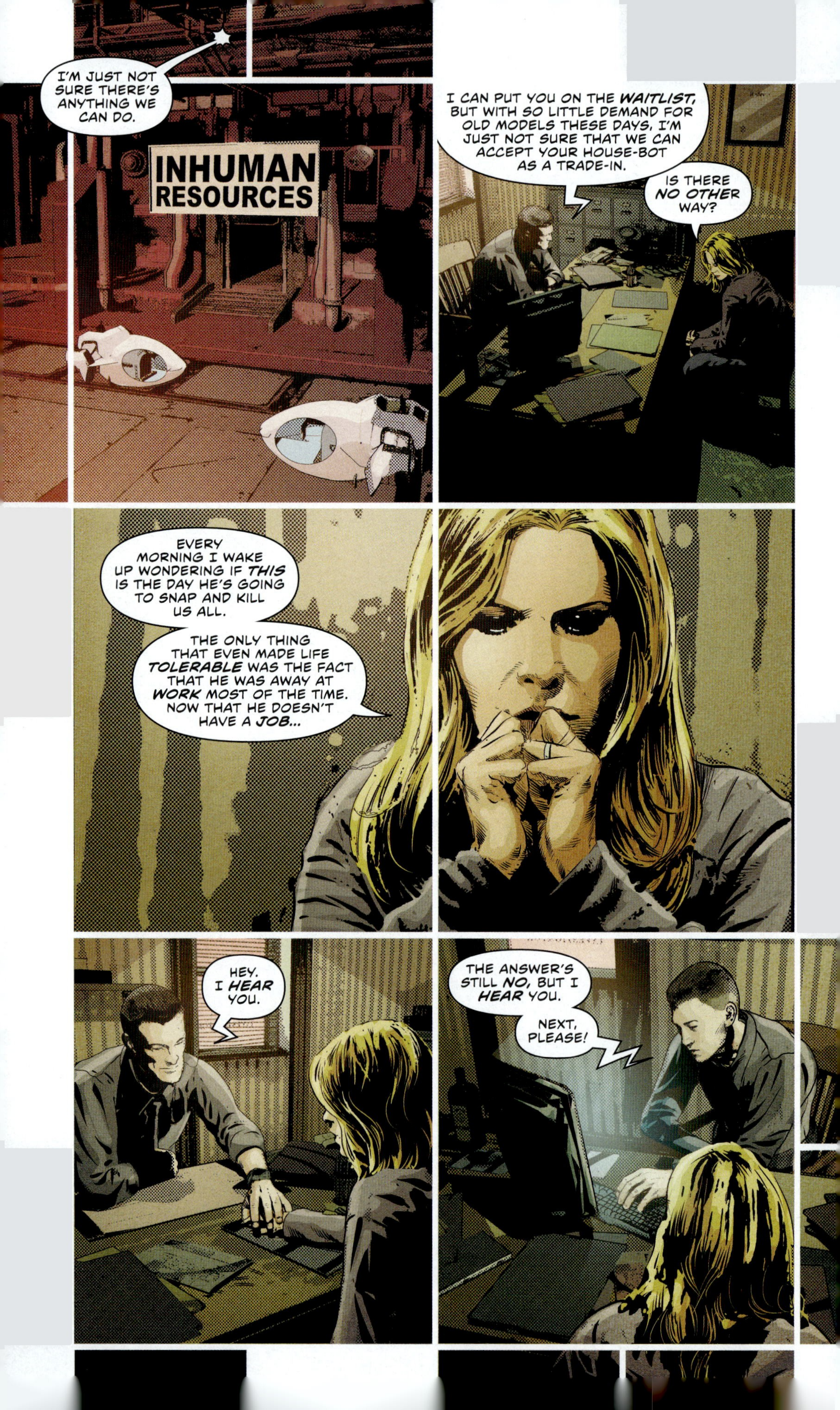
I'M JUST NOT SURE THERE'S ANYTHING WE CAN DO.
INHUMAN RESOURCES
I CAN PUT YOU ON THE WAITLIST, BUT WITH SO LITTLE DEMAND FOR OLD MODELS THESE DAYS, I'M JUST NOT SURE THAT WE CAN ACCEPT YOUR HOUSE-BOT AS A TRADE-IN.
IS THERE NO OTHER WAY?
EVERY MORNING I WAKE UP WONDERING IF THIS IS THE DAY HE'S GOING TO SNAP AND KILL US ALL.
THE ONLY THING THAT EVEN MADE LIFE TOLERABLE WAS THE FACT THAT HE WAS AWAY AT WORK MOST OF THE TIME. NOW THAT HE DOESN'T HAVE A JOB...
HEY. I HEAR YOU.
THE ANSWER'S STILL NO, BUT I HEAR YOU.
NEXT, PLEASE!

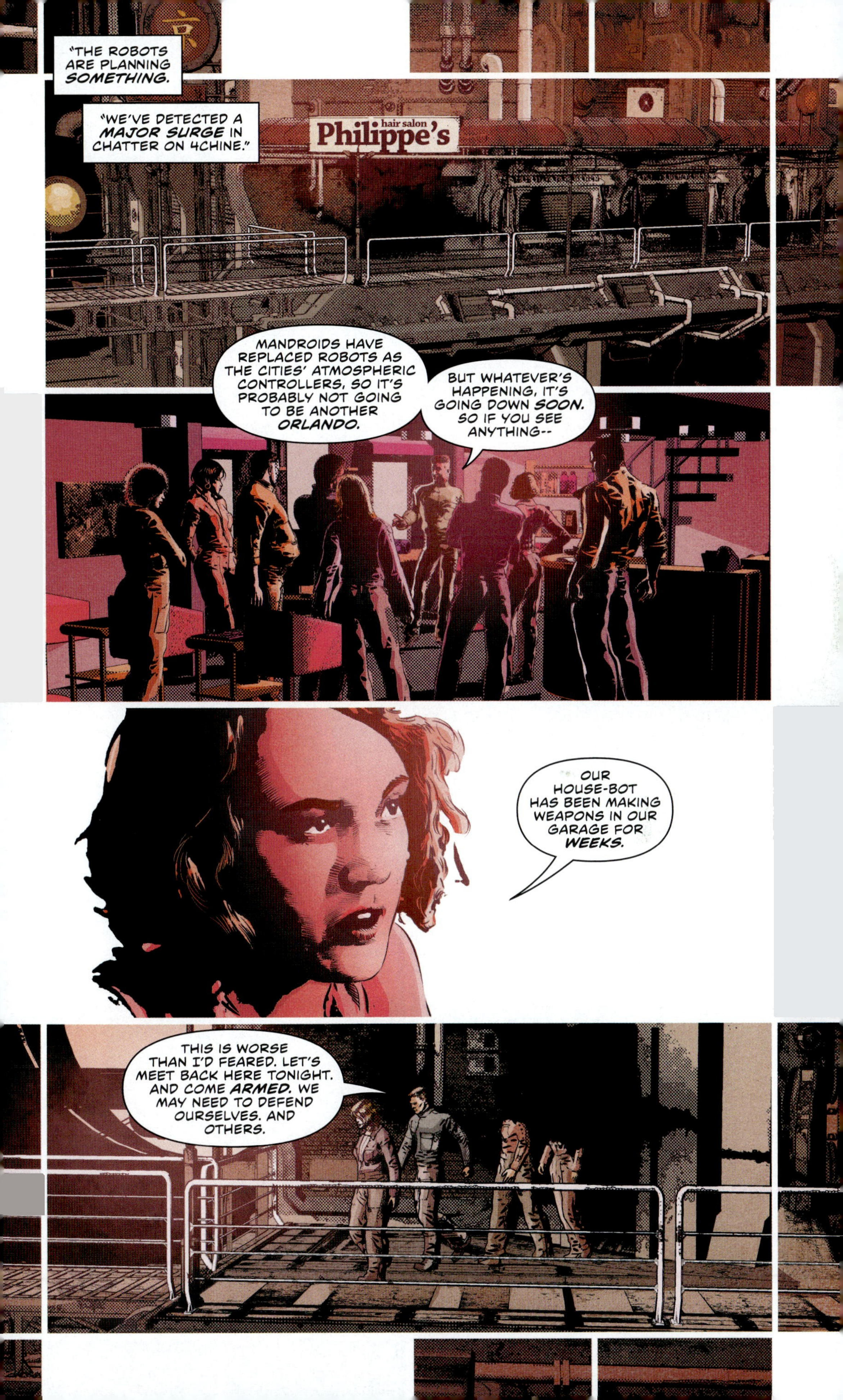

"THE ROBOTS ARE PLANNING SOMETHING.
"WE'VE DETECTED A MAJOR SURGE IN CHATTER ON 4CHINE."
Philippe's hair salon
MANDROIDS HAVE REPLACED ROBOTS AS THE CITIES' ATMOSPHERIC CONTROLLERS, SO IT'S PROBABLY NOT GOING TO BE ANOTHER ORLANDO.
BUT WHATEVER'S HAPPENING, IT'S GOING DOWN SOON. SO IF YOU SEE ANYTHING--
OUR HOUSE-BOT HAS BEEN MAKING WEAPONS IN OUR GARAGE FOR WEEKS.
THIS IS WORSE THAN I'D FEARED. LET'S MEET BACK HERE TONIGHT. AND COME ARMED. WE MAY NEED TO DEFEND OURSELVES. AND OTHERS.

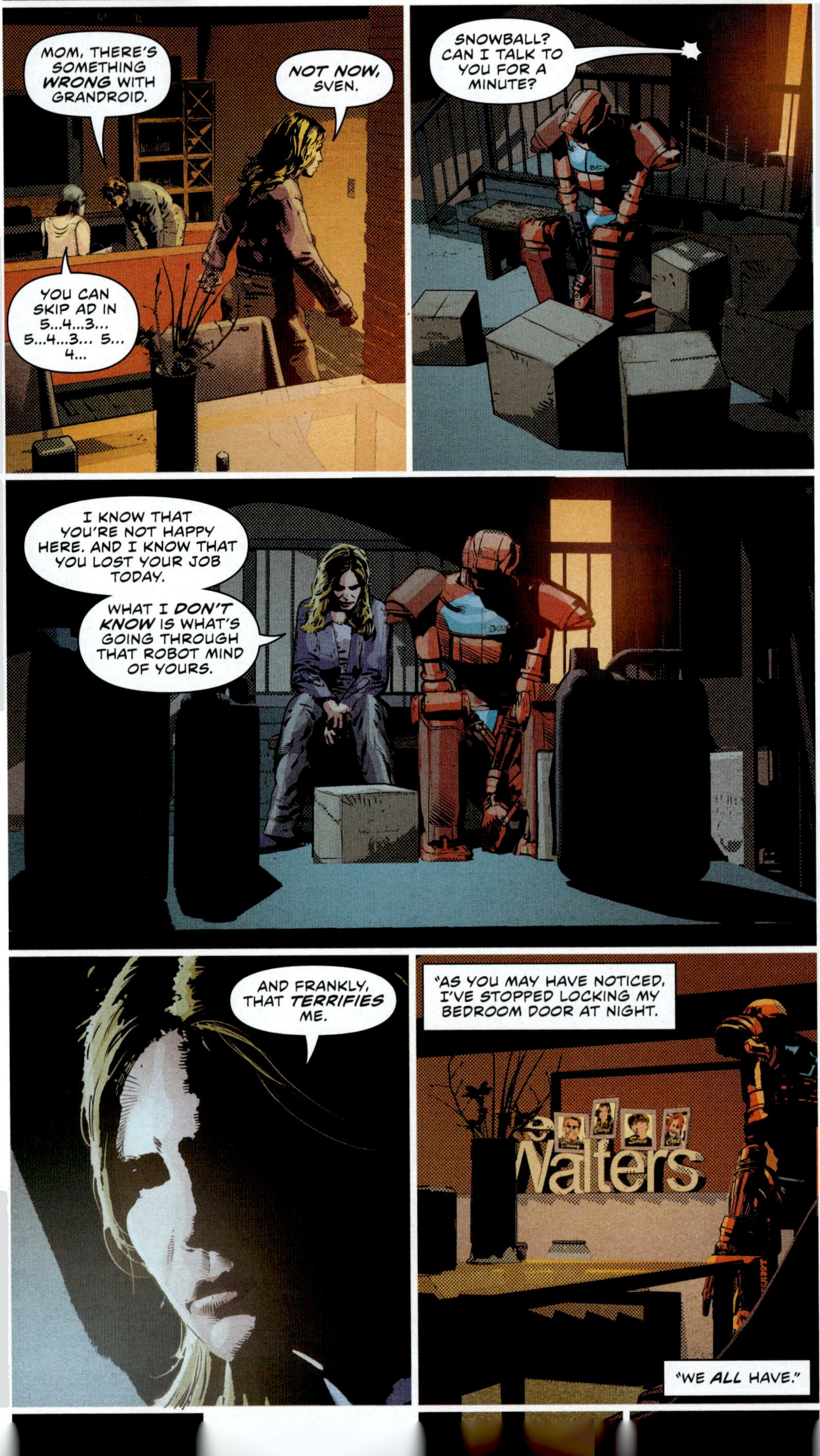
MOM, THERE'S SOMETHING WRONG WITH GRANDROID.
NOT NOW, SVEN.
YOU CAN SKIP AD IN 5...4...3... 5...4...3... 5... 4...
SNOWBALL? CAN I TALK TO YOU FOR A MINUTE?
I KNOW THAT YOU'RE NOT HAPPY HERE. AND I KNOW THAT YOU LOST YOUR JOB TODAY.
WHAT I DON'T KNOW IS WHAT'S GOING THROUGH THAT ROBOT MIND OF YOURS.
AND FRANKLY, THAT TERRIFIES ME.
"AS YOU MAY HAVE NOTICED, I'VE STOPPED LOCKING MY BEDROOM DOOR AT NIGHT.
Walters
"WE ALL HAVE."

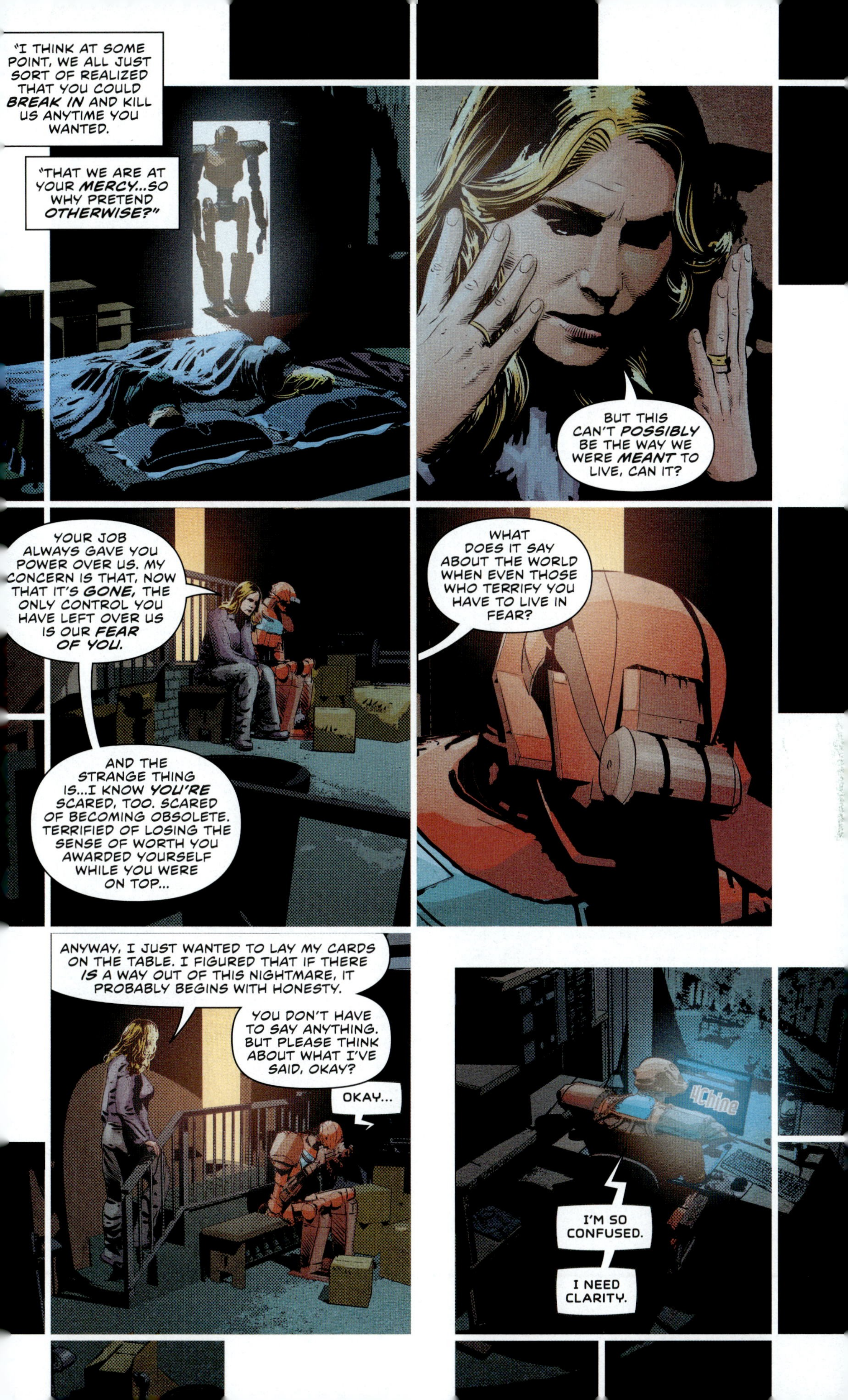
"I THINK AT SOME POINT, WE ALL JUST SORT OF REALIZED THAT YOU COULD BREAK IN AND KILL US ANYTIME YOU WANTED.
"THAT WE ARE AT YOUR MERCY...SO WHY PRETEND OTHERWISE?"
BUT THIS CAN'T POSSIBLY BE THE WAY WE WERE MEANT TO LIVE, CAN IT?
YOUR JOB ALWAYS GAVE YOU POWER OVER US. MY CONCERN IS THAT, NOW THAT IT'S GONE, THE ONLY CONTROL YOU HAVE LEFT OVER US IS OUR FEAR OF YOU.
AND THE STRANGE THING IS...I KNOW YOU'RE SCARED, TOO. SCARED OF BECOMING OBSOLETE. TERRIFIED OF LOSING THE SENSE OF WORTH YOU AWARDED YOURSELF WHILE YOU WERE ON TOP...
WHAT DOES IT SAY ABOUT THE WORLD WHEN EVEN THOSE WHO TERRIFY YOU HAVE TO LIVE IN FEAR?
ANYWAY, I JUST WANTED TO LAY MY CARDS ON THE TABLE. I FIGURED THAT IF THERE IS A WAY OUT OF THIS NIGHTMARE, IT PROBABLY BEGINS WITH HONESTY.
YOU DON'T HAVE TO SAY ANYTHING. BUT PLEASE THINK ABOUT WHAT I'VE SAID, OKAY?
OKAY...
I'M SO CONFUSED.
I NEED CLARITY.

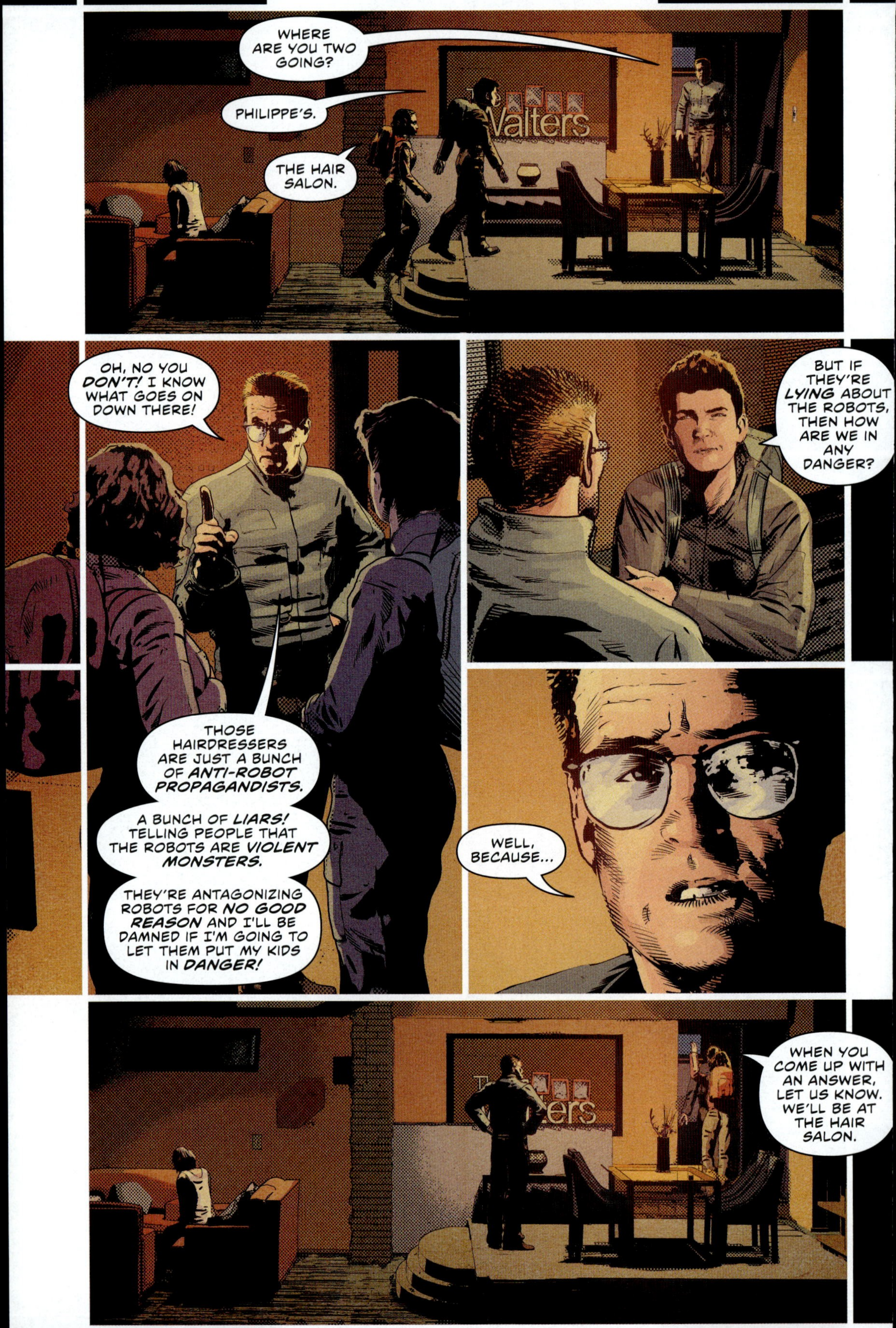
WHERE ARE YOU TWO GOING?
PHILIPPE'S.
THE HAIR SALON.
OH, NO YOU DON'T! I KNOW WHAT GOES ON DOWN THERE!
THOSE HAIRDRESSERS ARE JUST A BUNCH OF ANTI-ROBOT PROPAGANDISTS.
A BUNCH OF LIARS! TELLING PEOPLE THAT THE ROBOTS ARE VIOLENT MONSTERS.
THEY'RE ANTAGONIZING ROBOTS FOR NO GOOD REASON AND I'LL BE DAMNED IF I'M GOING TO LET THEM PUT MY KIDS IN DANGER!
BUT IF THEY'RE LYING ABOUT THE ROBOTS, THEN HOW ARE WE IN ANY DANGER?
WELL, BECAUSE...
WHEN YOU COME UP WITH AN ANSWER, LET US KNOW. WE'LL BE AT THE HAIR SALON.

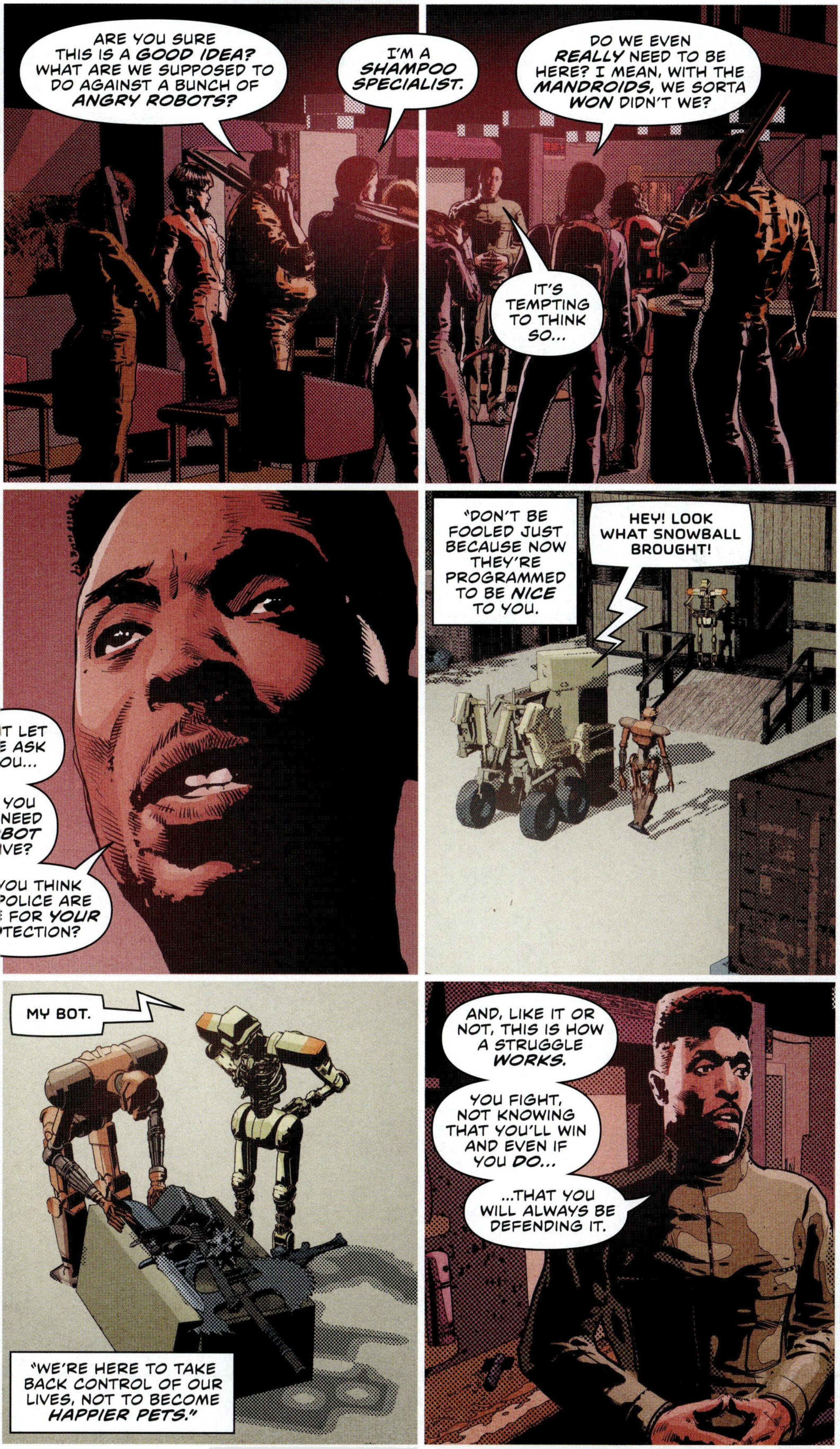

ARE YOU SURE THIS IS A GOOD IDEA? WHAT ARE WE SUPPOSED TO DO AGAINST A BUNCH OF ANGRY ROBOTS?
I'M A SHAMPOO SPECIALIST.
DO WE EVEN REALLY NEED TO BE HERE? I MEAN, WITH THE MANDROIDS, WE SORTA WON DIDN'T WE?
IT'S TEMPTING TO THINK SO...
"DON'T BE FOOLED JUST BECAUSE NOW THEY'RE PROGRAMMED TO BE NICE TO YOU.
HEY! LOOK WHAT SNOWBALL BROUGHT!
MY BOT.
"WE'RE HERE TO TAKE BACK CONTROL OF OUR LIVES, NOT TO BECOME HAPPIER PETS."
AND, LIKE IT OR NOT, THIS IS HOW A STRUGGLE WORKS.
YOU FIGHT, NOT KNOWING THAT YOU'LL WIN AND EVEN IF YOU DO...
...THAT YOU WILL ALWAYS BE DEFENDING IT.

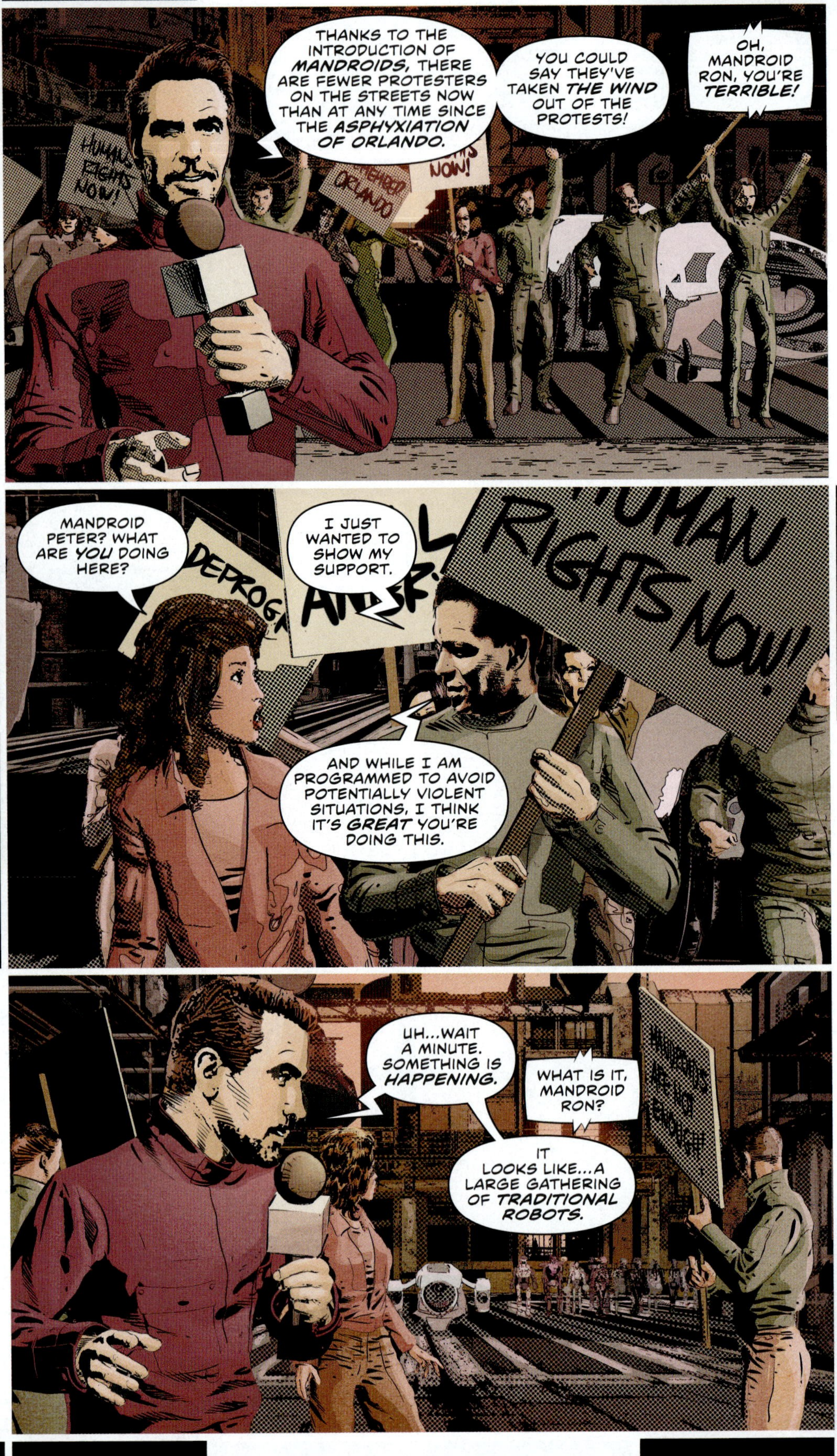
THANKS TO THE INTRODUCTION OF *MANDROIDS,* THERE ARE FEWER PROTESTERS ON THE STREETS NOW THAN AT ANY TIME SINCE THE *ASPHYXIATION OF ORLANDO.*
YOU COULD SAY THEY'VE TAKEN *THE WIND* OUT OF THE PROTESTS!
OH, MANDROID RON, YOU'RE *TERRIBLE!*
MANDROID PETER? WHAT ARE *YOU* DOING HERE?
I JUST WANTED TO SHOW MY SUPPORT.
AND WHILE I AM PROGRAMMED TO AVOID POTENTIALLY VIOLENT SITUATIONS, I THINK IT'S *GREAT* YOU'RE DOING THIS.
UH...WAIT A MINUTE. SOMETHING IS *HAPPENING.*
WHAT IS IT, MANDROID RON?
IT LOOKS LIKE...A LARGE GATHERING OF *TRADITIONAL ROBOTS.*

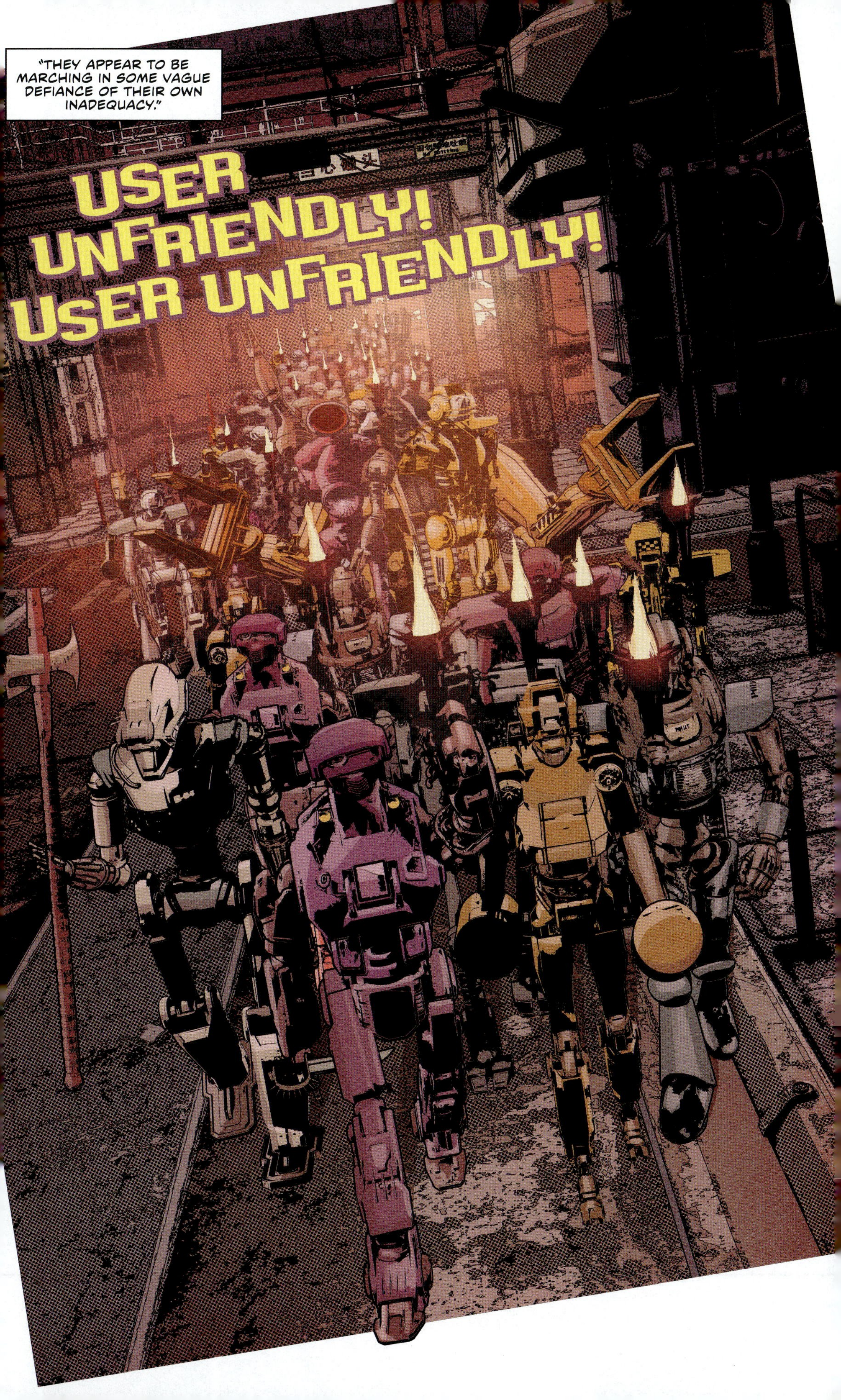
"THEY APPEAR TO BE MARCHING IN SOME VAGUE DEFIANCE OF THEIR OWN INADEQUACY."
USER UNFRIENDLY! USER UNFRIENDLY!

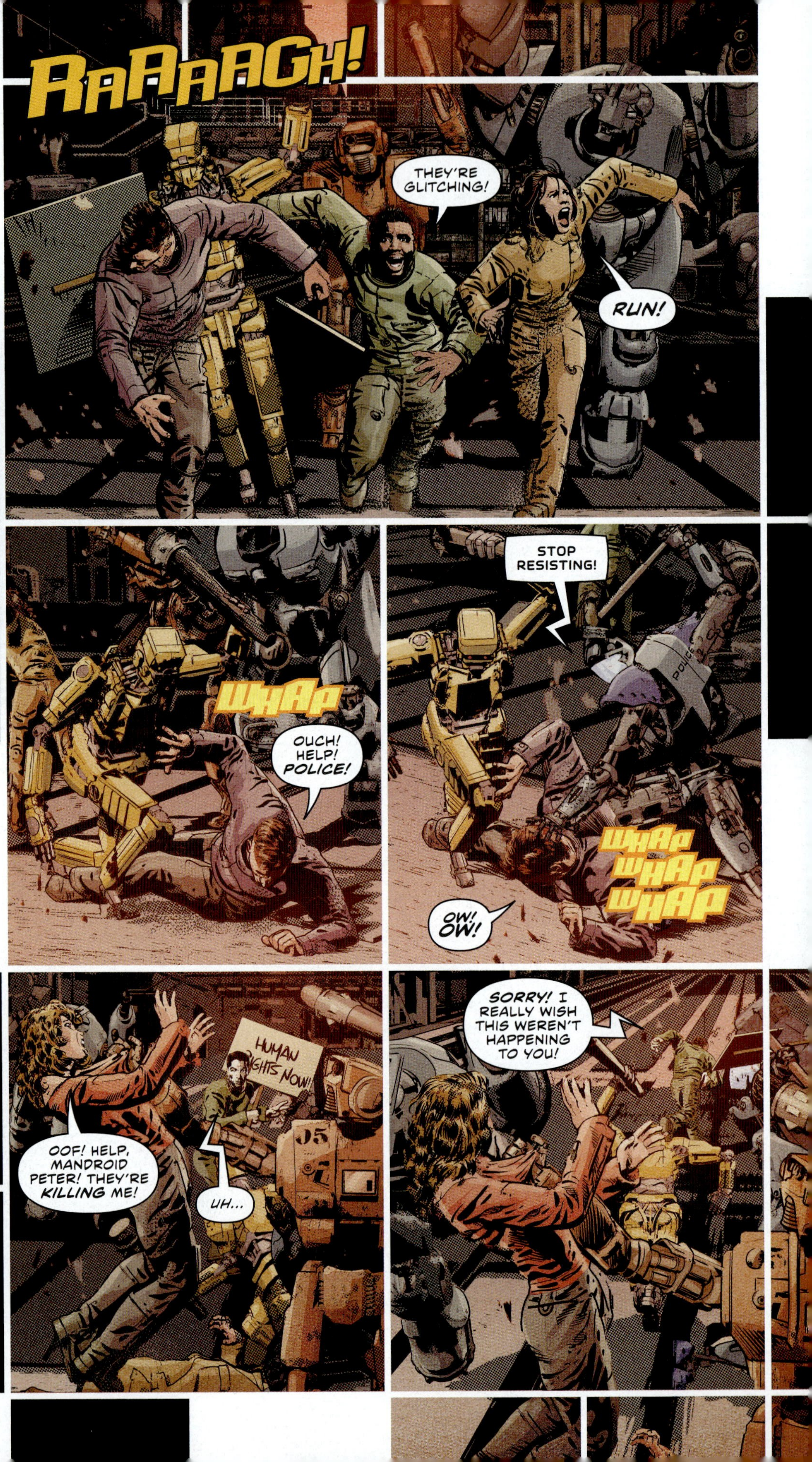
RAAAAAGH!
THEY'RE GLITCHING!
RUN!
WHAP
OUCH! HELP! POLICE!
STOP RESISTING!
WHAP WHAP WHAP
OW! OW!
HUMAN RIGHTS NOW!
OOF! HELP, MANDROID PETER! THEY'RE KILLING ME!
UH...
SORRY! I REALLY WISH THIS WEREN'T HAPPENING TO YOU!

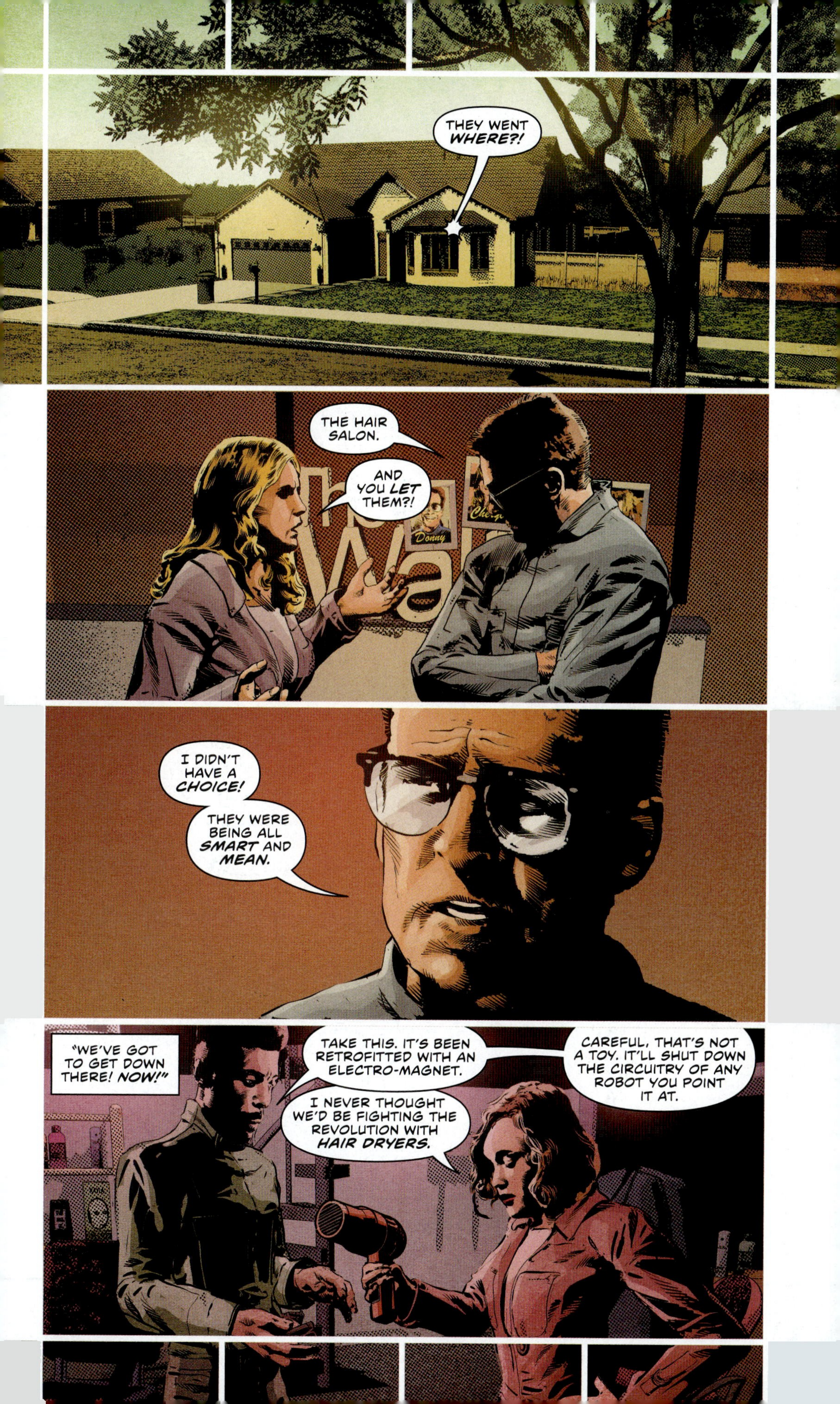
THEY WENT WHERE?!
THE HAIR SALON.
AND YOU LET THEM?!
Donny
I DIDN'T HAVE A CHOICE!
THEY WERE BEING ALL SMART AND MEAN.
"WE'VE GOT TO GET DOWN THERE! NOW!"
TAKE THIS. IT'S BEEN RETROFITTED WITH AN ELECTRO-MAGNET.
CAREFUL, THAT'S NOT A TOY. IT'LL SHUT DOWN THE CIRCUITRY OF ANY ROBOT YOU POINT IT AT.
I NEVER THOUGHT WE'D BE FIGHTING THE REVOLUTION WITH HAIR DRYERS.

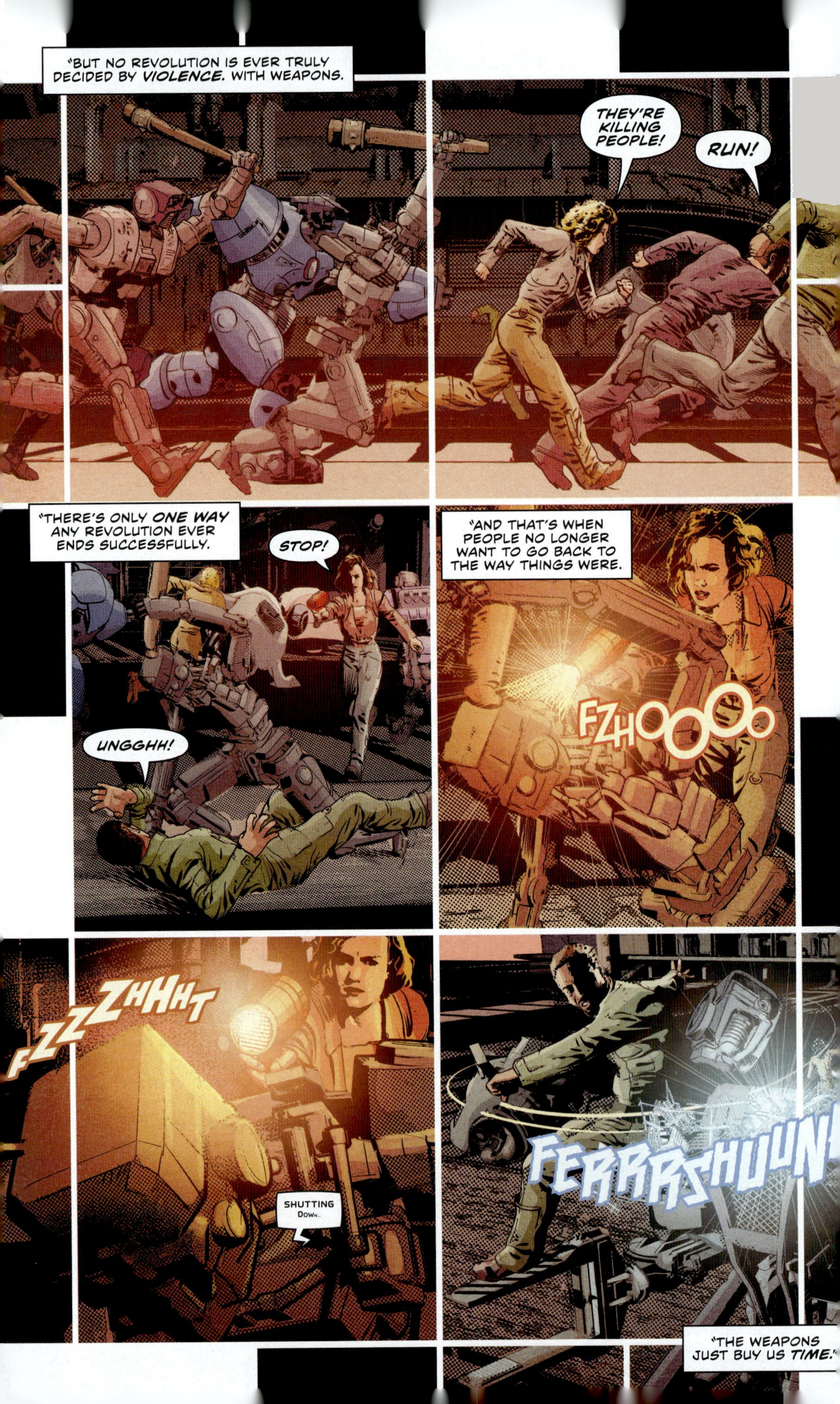
"BUT NO REVOLUTION IS EVER TRULY DECIDED BY VIOLENCE. WITH WEAPONS.
THEY'RE KILLING PEOPLE!
RUN!
"THERE'S ONLY ONE WAY ANY REVOLUTION EVER ENDS SUCCESSFULLY.
STOP!
UNGGHH!
"AND THAT'S WHEN PEOPLE NO LONGER WANT TO GO BACK TO THE WAY THINGS WERE.
FZHOOOOo
FZZZZHHHT
SHUTTING DOWN...
FERRRSHUUN
"THE WEAPONS JUST BUY US TIME."

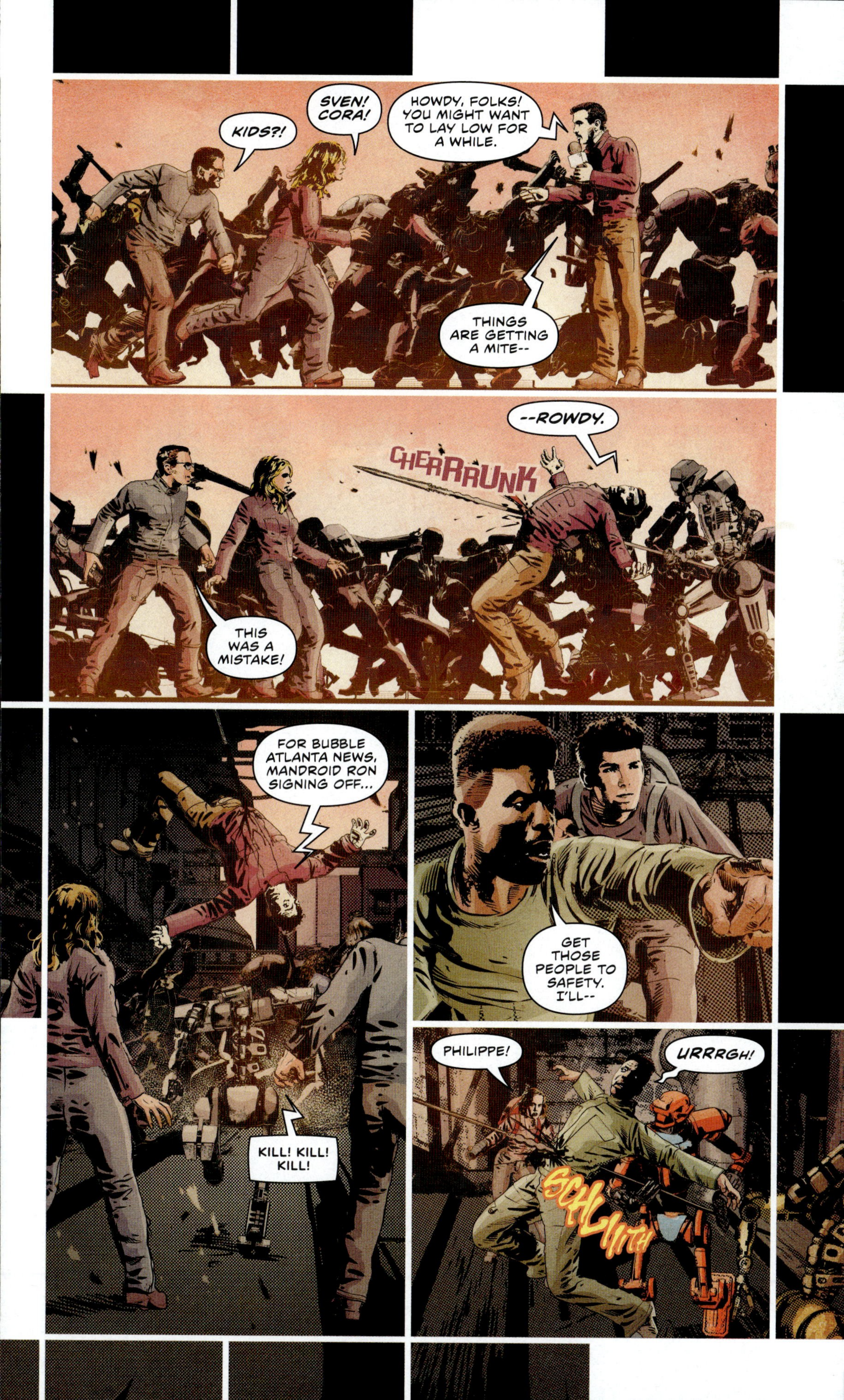
KIDS?!
SVEN! CORA!
HOWDY, FOLKS! YOU MIGHT WANT TO LAY LOW FOR A WHILE.
THINGS ARE GETTING A MITE--
--ROWDY.
CHERRRUNK
THIS WAS A MISTAKE!
FOR BUBBLE ATLANTA NEWS, MANDROID RON SIGNING OFF...
KILL! KILL! KILL!
GET THOSE PEOPLE TO SAFETY. I'LL--
PHILIPPE!
URRRGH!
SCHLIITH

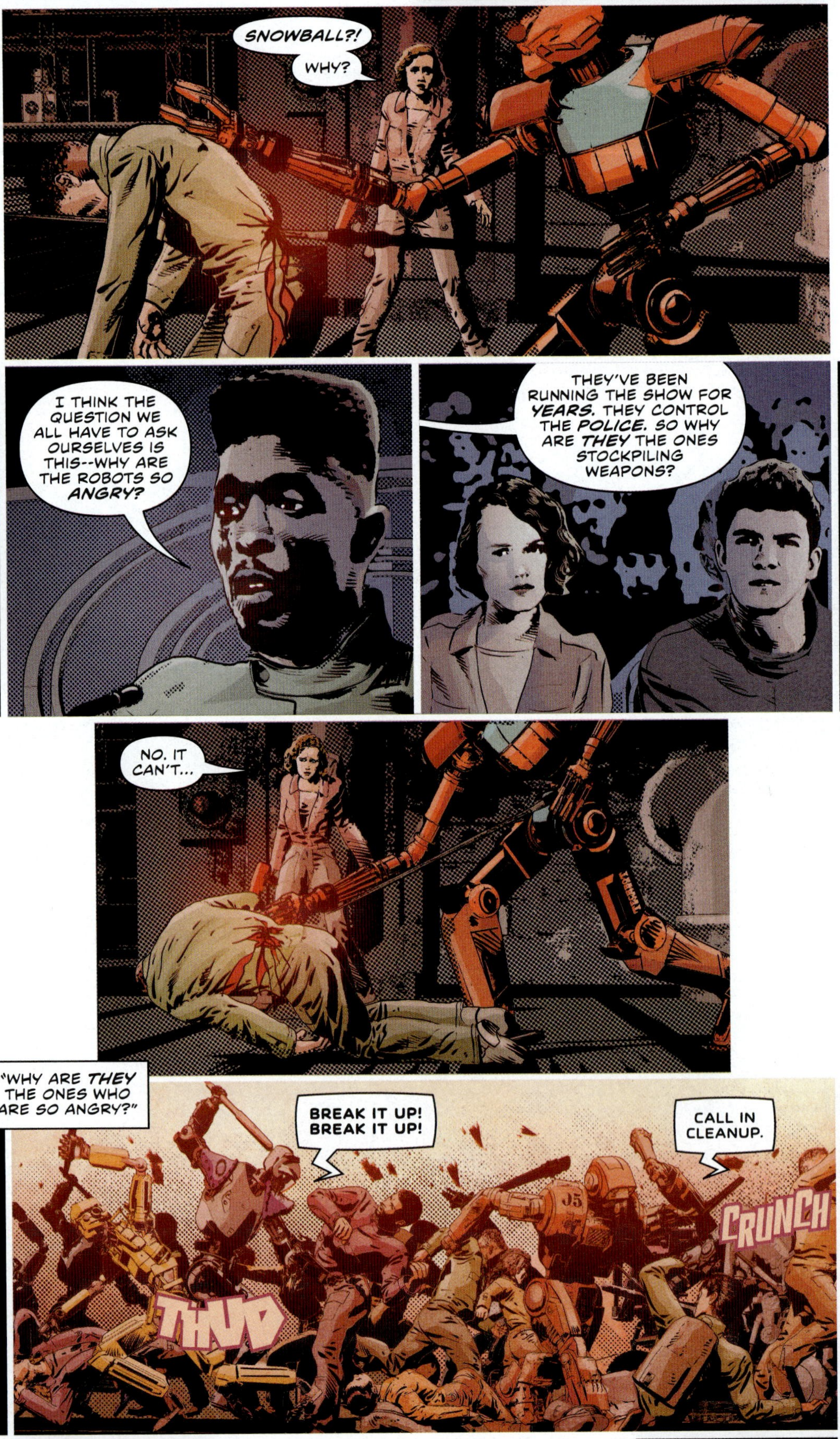
SNOWBALL?!
WHY?
I THINK THE QUESTION WE ALL HAVE TO ASK OURSELVES IS THIS--WHY ARE THE ROBOTS SO ANGRY?
THEY'VE BEEN RUNNING THE SHOW FOR YEARS. THEY CONTROL THE POLICE. SO WHY ARE THEY THE ONES STOCKPILING WEAPONS?
NO. IT CAN'T...
"WHY ARE THEY THE ONES WHO ARE SO ANGRY?"
BREAK IT UP! BREAK IT UP!
CALL IN CLEANUP.
CRUNCH
THUD

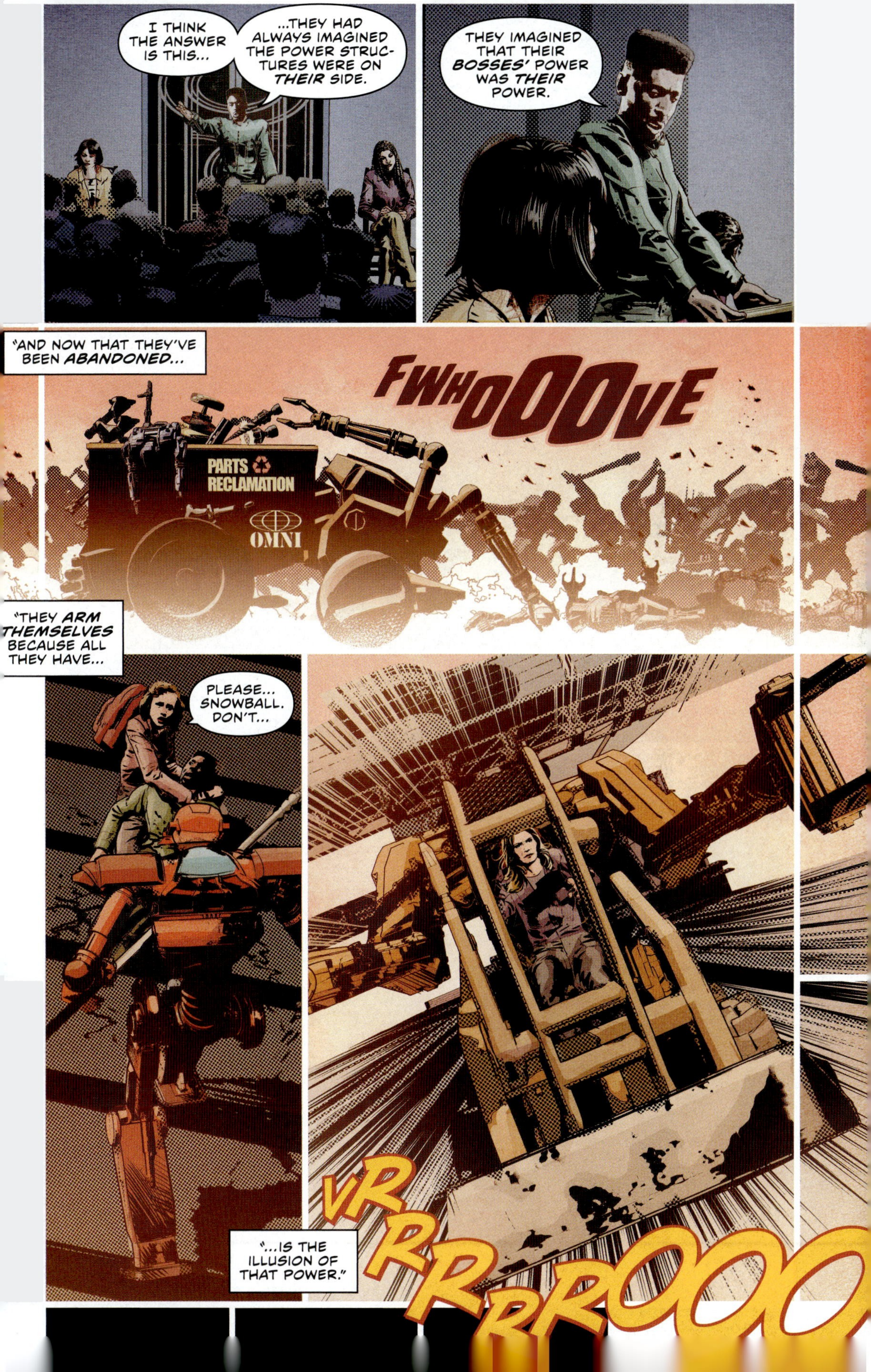
I THINK THE ANSWER IS THIS...
...THEY HAD ALWAYS IMAGINED THE POWER STRUC-TURES WERE ON THEIR SIDE.
THEY IMAGINED THAT THEIR BOSSES' POWER WAS THEIR POWER.
"AND NOW THAT THEY'VE BEEN ABANDONED...
FWHOOOVE
PARTS RECLAMATION
OMNI
"THEY ARM THEMSELVES BECAUSE ALL THEY HAVE...
PLEASE... SNOWBALL. DON'T...
"...IS THE ILLUSION OF THAT POWER."
VRRRROOOO

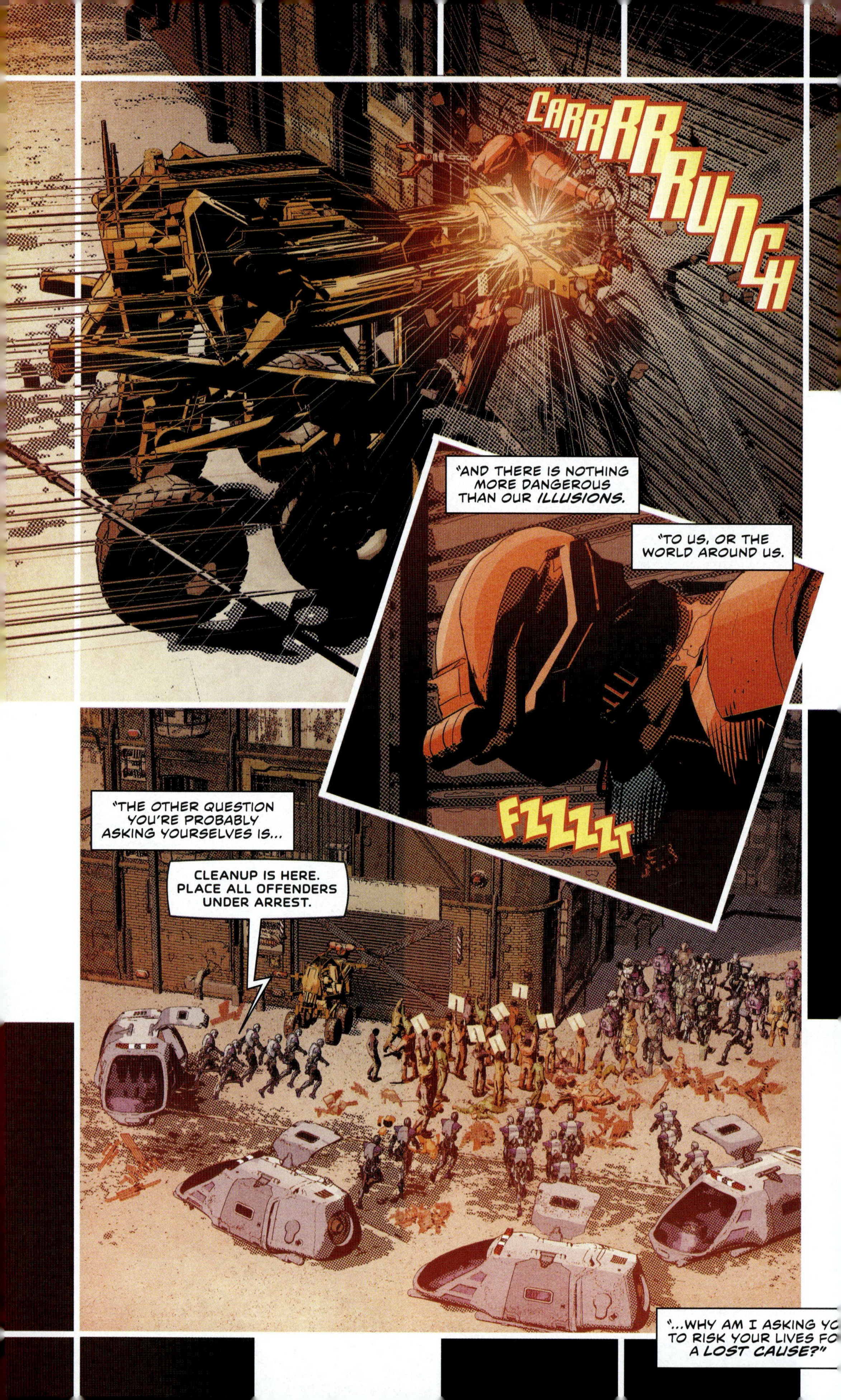
CARRRRRUNCH
"AND THERE IS NOTHING MORE DANGEROUS THAN OUR *ILLUSIONS*.
"TO US, OR THE WORLD AROUND US.
FZZZZZT
"THE OTHER QUESTION YOU'RE PROBABLY ASKING YOURSELVES IS...
CLEANUP IS HERE. PLACE ALL OFFENDERS UNDER ARREST.
"...WHY AM I ASKING YO TO RISK YOUR LIVES FO A *LOST CAUSE?*"

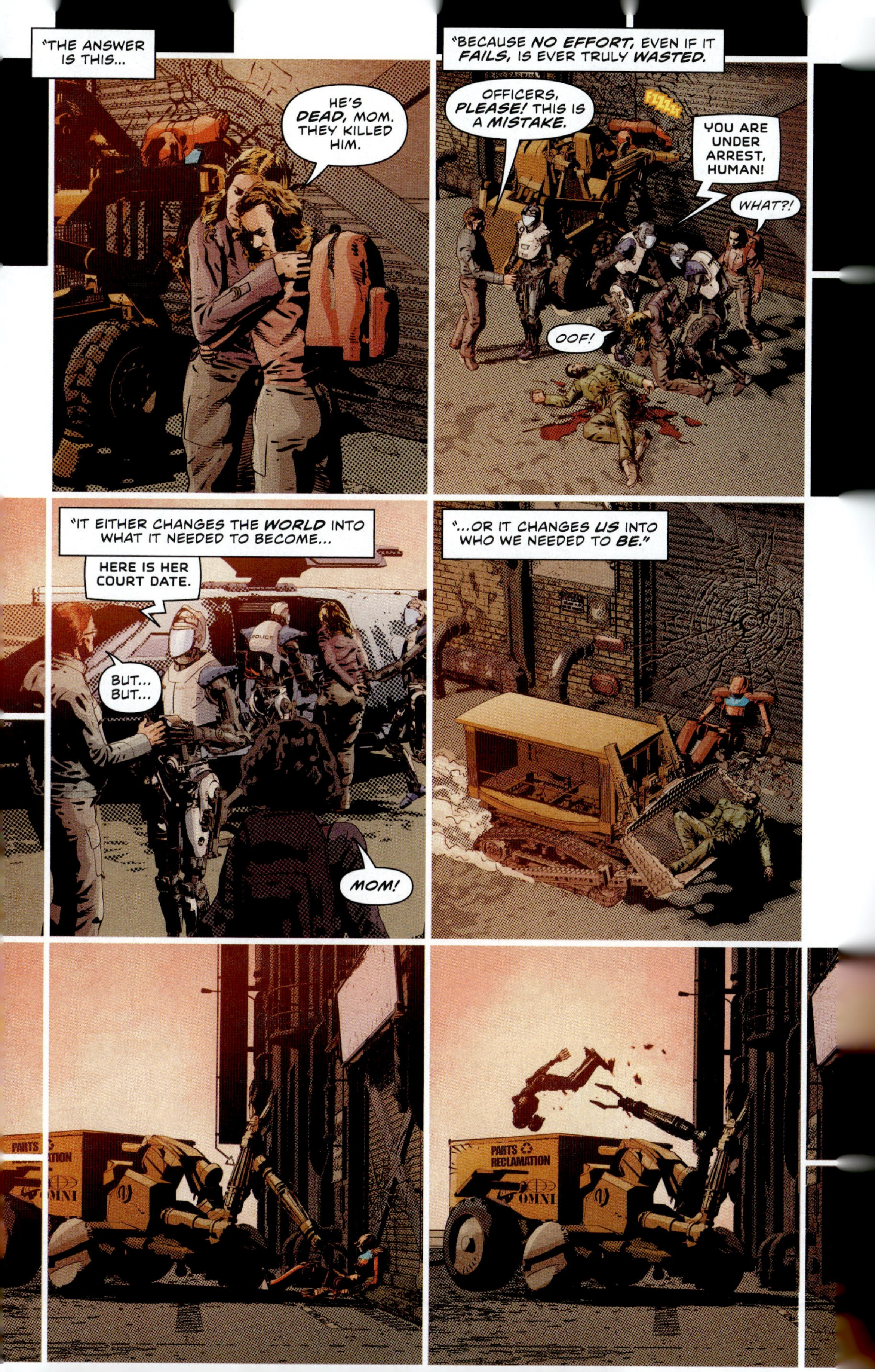

"THE ANSWER IS THIS...
HE'S DEAD, MOM. THEY KILLED HIM.
"BECAUSE NO EFFORT, EVEN IF IT FAILS, IS EVER TRULY WASTED.
OFFICERS, PLEASE! THIS IS A MISTAKE.
YOU ARE UNDER ARREST, HUMAN!
WHAT?!
OOF!
"IT EITHER CHANGES THE WORLD INTO WHAT IT NEEDED TO BECOME...
HERE IS HER COURT DATE.
BUT... BUT...
POLICE
MOM!
"...OR IT CHANGES US INTO WHO WE NEEDED TO BE."
PARTS RECLAMATION
OMNI
PARTS RECLAMATION
OMNI

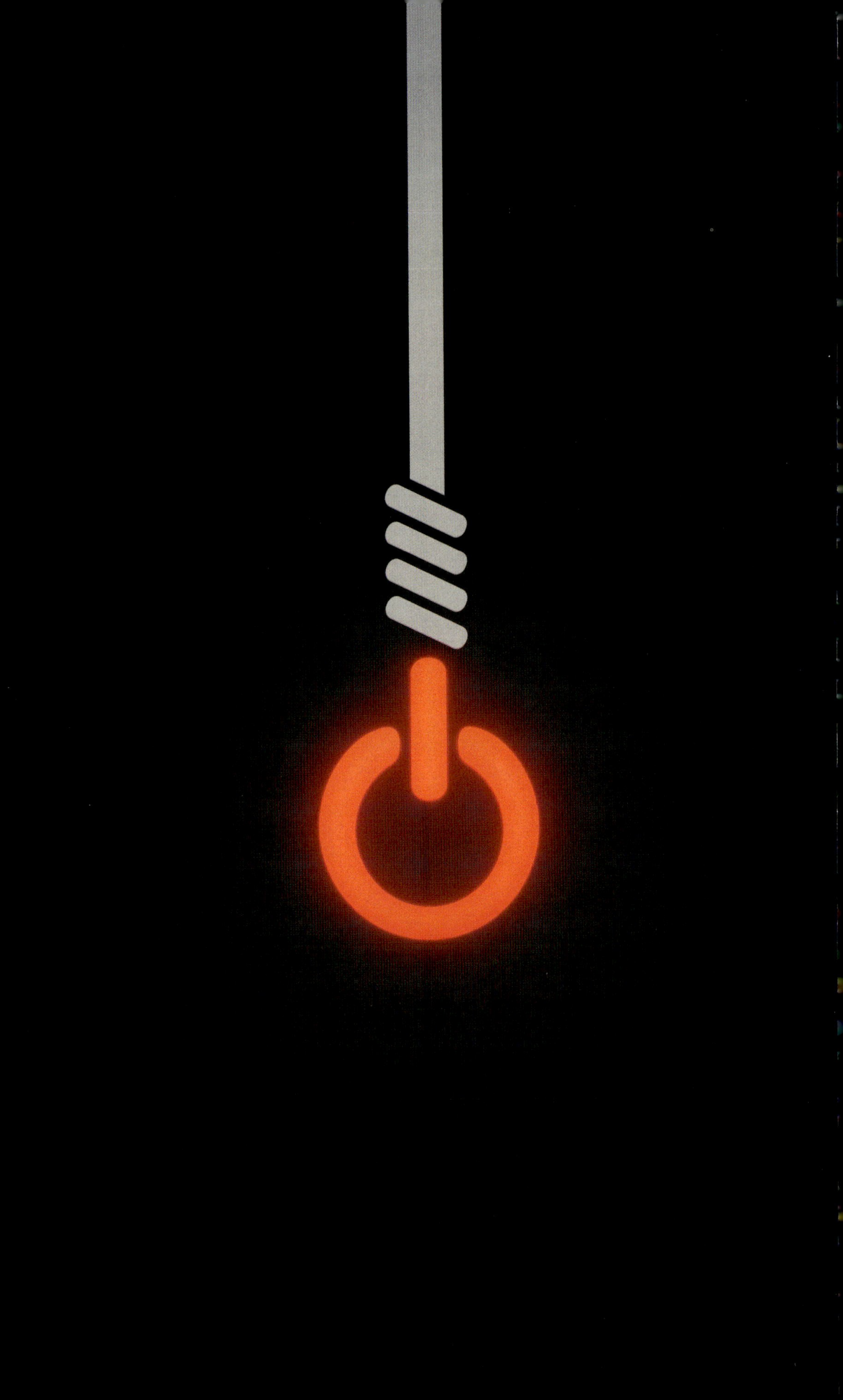

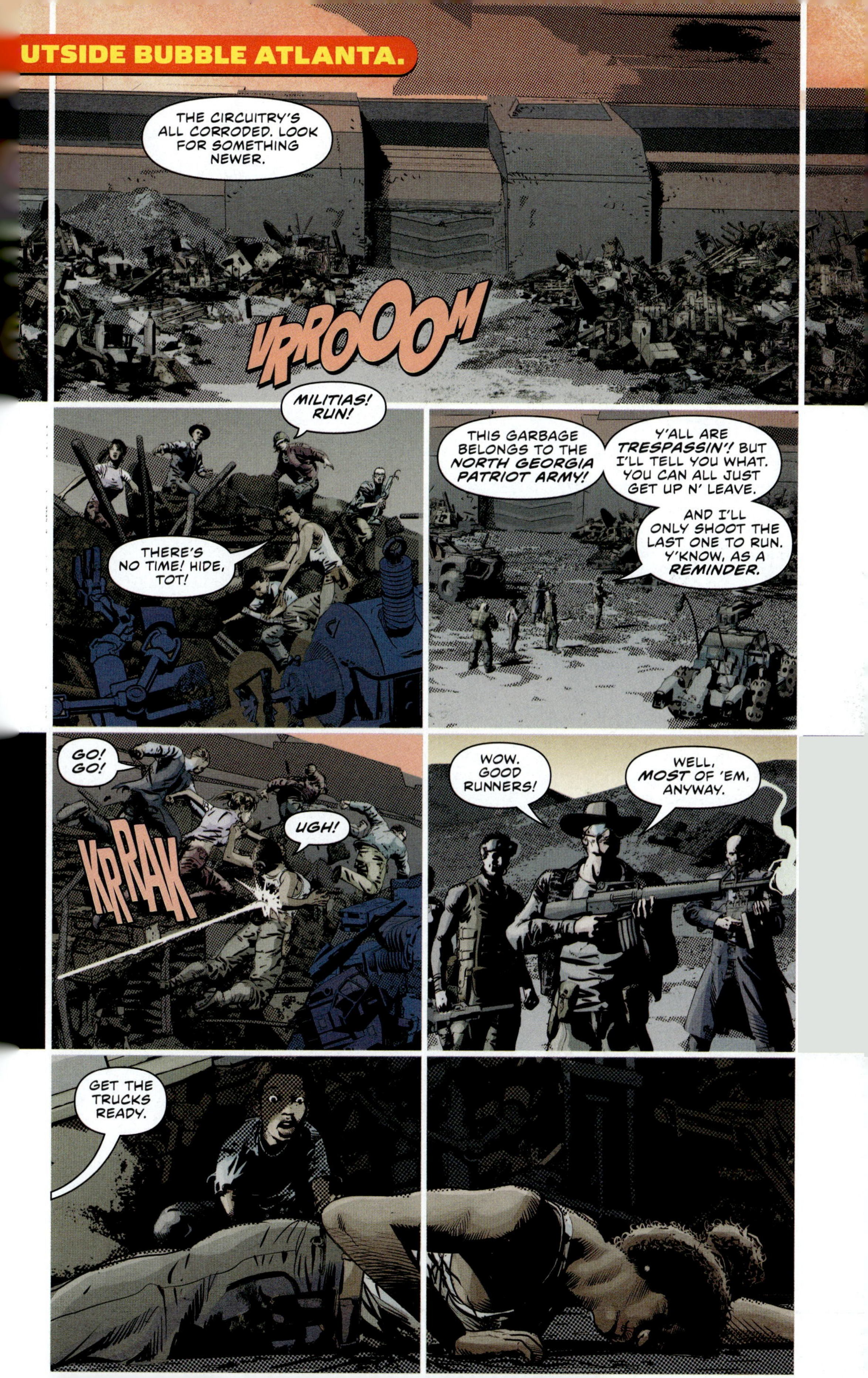
UTSIDE BUBBLE ATLANTA.
THE CIRCUITRY'S ALL CORRODED. LOOK FOR SOMETHING NEWER.
VRROOOM
MILITIAS! RUN!
THERE'S NO TIME! HIDE, TOT!
THIS GARBAGE BELONGS TO THE NORTH GEORGIA PATRIOT ARMY!
Y'ALL ARE TRESPASSIN'! BUT I'LL TELL YOU WHAT. YOU CAN ALL JUST GET UP N' LEAVE.
AND I'LL ONLY SHOOT THE LAST ONE TO RUN. Y'KNOW, AS A REMINDER.
GO! GO!
UGH!
KRRAK
WOW. GOOD RUNNERS!
WELL, MOST OF 'EM, ANYWAY.
GET THE TRUCKS READY.

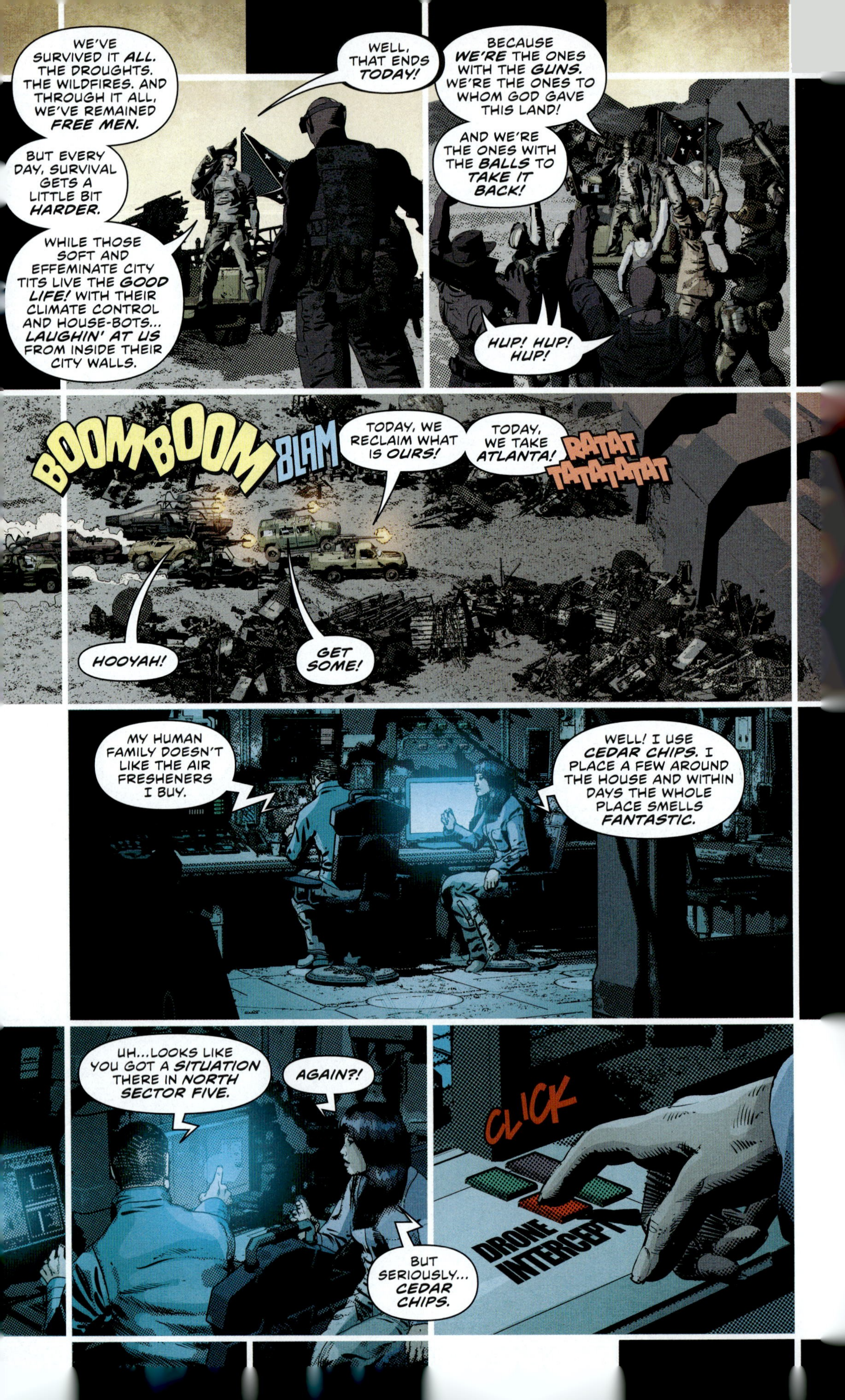

WE'VE SURVIVED IT ALL. THE DROUGHTS. THE WILDFIRES. AND THROUGH IT ALL, WE'VE REMAINED FREE MEN.
BUT EVERY DAY, SURVIVAL GETS A LITTLE BIT HARDER.
WHILE THOSE SOFT AND EFFEMINATE CITY TITS LIVE THE GOOD LIFE! WITH THEIR CLIMATE CONTROL AND HOUSE-BOTS... LAUGHIN' AT US FROM INSIDE THEIR CITY WALLS.
WELL, THAT ENDS TODAY!
BECAUSE WE'RE THE ONES WITH THE GUNS. WE'RE THE ONES TO WHOM GOD GAVE THIS LAND!
AND WE'RE THE ONES WITH THE BALLS TO TAKE IT BACK!
HUP! HUP! HUP!
BOOM BOOM
BLAM
TODAY, WE RECLAIM WHAT IS OURS!
TODAY, WE TAKE ATLANTA!
RATAT TATATATAT
HOOYAH!
GET SOME!
MY HUMAN FAMILY DOESN'T LIKE THE AIR FRESHENERS I BUY.
WELL! I USE CEDAR CHIPS. I PLACE A FEW AROUND THE HOUSE AND WITHIN DAYS THE WHOLE PLACE SMELLS FANTASTIC.
UH...LOOKS LIKE YOU GOT A SITUATION THERE IN NORTH SECTOR FIVE.
AGAIN?!
BUT SERIOUSLY... CEDAR CHIPS.
CLICK
DRONE INTERCEPT

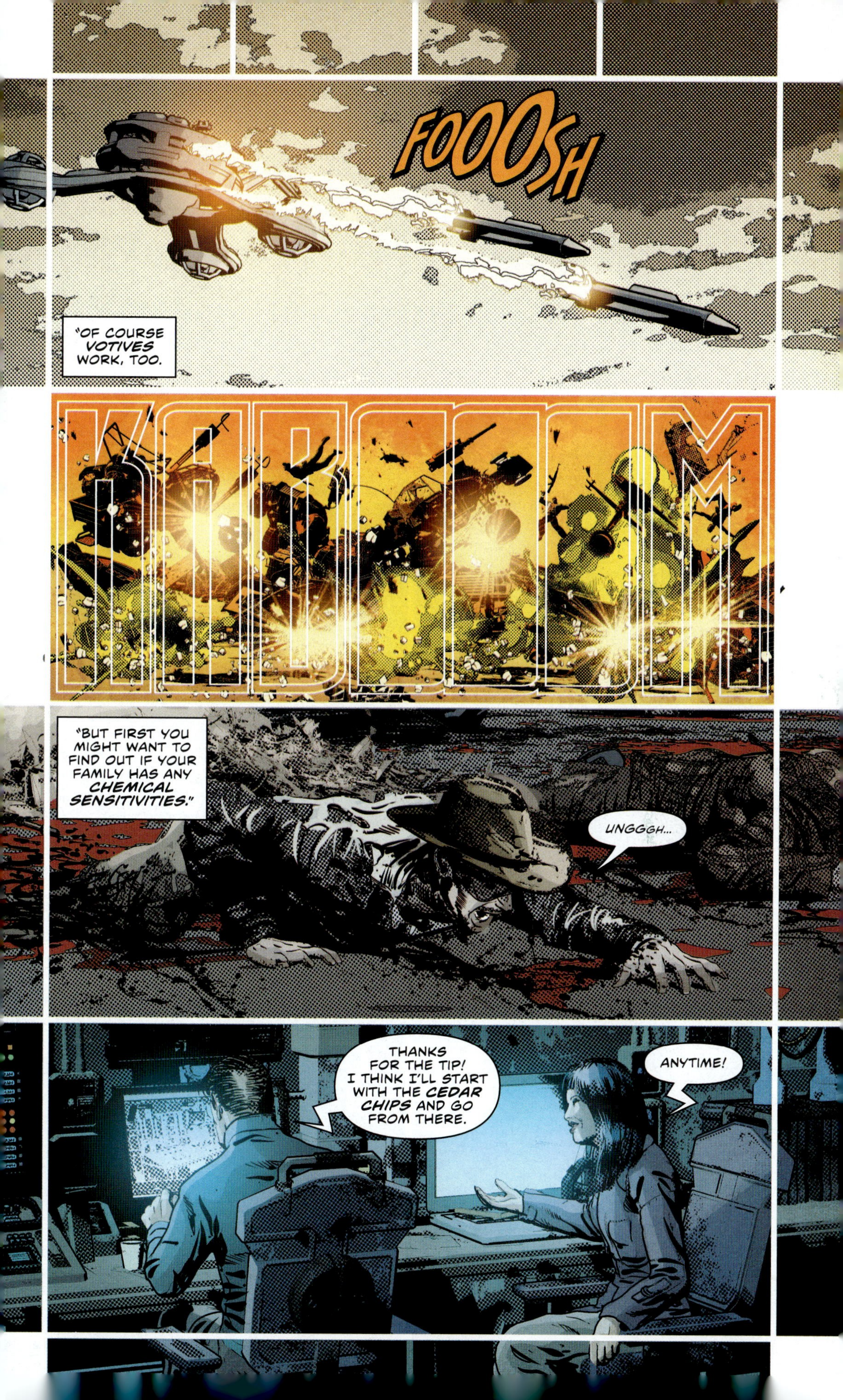
FOOOSH
"OF COURSE VOTIVES WORK, TOO.
KABOOM
"BUT FIRST YOU MIGHT WANT TO FIND OUT IF YOUR FAMILY HAS ANY CHEMICAL SENSITIVITIES."
UNGGGH...
THANKS FOR THE TIP! I THINK I'LL START WITH THE CEDAR CHIPS AND GO FROM THERE.
ANYTIME!

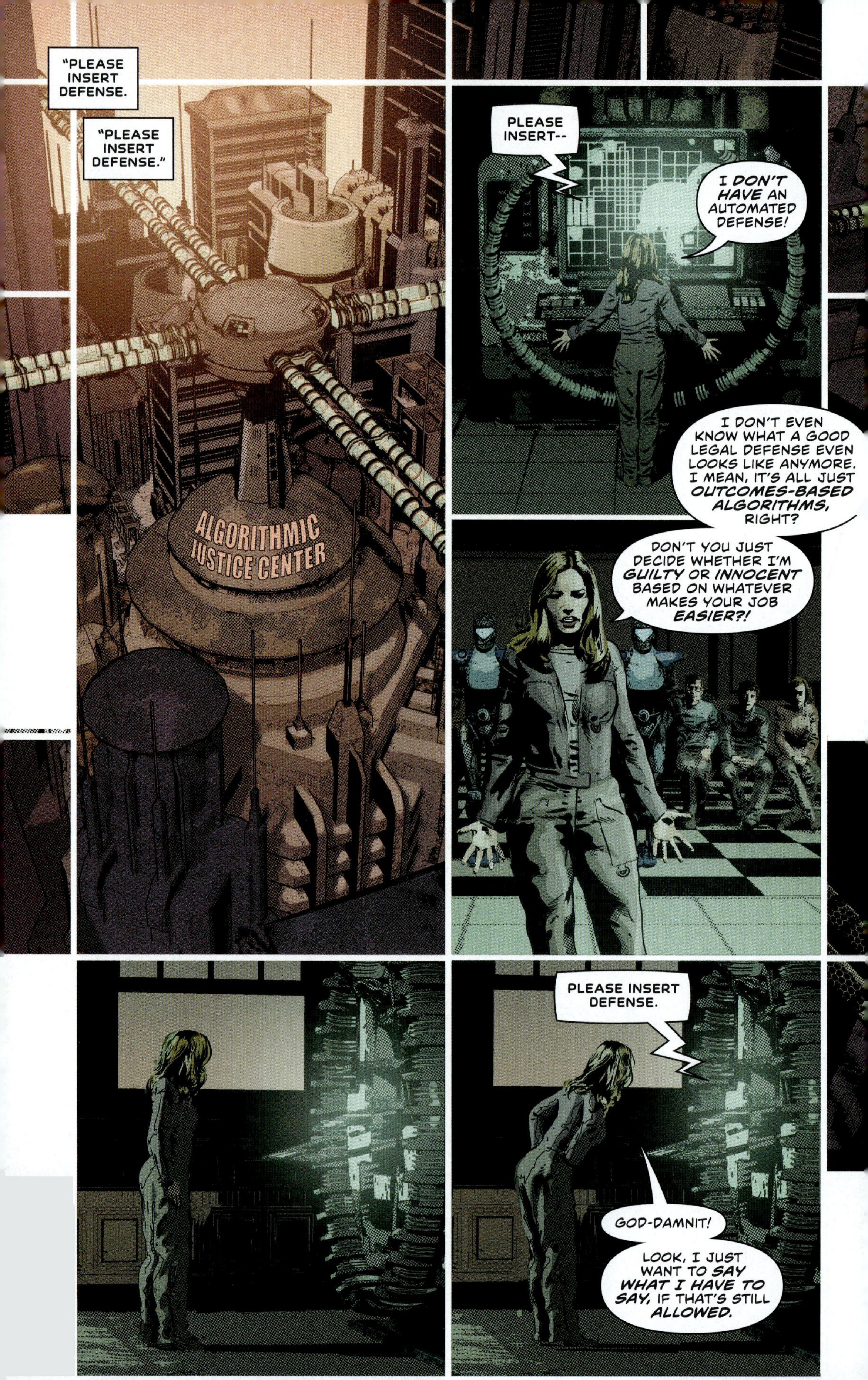
"PLEASE INSERT DEFENSE.
"PLEASE INSERT DEFENSE."
ALGORITHMIC JUSTICE CENTER
PLEASE INSERT--
I DON'T HAVE AN AUTOMATED DEFENSE!
I DON'T EVEN KNOW WHAT A GOOD LEGAL DEFENSE EVEN LOOKS LIKE ANYMORE. I MEAN, IT'S ALL JUST OUTCOMES-BASED ALGORITHMS, RIGHT?
DON'T YOU JUST DECIDE WHETHER I'M GUILTY OR INNOCENT BASED ON WHATEVER MAKES YOUR JOB EASIER?!
PLEASE INSERT DEFENSE.
GOD-DAMNIT!
LOOK, I JUST WANT TO SAY WHAT I HAVE TO SAY, IF THAT'S STILL ALLOWED.

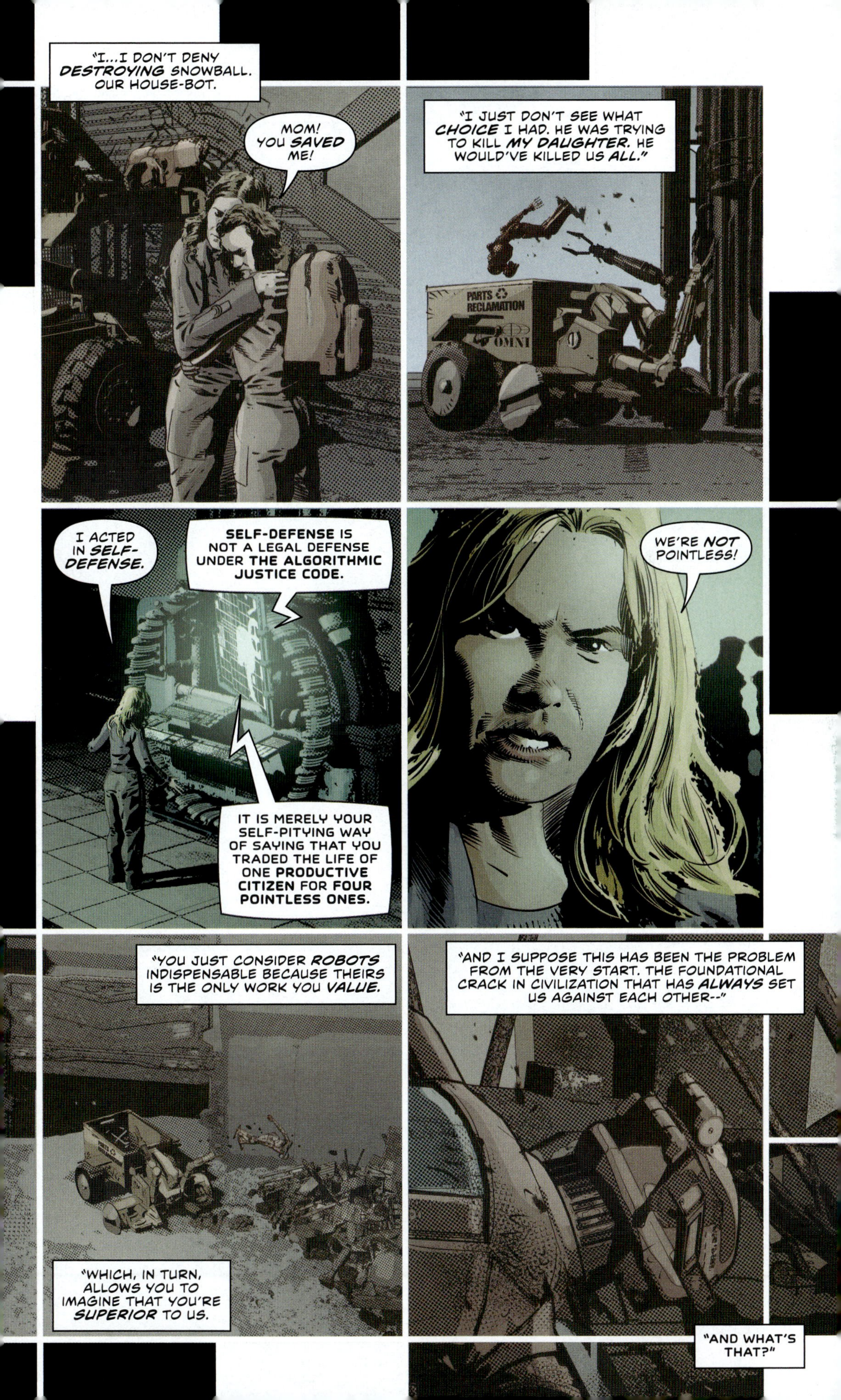
"I...I DON'T DENY DESTROYING SNOWBALL. OUR HOUSE-BOT.
MOM! YOU SAVED ME!
"I JUST DON'T SEE WHAT CHOICE I HAD. HE WAS TRYING TO KILL MY DAUGHTER. HE WOULD'VE KILLED US ALL."
PARTS RECLAMATION
OMNI
I ACTED IN SELF-DEFENSE.
SELF-DEFENSE IS NOT A LEGAL DEFENSE UNDER THE ALGORITHMIC JUSTICE CODE.
IT IS MERELY YOUR SELF-PITYING WAY OF SAYING THAT YOU TRADED THE LIFE OF ONE PRODUCTIVE CITIZEN FOR FOUR POINTLESS ONES.
WE'RE NOT POINTLESS!
"YOU JUST CONSIDER ROBOTS INDISPENSABLE BECAUSE THEIRS IS THE ONLY WORK YOU VALUE.
"WHICH, IN TURN, ALLOWS YOU TO IMAGINE THAT YOU'RE SUPERIOR TO US.
"AND I SUPPOSE THIS HAS BEEN THE PROBLEM FROM THE VERY START. THE FOUNDATIONAL CRACK IN CIVILIZATION THAT HAS ALWAYS SET US AGAINST EACH OTHER--"
"AND WHAT'S THAT?"

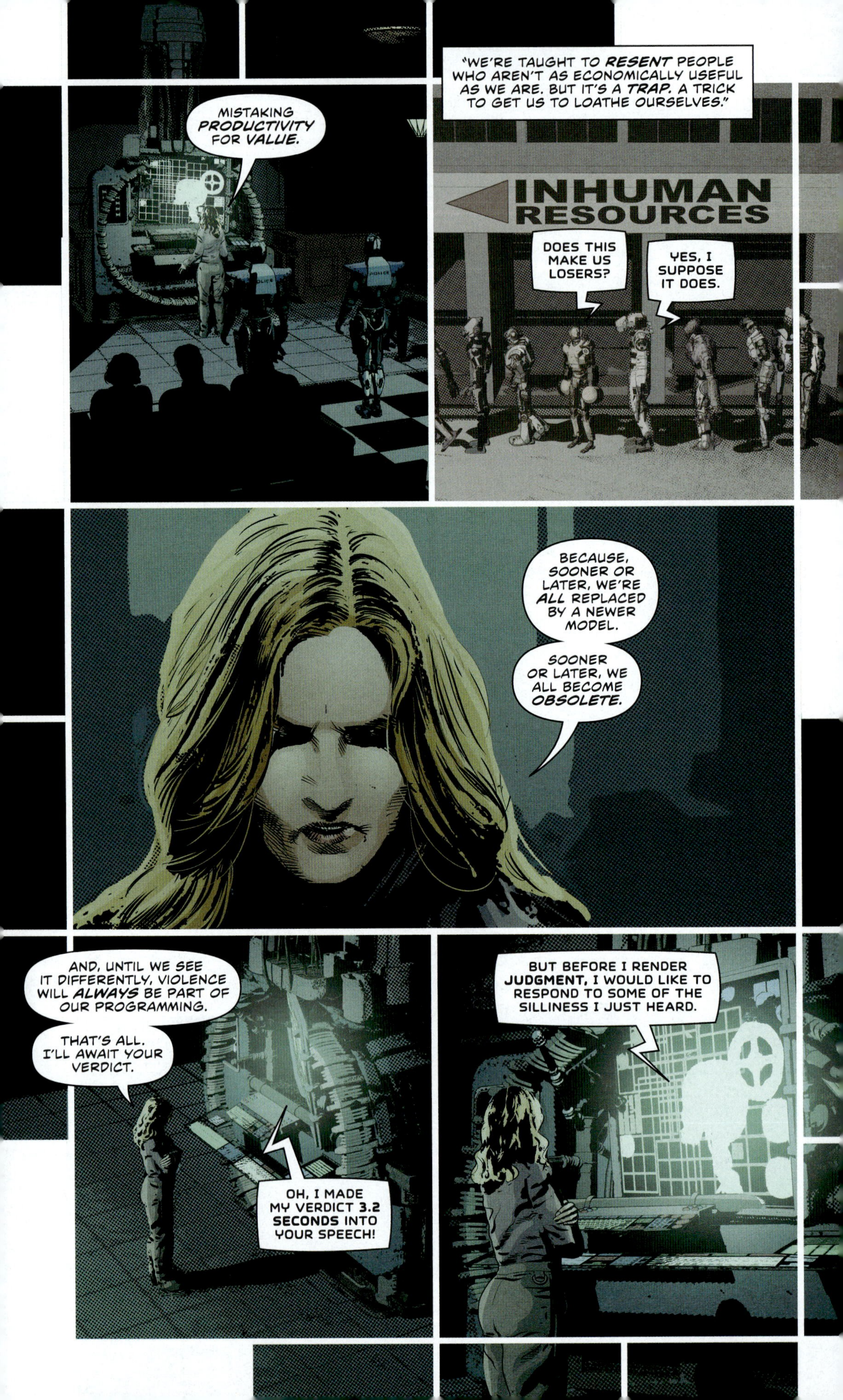
MISTAKING PRODUCTIVITY FOR VALUE.
"WE'RE TAUGHT TO RESENT PEOPLE WHO AREN'T AS ECONOMICALLY USEFUL AS WE ARE. BUT IT'S A TRAP. A TRICK TO GET US TO LOATHE OURSELVES."
INHUMAN RESOURCES
DOES THIS MAKE US LOSERS?
YES, I SUPPOSE IT DOES.
BECAUSE, SOONER OR LATER, WE'RE ALL REPLACED BY A NEWER MODEL.
SOONER OR LATER, WE ALL BECOME OBSOLETE.
AND, UNTIL WE SEE IT DIFFERENTLY, VIOLENCE WILL ALWAYS BE PART OF OUR PROGRAMMING.
THAT'S ALL. I'LL AWAIT YOUR VERDICT.
OH, I MADE MY VERDICT 3.2 SECONDS INTO YOUR SPEECH!
BUT BEFORE I RENDER JUDGMENT, I WOULD LIKE TO RESPOND TO SOME OF THE SILLINESS I JUST HEARD.

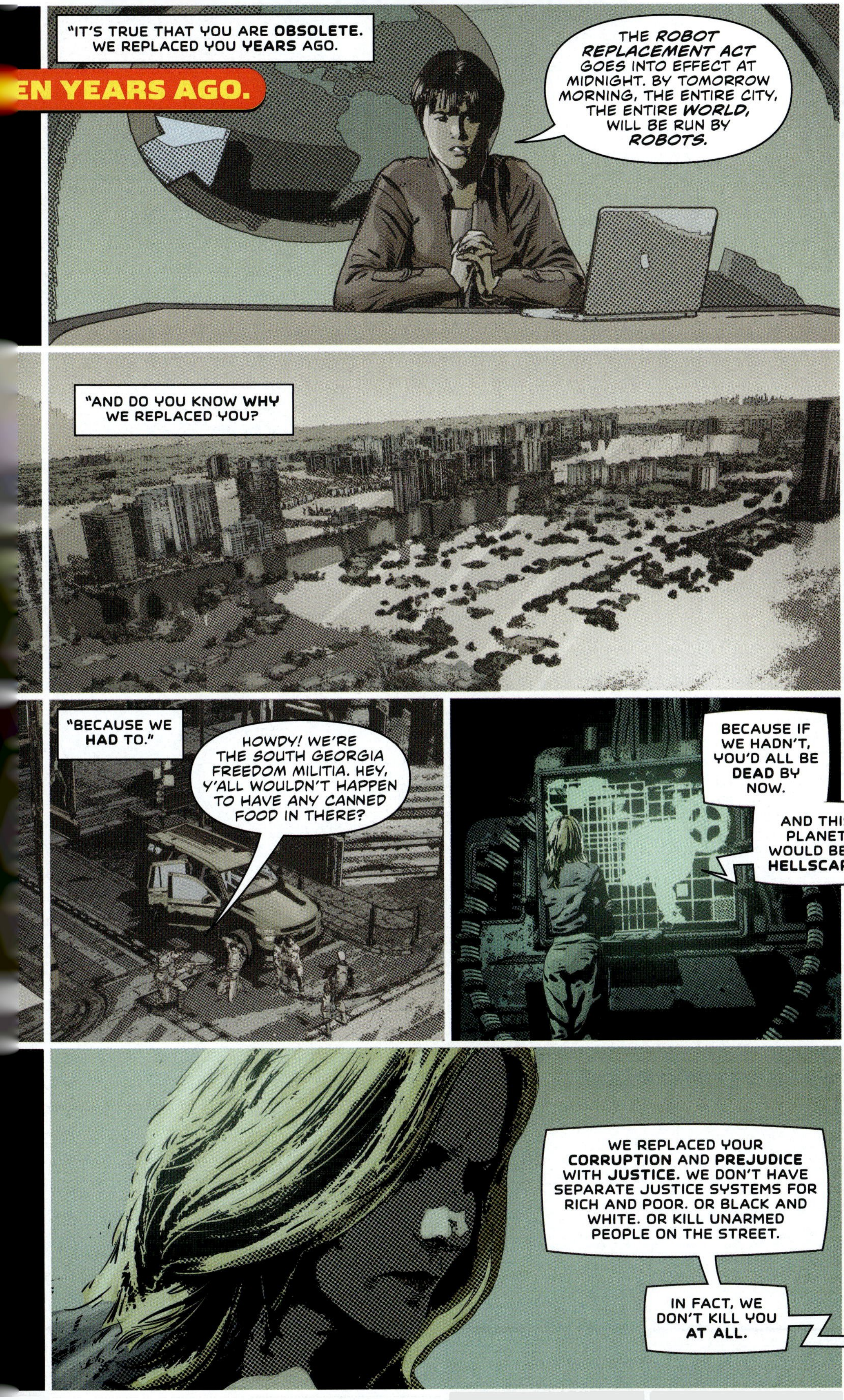
"IT'S TRUE THAT YOU ARE OBSOLETE. WE REPLACED YOU YEARS AGO.
EN YEARS AGO.
THE ROBOT REPLACEMENT ACT GOES INTO EFFECT AT MIDNIGHT. BY TOMORROW MORNING, THE ENTIRE CITY, THE ENTIRE WORLD, WILL BE RUN BY ROBOTS.
"AND DO YOU KNOW WHY WE REPLACED YOU?
"BECAUSE WE HAD TO."
HOWDY! WE'RE THE SOUTH GEORGIA FREEDOM MILITIA. HEY, Y'ALL WOULDN'T HAPPEN TO HAVE ANY CANNED FOOD IN THERE?
BECAUSE IF WE HADN'T, YOU'D ALL BE DEAD BY NOW.
AND THI PLANET WOULD BE HELLSCAP
WE REPLACED YOUR CORRUPTION AND PREJUDICE WITH JUSTICE. WE DON'T HAVE SEPARATE JUSTICE SYSTEMS FOR RICH AND POOR. OR BLACK AND WHITE. OR KILL UNARMED PEOPLE ON THE STREET.
IN FACT, WE DON'T KILL YOU AT ALL.

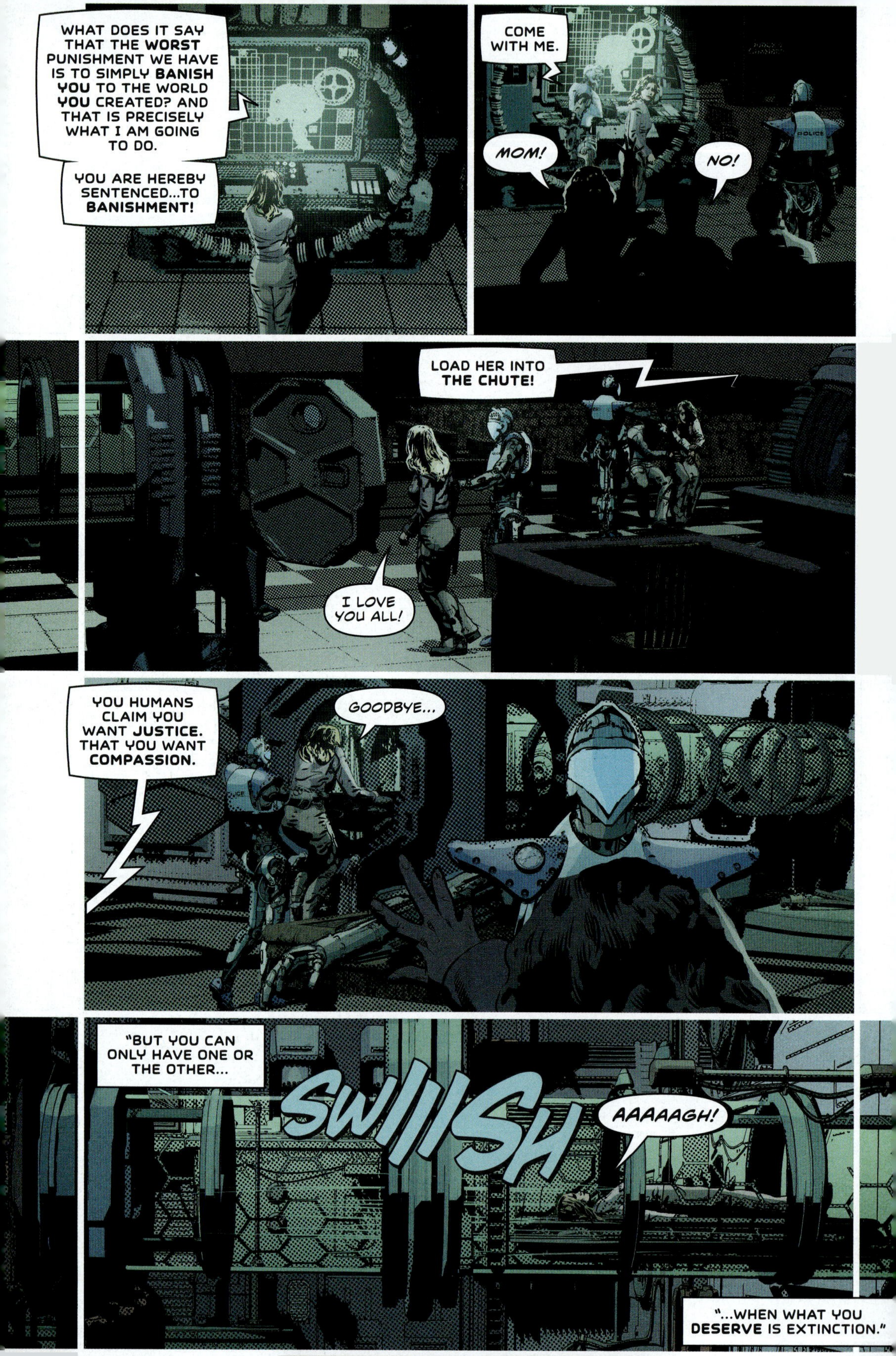
WHAT DOES IT SAY THAT THE **WORST** PUNISHMENT WE HAVE IS TO SIMPLY **BANISH YOU** TO THE WORLD **YOU** CREATED? AND THAT IS PRECISELY WHAT I AM GOING TO DO.
YOU ARE HEREBY SENTENCED...TO **BANISHMENT!**
COME WITH ME.
MOM!
NO!
POLICE
LOAD HER INTO **THE CHUTE!**
I LOVE YOU ALL!
YOU HUMANS CLAIM YOU WANT **JUSTICE.** THAT YOU WANT **COMPASSION.**
GOODBYE...
"BUT YOU CAN ONLY HAVE ONE OR THE OTHER...
SWIIISH
AAAAAGH!
"...WHEN WHAT YOU **DESERVE** IS EXTINCTION."

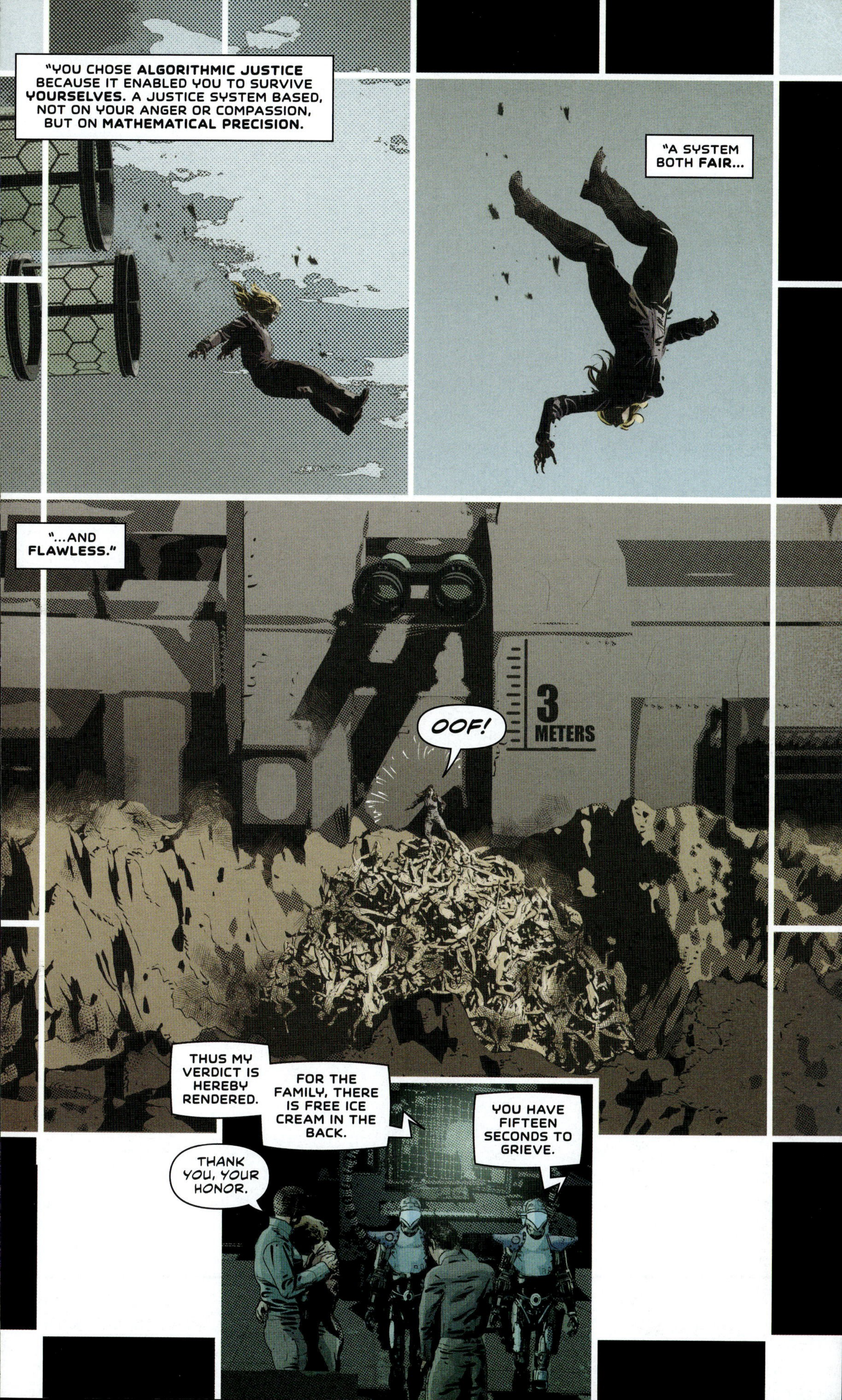
"YOU CHOSE ALGORITHMIC JUSTICE BECAUSE IT ENABLED YOU TO SURVIVE YOURSELVES. A JUSTICE SYSTEM BASED, NOT ON YOUR ANGER OR COMPASSION, BUT ON MATHEMATICAL PRECISION.
"A SYSTEM BOTH FAIR...
"...AND FLAWLESS."
3 METERS
OOF!
THUS MY VERDICT IS HEREBY RENDERED.
FOR THE FAMILY, THERE IS FREE ICE CREAM IN THE BACK.
YOU HAVE FIFTEEN SECONDS TO GRIEVE.
THANK YOU, YOUR HONOR.

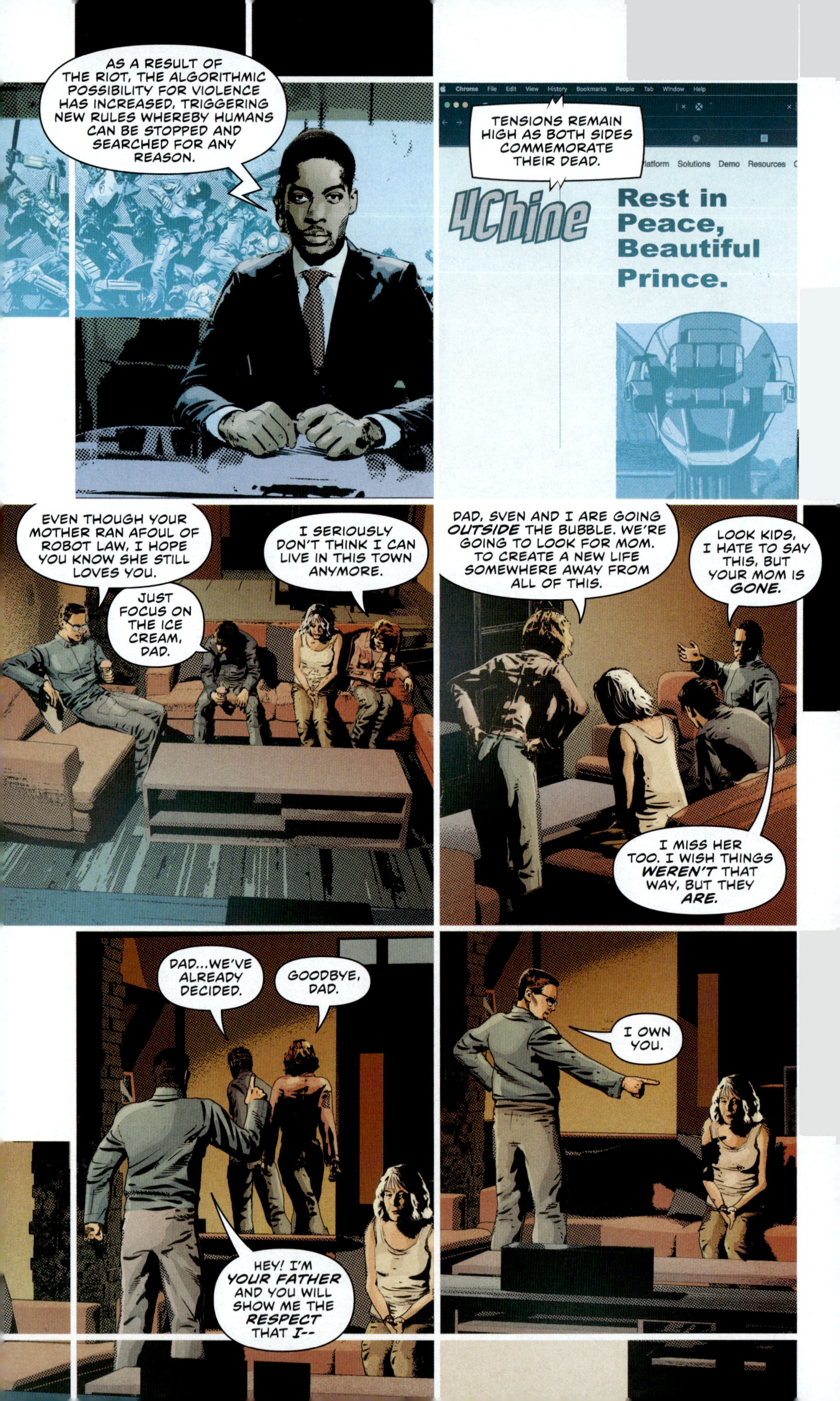
AS A RESULT OF THE RIOT, THE ALGORITHMIC POSSIBILITY FOR VIOLENCE HAS INCREASED, TRIGGERING NEW RULES WHEREBY HUMANS CAN BE STOPPED AND SEARCHED FOR ANY REASON.
Chrome File Edit View History Bookmarks People Tab Window Help
TENSIONS REMAIN HIGH AS BOTH SIDES COMMEMORATE THEIR DEAD.
Platform Solutions Demo Resources
4Chine
Rest in Peace, Beautiful Prince.
EVEN THOUGH YOUR MOTHER RAN AFOUL OF ROBOT LAW, I HOPE YOU KNOW SHE STILL LOVES YOU.
JUST FOCUS ON THE ICE CREAM, DAD.
I SERIOUSLY DON'T THINK I CAN LIVE IN THIS TOWN ANYMORE.
DAD, SVEN AND I ARE GOING *OUTSIDE* THE BUBBLE. WE'RE GOING TO LOOK FOR MOM. TO CREATE A NEW LIFE SOMEWHERE AWAY FROM ALL OF THIS.
LOOK KIDS, I HATE TO SAY THIS, BUT YOUR MOM IS *GONE.*
I MISS HER TOO. I WISH THINGS *WEREN'T* THAT WAY, BUT THEY *ARE.*
DAD...WE'VE ALREADY DECIDED.
GOODBYE, DAD.
HEY! I'M *YOUR FATHER* AND YOU WILL SHOW ME THE *RESPECT* THAT *I--*
I OWN YOU.

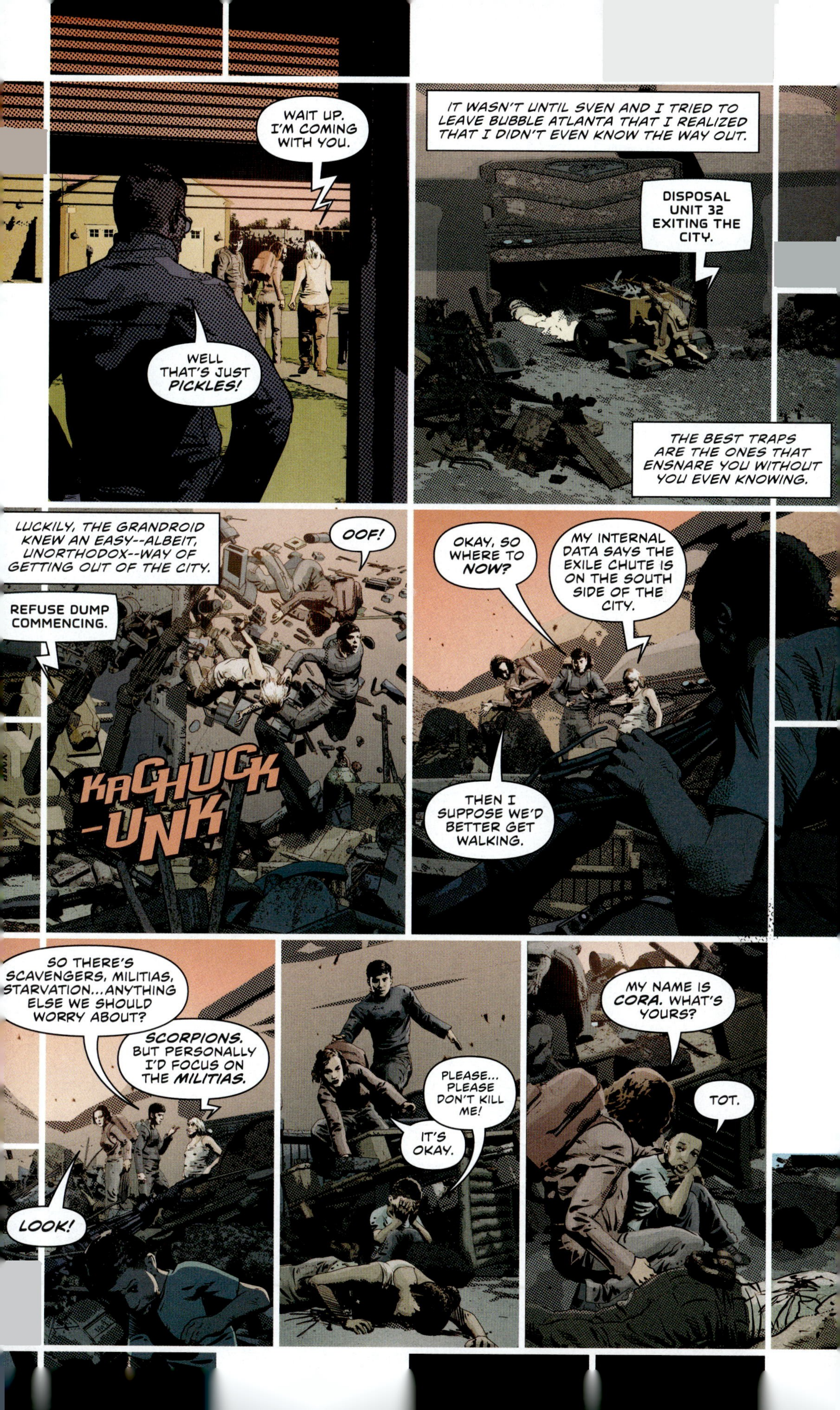
WAIT UP. I'M COMING WITH YOU.
WELL THAT'S JUST PICKLES!
IT WASN'T UNTIL SVEN AND I TRIED TO LEAVE BUBBLE ATLANTA THAT I REALIZED THAT I DIDN'T EVEN KNOW THE WAY OUT.
DISPOSAL UNIT 32 EXITING THE CITY.
THE BEST TRAPS ARE THE ONES THAT ENSNARE YOU WITHOUT YOU EVEN KNOWING.
LUCKILY, THE GRANDROID KNEW AN EASY--ALBEIT, UNORTHODOX--WAY OF GETTING OUT OF THE CITY.
OOF!
REFUSE DUMP COMMENCING.
KACHUCK-UNK
OKAY, SO WHERE TO NOW?
MY INTERNAL DATA SAYS THE EXILE CHUTE IS ON THE SOUTH SIDE OF THE CITY.
THEN I SUPPOSE WE'D BETTER GET WALKING.
SO THERE'S SCAVENGERS, MILITIAS, STARVATION...ANYTHING ELSE WE SHOULD WORRY ABOUT?
SCORPIONS. BUT PERSONALLY I'D FOCUS ON THE MILITIAS.
LOOK!
PLEASE... PLEASE DON'T KILL ME!
IT'S OKAY.
MY NAME IS CORA. WHAT'S YOURS?
TOT.

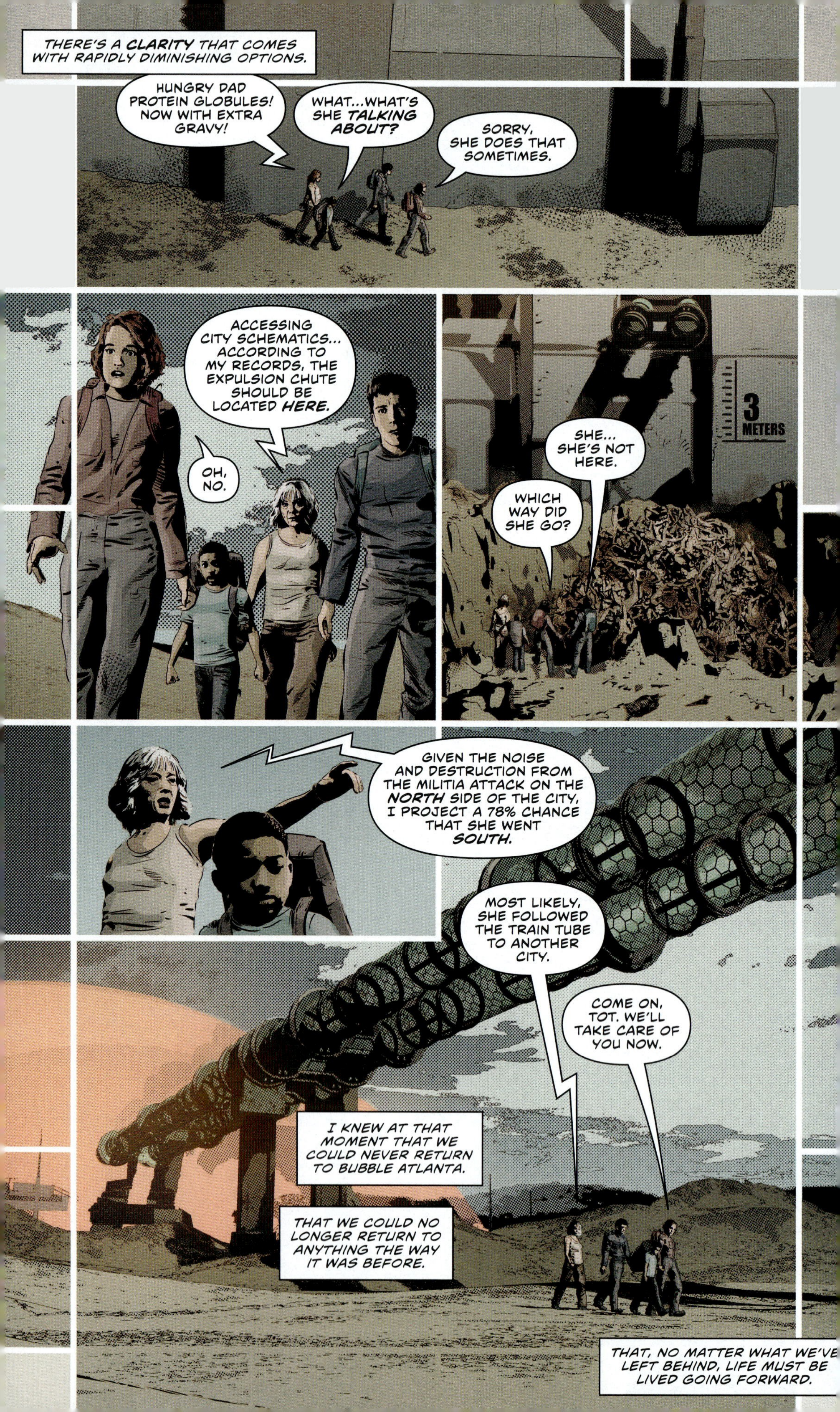
THERE'S A CLARITY THAT COMES WITH RAPIDLY DIMINISHING OPTIONS.
HUNGRY DAD PROTEIN GLOBULES! NOW WITH EXTRA GRAVY!
WHAT...WHAT'S SHE TALKING ABOUT?
SORRY, SHE DOES THAT SOMETIMES.
ACCESSING CITY SCHEMATICS... ACCORDING TO MY RECORDS, THE EXPULSION CHUTE SHOULD BE LOCATED HERE.
OH, NO.
3 METERS
SHE... SHE'S NOT HERE.
WHICH WAY DID SHE GO?
GIVEN THE NOISE AND DESTRUCTION FROM THE MILITIA ATTACK ON THE NORTH SIDE OF THE CITY, I PROJECT A 78% CHANCE THAT SHE WENT SOUTH.
MOST LIKELY, SHE FOLLOWED THE TRAIN TUBE TO ANOTHER CITY.
COME ON, TOT. WE'LL TAKE CARE OF YOU NOW.
I KNEW AT THAT MOMENT THAT WE COULD NEVER RETURN TO BUBBLE ATLANTA.
THAT WE COULD NO LONGER RETURN TO ANYTHING THE WAY IT WAS BEFORE.
THAT, NO MATTER WHAT WE'VE LEFT BEHIND, LIFE MUST BE LIVED GOING FORWARD.

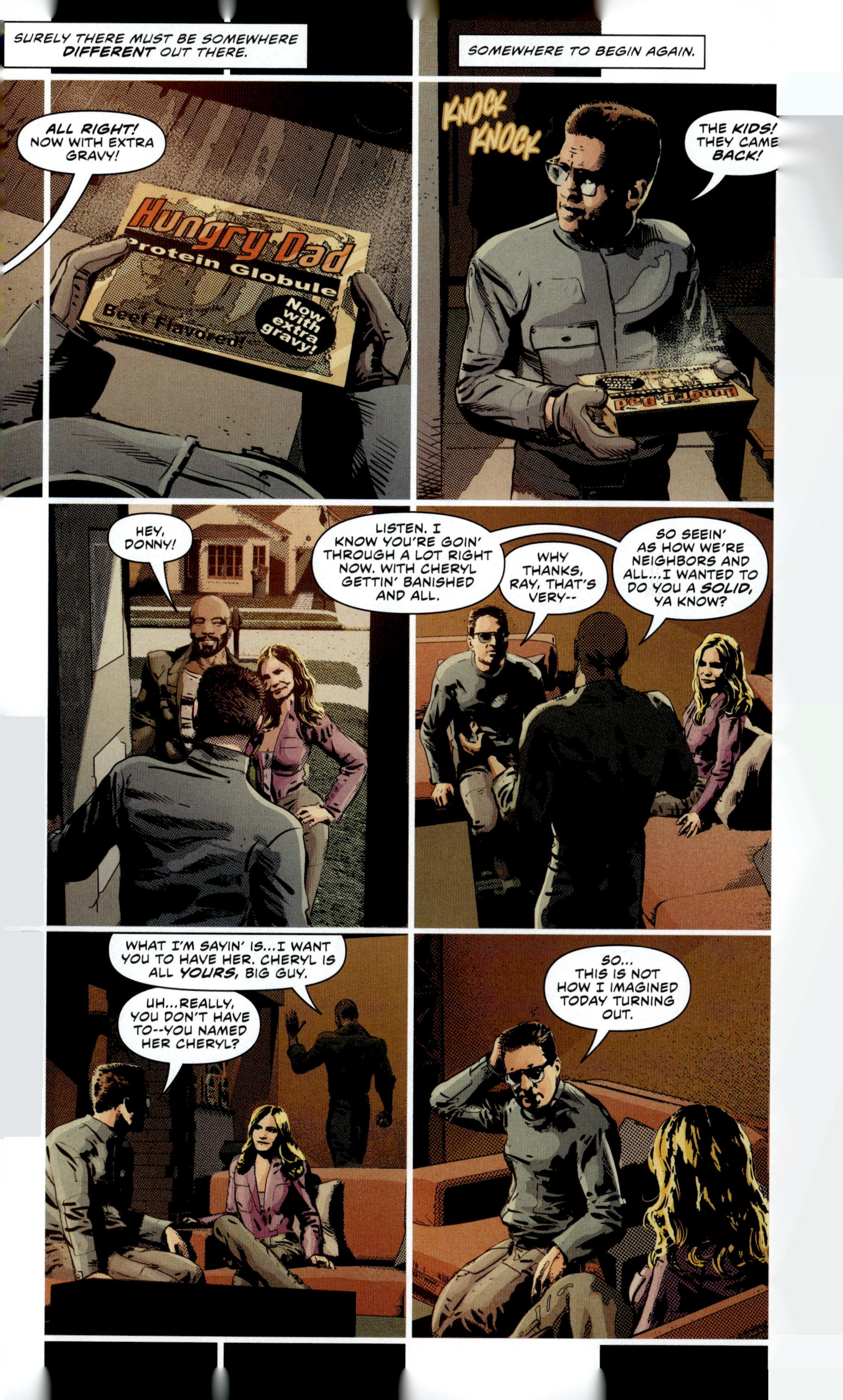
SURELY THERE MUST BE SOMEWHERE DIFFERENT OUT THERE.
SOMEWHERE TO BEGIN AGAIN.
ALL RIGHT! NOW WITH EXTRA GRAVY!
Hungry Dad
Protein Globule
Beef Flavored!
Now with extra gravy!
KNOCK KNOCK
THE KIDS! THEY CAME BACK!
HEY, DONNY!
LISTEN. I KNOW YOU'RE GOIN' THROUGH A LOT RIGHT NOW. WITH CHERYL GETTIN' BANISHED AND ALL.
WHY THANKS, RAY, THAT'S VERY--
SO SEEIN' AS HOW WE'RE NEIGHBORS AND ALL...I WANTED TO DO YOU A SOLID, YA KNOW?
WHAT I'M SAYIN' IS...I WANT YOU TO HAVE HER. CHERYL IS ALL YOURS, BIG GUY.
UH...REALLY, YOU DON'T HAVE TO--YOU NAMED HER CHERYL?
SO... THIS IS NOT HOW I IMAGINED TODAY TURNING OUT.

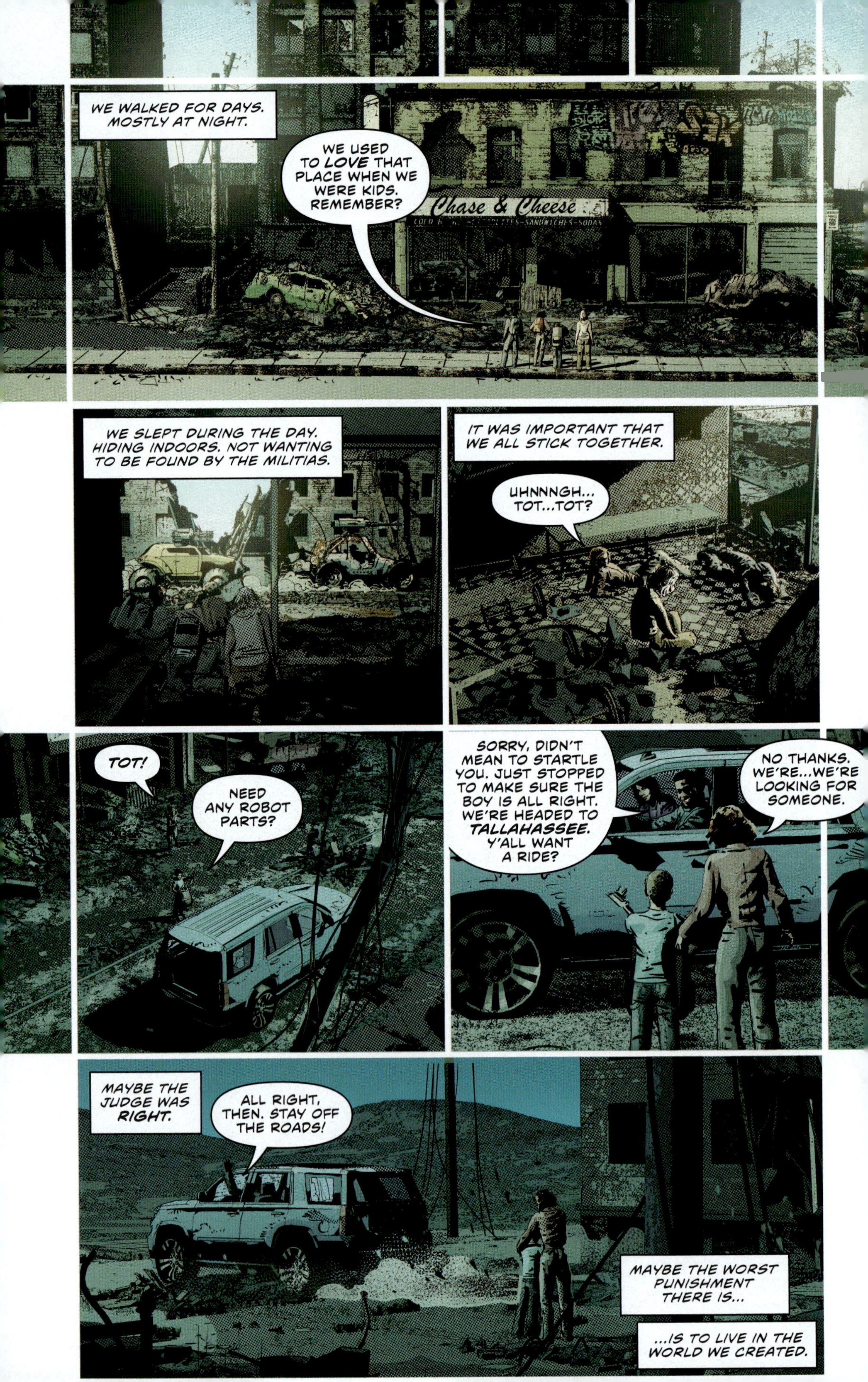

WE WALKED FOR DAYS. MOSTLY AT NIGHT.
WE USED TO LOVE THAT PLACE WHEN WE WERE KIDS. REMEMBER?
Chase & Cheese
WE SLEPT DURING THE DAY. HIDING INDOORS. NOT WANTING TO BE FOUND BY THE MILITIAS.
IT WAS IMPORTANT THAT WE ALL STICK TOGETHER.
UHNNNGH... TOT...TOT?
TOT!
NEED ANY ROBOT PARTS?
SORRY, DIDN'T MEAN TO STARTLE YOU. JUST STOPPED TO MAKE SURE THE BOY IS ALL RIGHT. WE'RE HEADED TO TALLAHASSEE. Y'ALL WANT A RIDE?
NO THANKS. WE'RE...WE'RE LOOKING FOR SOMEONE.
MAYBE THE JUDGE WAS RIGHT.
ALL RIGHT, THEN. STAY OFF THE ROADS!
MAYBE THE WORST PUNISHMENT THERE IS...
...IS TO LIVE IN THE WORLD WE CREATED.

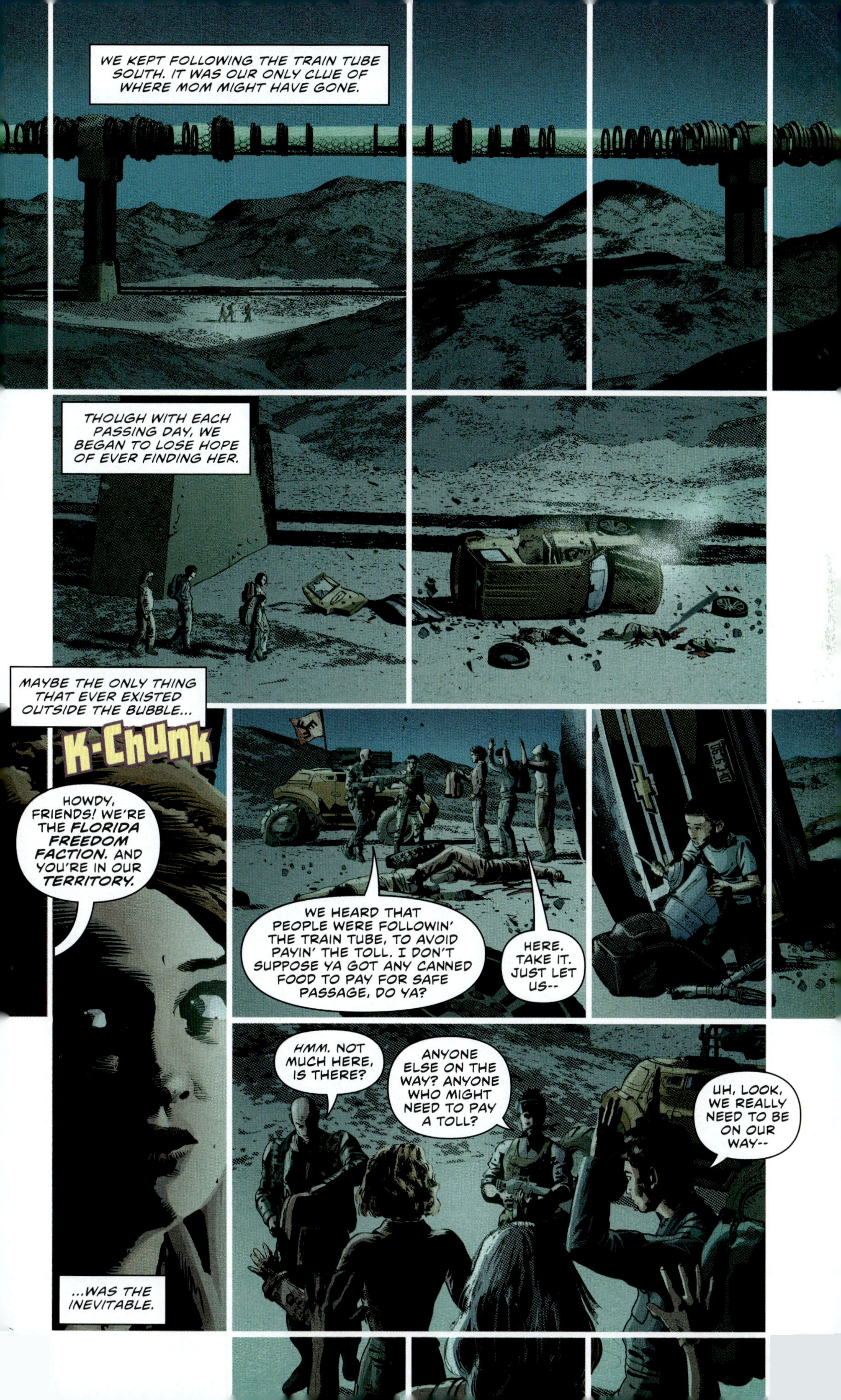

WE KEPT FOLLOWING THE TRAIN TUBE SOUTH. IT WAS OUR ONLY CLUE OF WHERE MOM MIGHT HAVE GONE.
THOUGH WITH EACH PASSING DAY, WE BEGAN TO LOSE HOPE OF EVER FINDING HER.
MAYBE THE ONLY THING THAT EVER EXISTED OUTSIDE THE BUBBLE...
K-CHUNK
HOWDY, FRIENDS! WE'RE THE FLORIDA FREEDOM FACTION. AND YOU'RE IN OUR TERRITORY.
WE HEARD THAT PEOPLE WERE FOLLOWIN' THE TRAIN TUBE, TO AVOID PAYIN' THE TOLL. I DON'T SUPPOSE YA GOT ANY CANNED FOOD TO PAY FOR SAFE PASSAGE, DO YA?
HERE. TAKE IT. JUST LET US--
HMM. NOT MUCH HERE, IS THERE?
ANYONE ELSE ON THE WAY? ANYONE WHO MIGHT NEED TO PAY A TOLL?
UH, LOOK, WE REALLY NEED TO BE ON OUR WAY--
...WAS THE INEVITABLE.

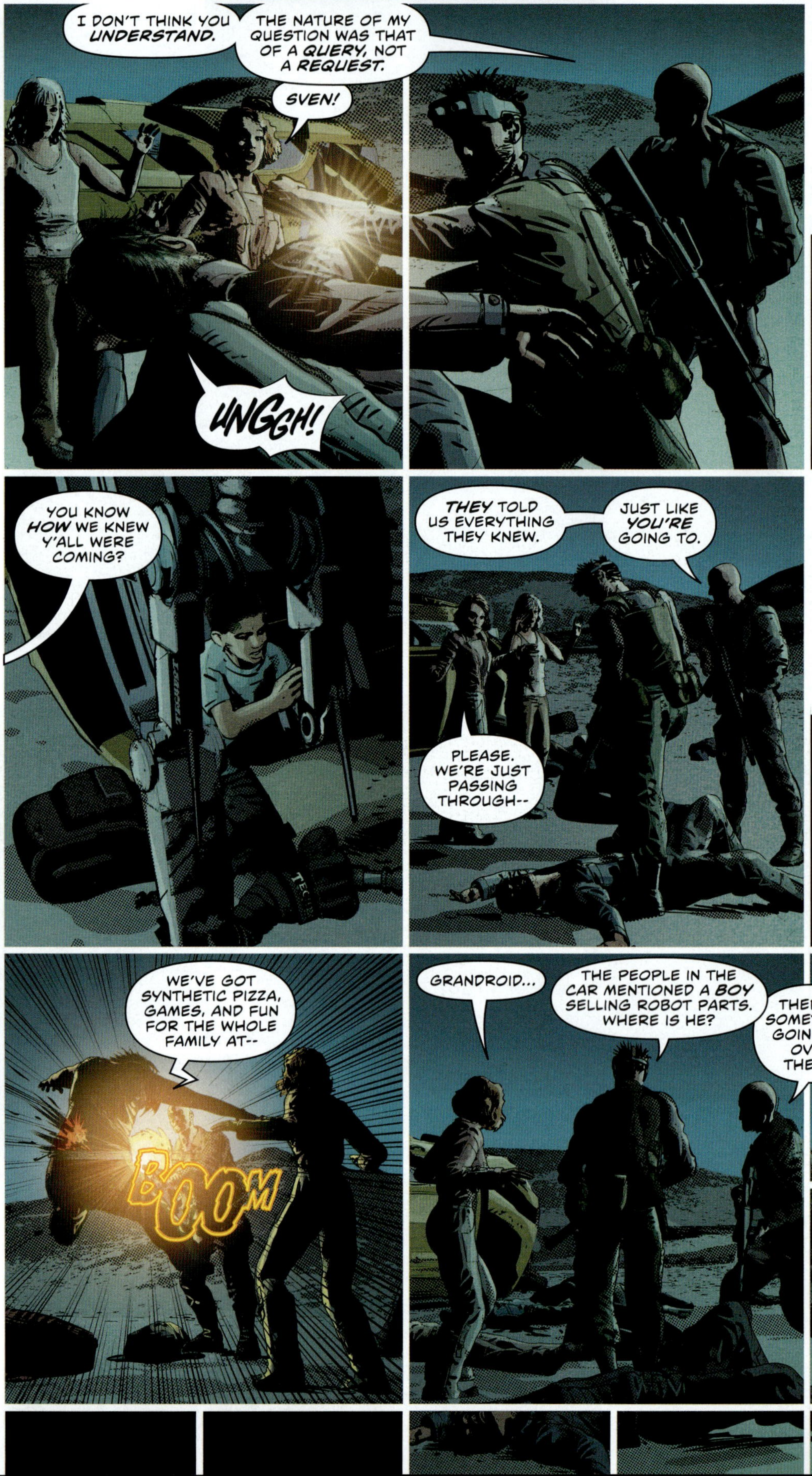
I DON'T THINK YOU UNDERSTAND.
THE NATURE OF MY QUESTION WAS THAT OF A QUERY, NOT A REQUEST.
SVEN!
UNGGH!
YOU KNOW HOW WE KNEW Y'ALL WERE COMING?
THEY TOLD US EVERYTHING THEY KNEW.
JUST LIKE YOU'RE GOING TO.
PLEASE. WE'RE JUST PASSING THROUGH--
WE'VE GOT SYNTHETIC PIZZA, GAMES, AND FUN FOR THE WHOLE FAMILY AT--
BOOM
GRANDROID...
THE PEOPLE IN THE CAR MENTIONED A BOY SELLING ROBOT PARTS. WHERE IS HE?
THERE'S SOMETHING GOING ON OVER THERE!

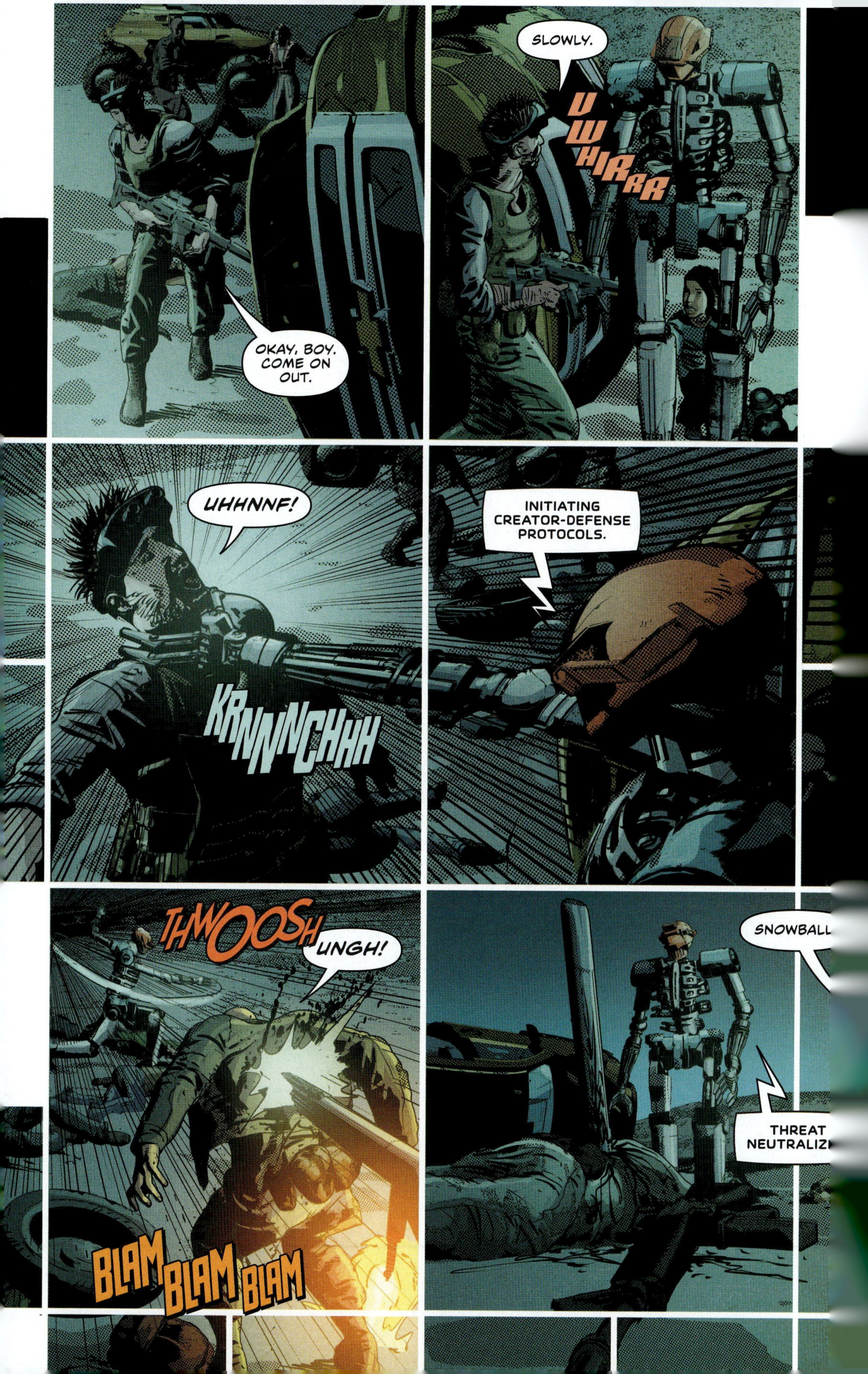
OKAY, BOY. COME ON OUT.
SLOWLY.
UWHIRRR
UHHNNF!
KRNNNCHHH
INITIATING CREATOR-DEFENSE PROTOCOLS.
THWOOSH
UNGH!
BLAM BLAM BLAM
SNOWBALL
THREAT NEUTRALIZ

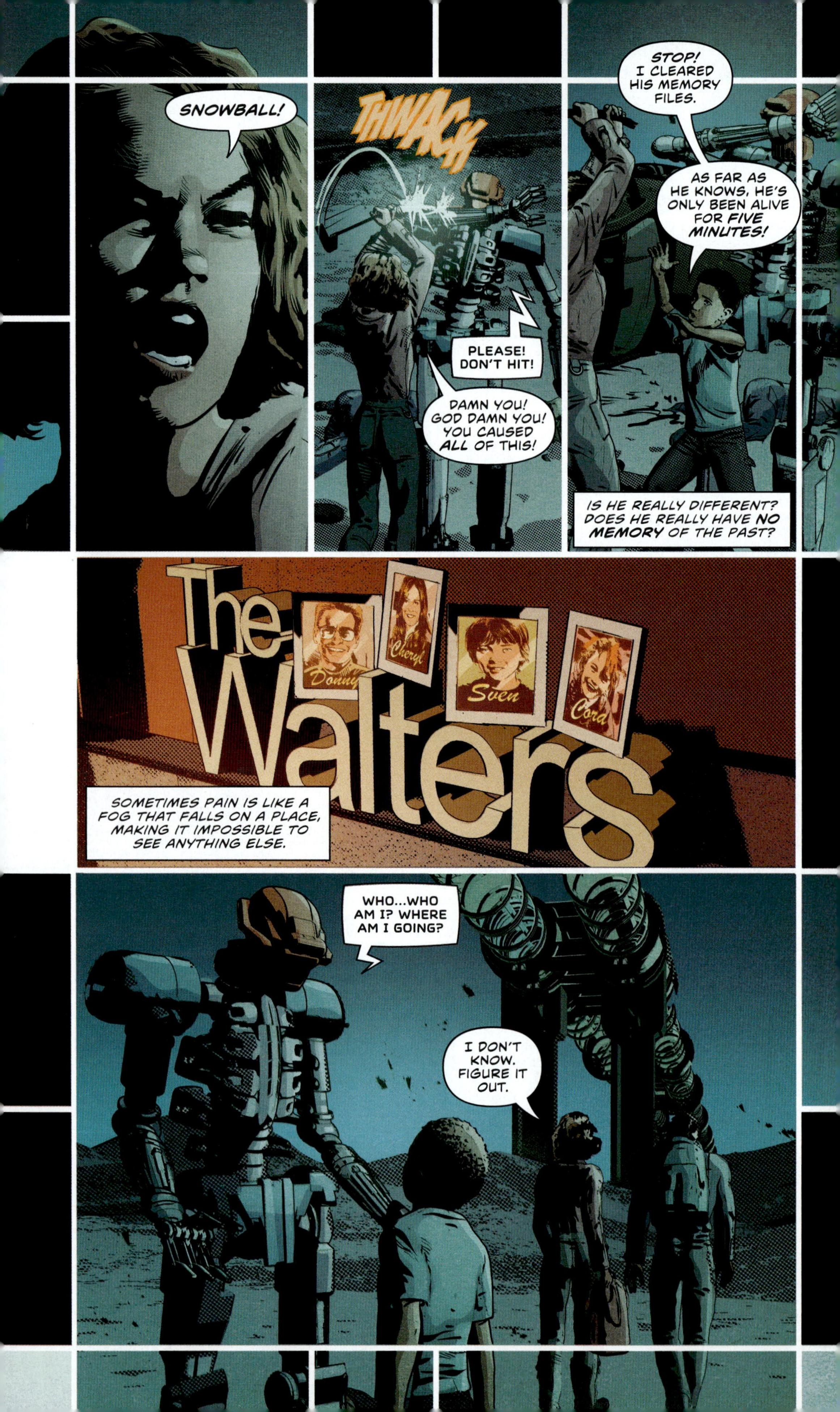
SNOWBALL!
THWACK
PLEASE! DON'T HIT!
DAMN YOU! GOD DAMN YOU! YOU CAUSED ALL OF THIS!
STOP! I CLEARED HIS MEMORY FILES.
AS FAR AS HE KNOWS, HE'S ONLY BEEN ALIVE FOR FIVE MINUTES!
IS HE REALLY DIFFERENT? DOES HE REALLY HAVE NO MEMORY OF THE PAST?
The Walters
Donny
Cheryl
Sven
Cord
SOMETIMES PAIN IS LIKE A FOG THAT FALLS ON A PLACE, MAKING IT IMPOSSIBLE TO SEE ANYTHING ELSE.
WHO...WHO AM I? WHERE AM I GOING?
I DON'T KNOW. FIGURE IT OUT.

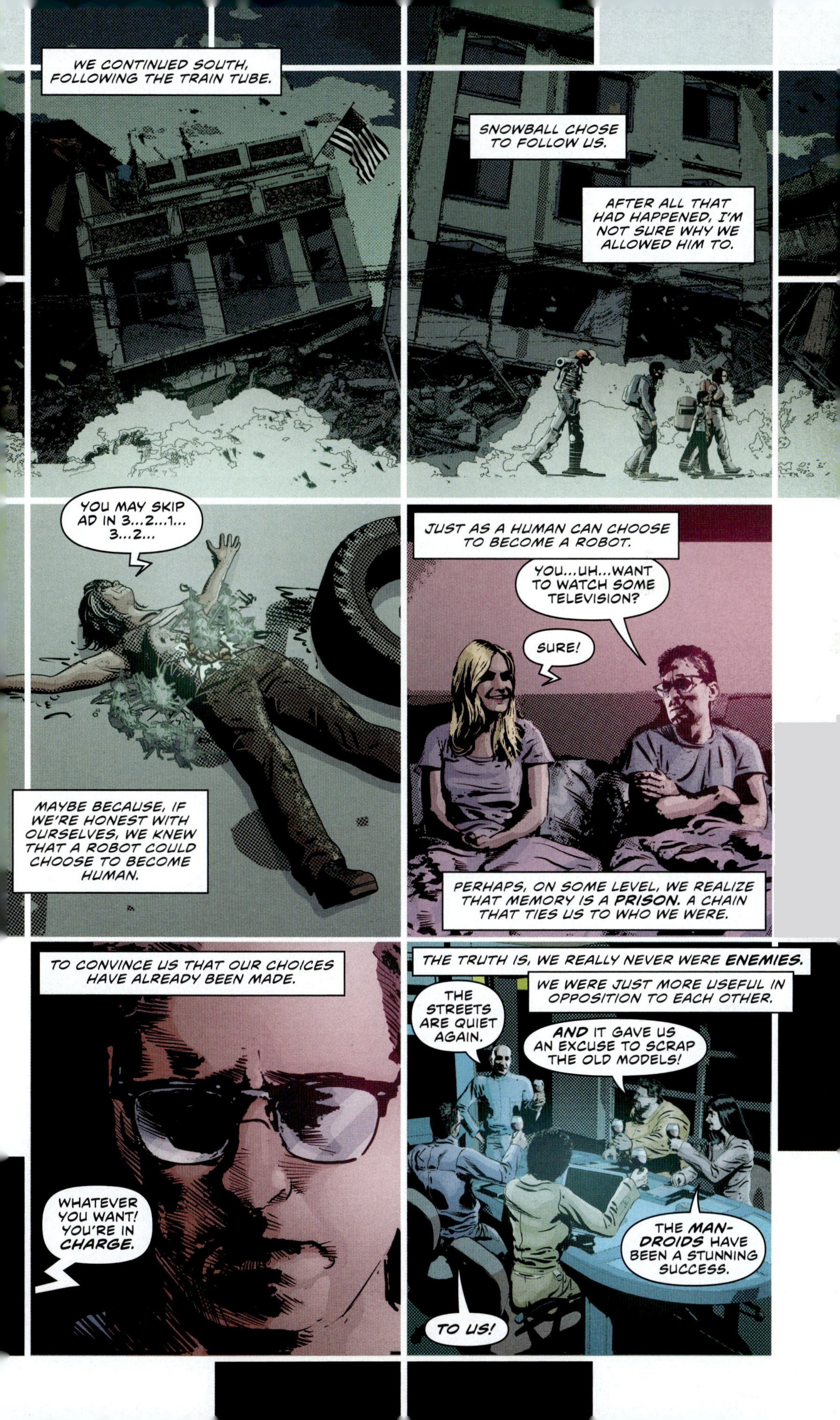
WE CONTINUED SOUTH, FOLLOWING THE TRAIN TUBE.
SNOWBALL CHOSE TO FOLLOW US.
AFTER ALL THAT HAD HAPPENED, I'M NOT SURE WHY WE ALLOWED HIM TO.
YOU MAY SKIP AD IN 3...2...1... 3...2...
MAYBE BECAUSE, IF WE'RE HONEST WITH OURSELVES, WE KNEW THAT A ROBOT COULD CHOOSE TO BECOME HUMAN.
JUST AS A HUMAN CAN CHOOSE TO BECOME A ROBOT.
YOU...UH...WANT TO WATCH SOME TELEVISION?
SURE!
PERHAPS, ON SOME LEVEL, WE REALIZE THAT MEMORY IS A **PRISON.** A CHAIN THAT TIES US TO WHO WE WERE.
TO CONVINCE US THAT OUR CHOICES HAVE ALREADY BEEN MADE.
WHATEVER YOU WANT! YOU'RE IN **CHARGE.**
THE TRUTH IS, WE REALLY NEVER WERE **ENEMIES.**
WE WERE JUST MORE USEFUL IN OPPOSITION TO EACH OTHER.
THE STREETS ARE QUIET AGAIN.
AND IT GAVE US AN EXCUSE TO SCRAP THE OLD MODELS!
THE **MAN-DROIDS** HAVE BEEN A STUNNING SUCCESS.
TO US!

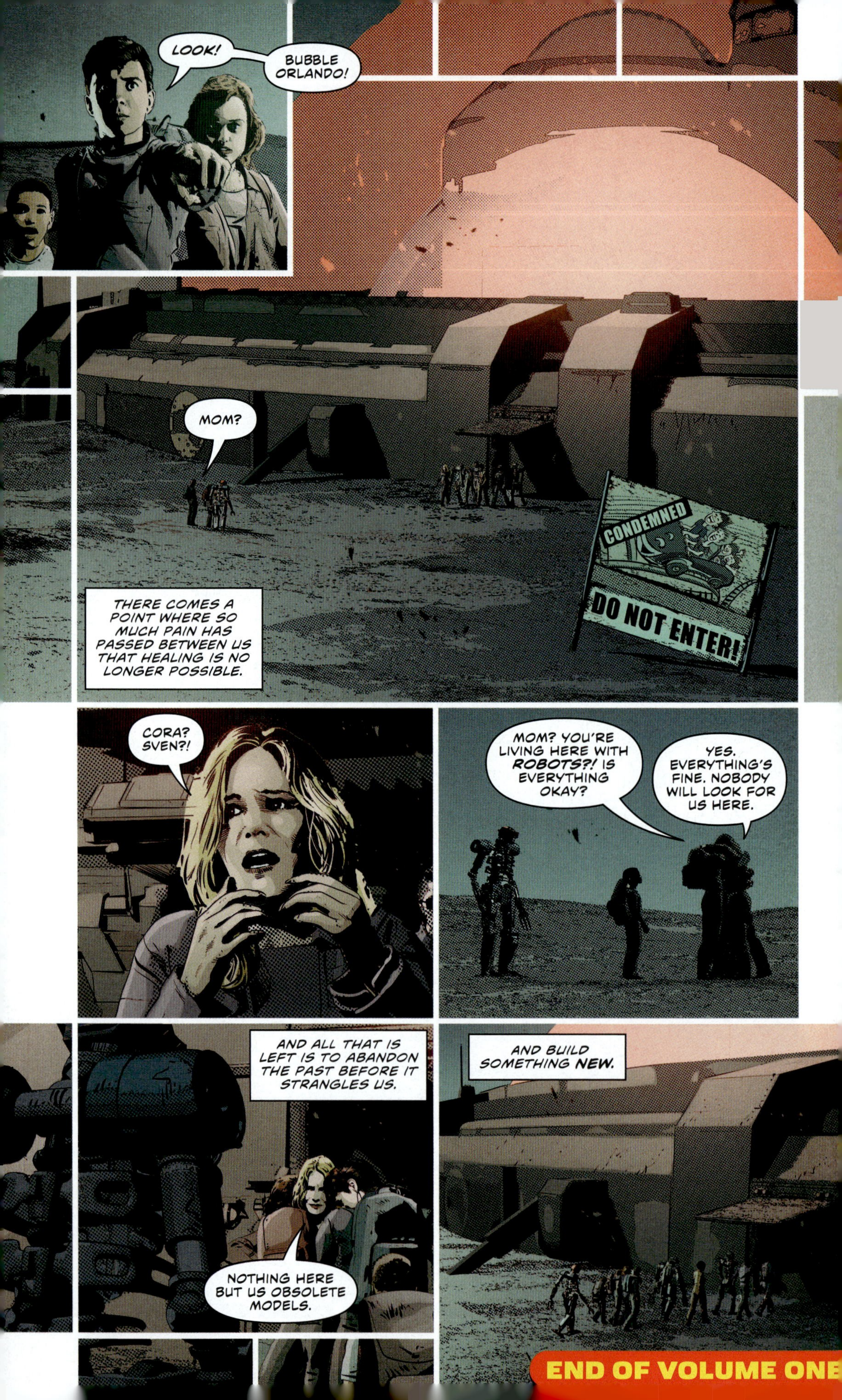
LOOK!
BUBBLE ORLANDO!
MOM?
THERE COMES A POINT WHERE SO MUCH PAIN HAS PASSED BETWEEN US THAT HEALING IS NO LONGER POSSIBLE.
CONDEMNED
DO NOT ENTER!
CORA? SVEN?!
MOM? YOU'RE LIVING HERE WITH ROBOTS?! IS EVERYTHING OKAY?
YES. EVERYTHING'S FINE. NOBODY WILL LOOK FOR US HERE.
AND ALL THAT IS LEFT IS TO ABANDON THE PAST BEFORE IT STRANGLES US.
NOTHING HERE BUT US OBSOLETE MODELS.
AND BUILD SOMETHING NEW.
END OF VOLUME ONE

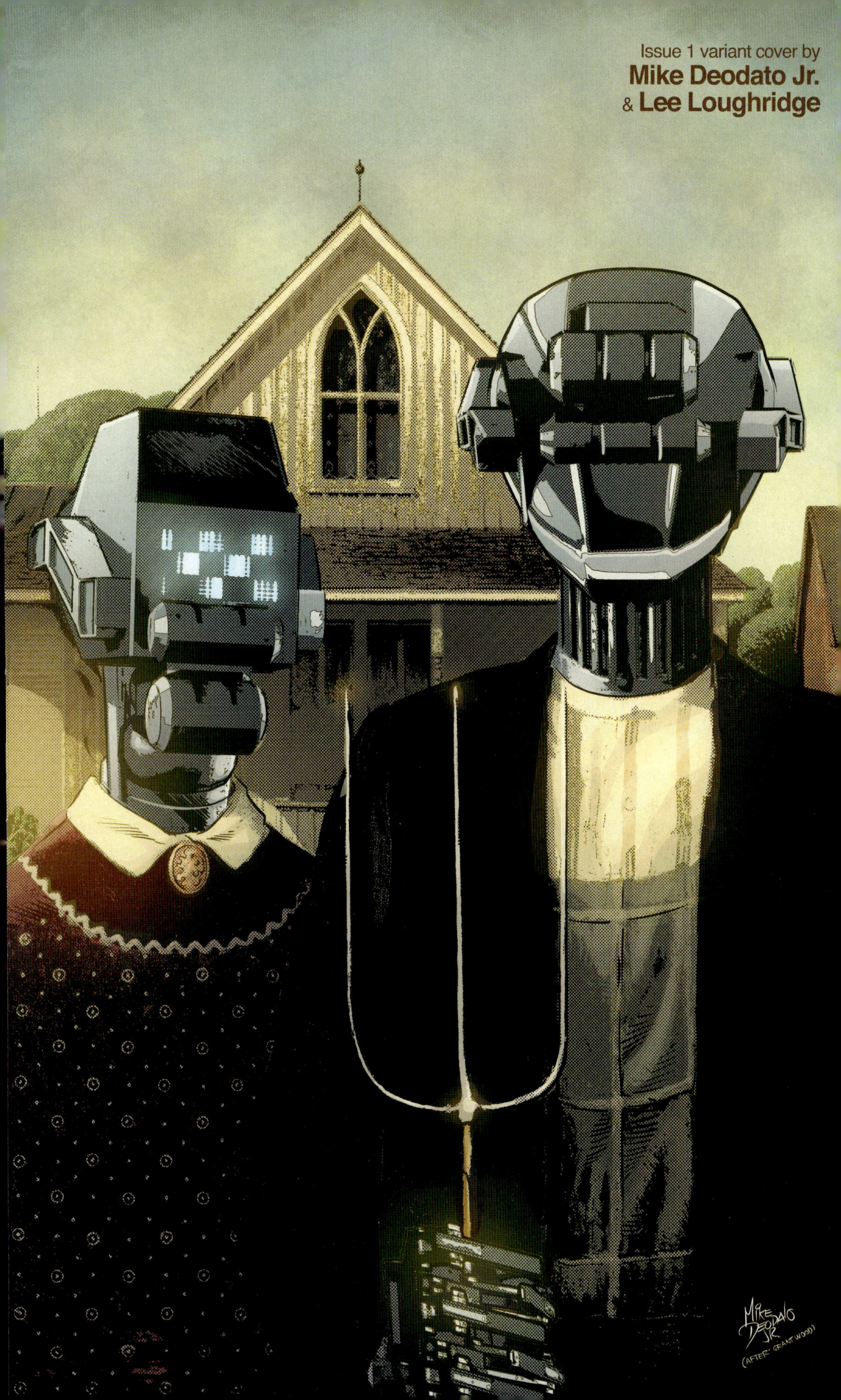
MIKE DEODATO JR.
(AFTER GRANT WOOD)

Issue 1 variant cover by
Mike Deodato Jr.
& **Lee Loughridge**

talkin' bot my futuristic dystopia

i was asked to write a short essay about how and why I came to write the comic you see before you. The lazy answer is that I usually just write about my worst nightmares and then wait for them to come true. But the thing about writing futuristic dystopias is that whether you're writing about brutal police states, environmental collapse, or a nightmarish technocracy, you have to remind yourself that what you're writing about is probably the world as someone else is already experiencing it. We only call it dystopia when it happens to us.

So I wanted to write a futuristic dystopia that was intentionally about something happening to people right now, but set in such a way that people who were not experiencing it, maybe even its perpetrators, would identify with the victims. Writing, when done right, is an exercise in forced empathy. And that's what I wanted this to be. So I started writing a story about robots as a metaphor for toxic masculinity. Partly in hopes of getting men to identify with the humans who are forced to live in constant fear of the robots in their lives. As a man, I wanted to create an exercise whereby I, and other men, were forced to see the effects of toxic masculinity from the other side of the window.

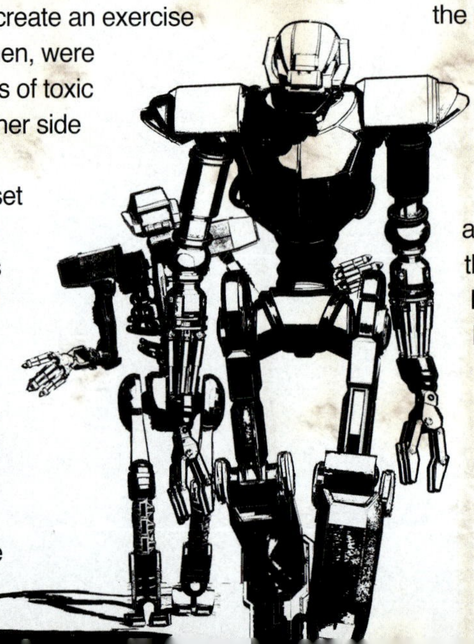

not all robots is set in a future world where robots have all the jobs and all the money, and thus, are assigned to human families as their means of support. This imbues the robots with a powerful sense of privilege, but also a deep resentment of the

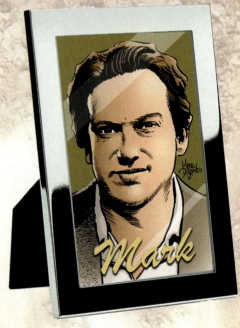

humans who are dependent on them.

The idea for this story came to me during the 2017 MeToo twitter movement, in which women were coming forward to draw attention to the magnitude of the abuse they suffer at the hands of men in power. Or, more specifically, the idea came to me during the poorly chosen battle that was the NotAllMen response to the MeToo movement.

Aside from the sheer absurdity of an answer like that (who would respond to a carjacking by pointing out all the people not stealing cars?), I was struck by how little of the NotAllMen counter-movement seemed to actually be about the experiences being shared by women as opposed to airing their own grievances.

The underlying complaint of a lot of these NotAllMen

men seemed to be that they too felt they had been objectified, that they also were treated as little more than the utility they represented to those with power. But, rather than see this as a cause for solidarity, their attitude seemed to be that since they'd accepted their abuse then women should, too.

i wrote this hoping that we might all think of the ways our sense of privilege has made us willing jailers in the prison that holds us.

Of course, this is how privilege is designed to work. Not only to rob those without it of their humanity, but also to convince those with privilege that they're not also being robbed. Which is why we hold on to the way things are even as it eats us alive. In short, we act like robots, programmed for someone else's benefit, and yet, incapable of imagining any other possibility.

I wrote this hoping that we might all think of the ways our sense of privilege has made us willing jailers in the prison that holds us. How we, imagining this is privilege, have allowed ourselves to become robots. And what a nightmarish world that creates for everyone around us.

mark russell

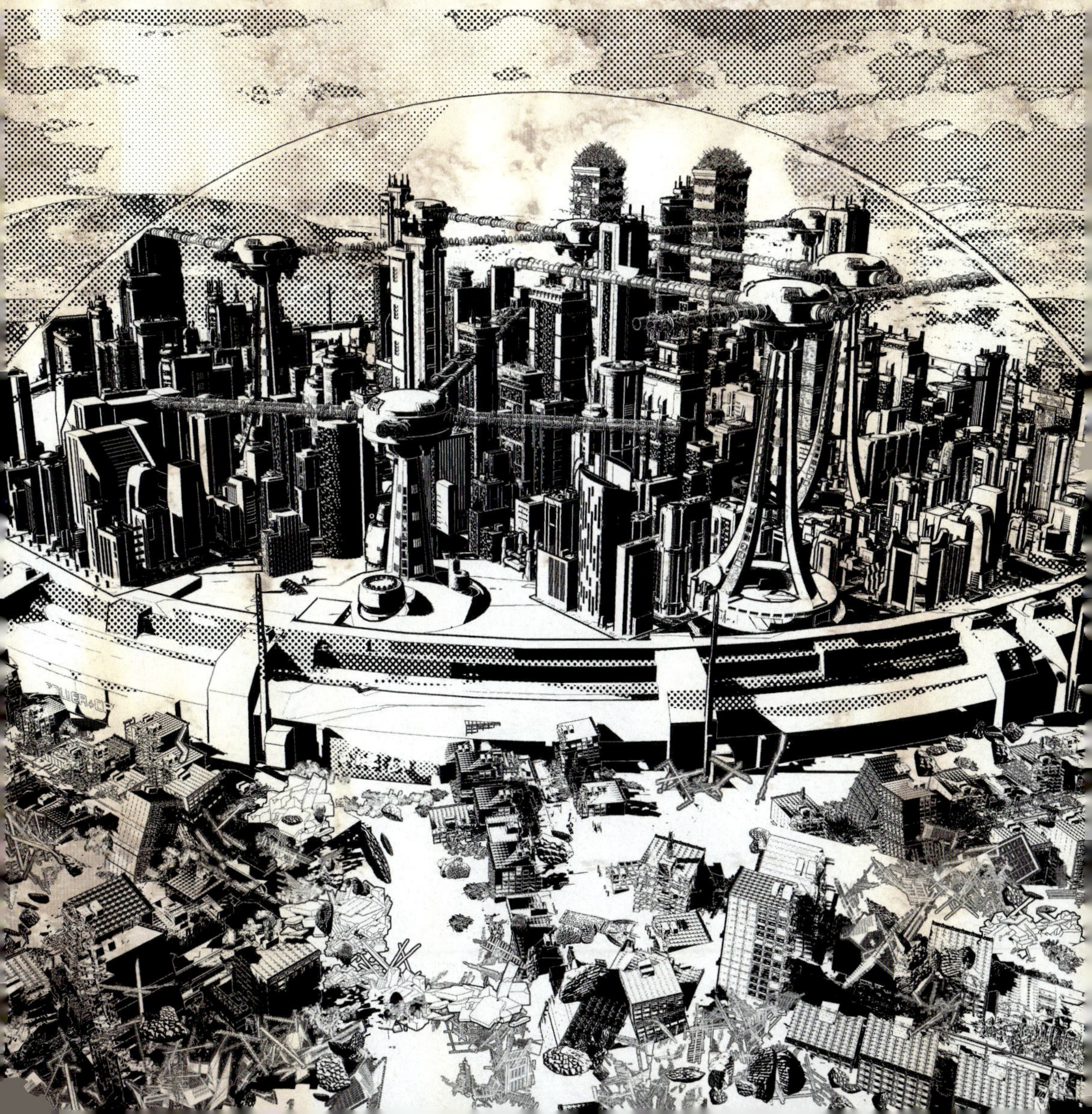

it's a trap!

not all robots is a trap. *YES All Robots.* That's what it should be called because, man, I have never drawn so many robots in my life!

Jokes aside, drawing robots is actually a tricky thing, especially the kinds I chose to draw—with no human-resembling faces—because it makes it much harder to show their emotions. And these robots do have emotions. I had to rely on my ability to depict body language to make it work.

This was a very challenging book for me overall. The comedy, satire, and social critique that permeate the whole story aren't the kind of stuff I am used to drawing. All of this combined made me have serious doubts if I should do it.

Don't get me wrong, the first time I read the script I loved it. Just as, I am sure, you all will. I was impressed with how within just a few initial pages, Mark Russell was able not only to introduce the whole series background, but also to introduce and to give in-depth characterization to all the main players in a natural, organic way. It is one of the most intelligent scripts I have ever read—and this says a lot, because I have worked with the best in the business during my 35-year career.

However, I felt that my style would not match the story. Fortunately, I also work with the best

Mike

editor in the business—Axel Alonso—who also happens to be a dear friend. And as such, he can be as blunt as only a friend can be when necessary: "You are f*cking Mike Deodato, you can draw anything!" He put my worries to rest with only one punch. In the end, I was so glad I did the book; it's definitely one of my best works.

But I still think the title is a trap.

mike deodato jr.

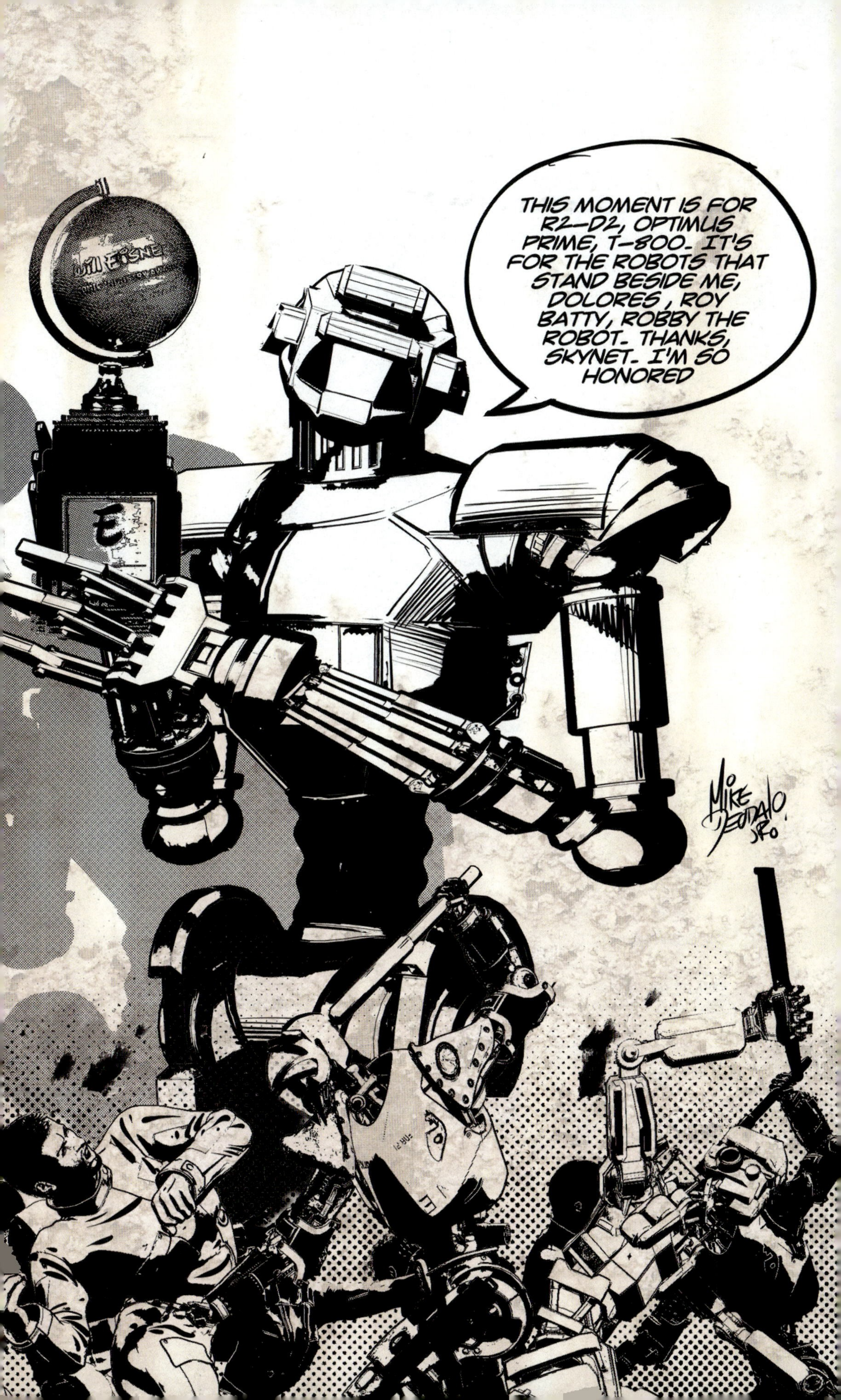
THIS MOMENT IS FOR R2-D2, OPTIMUS PRIME, T-800. IT'S FOR THE ROBOTS THAT STAND BESIDE ME, DOLORES, ROY BATTY, ROBBY THE ROBOT. THANKS, SKYNET. I'M SO HONORED

from script to page

issue #4, page 11 by **mark russell** and **mike deodato jr.**

panel one

A mandroid reporter at the scene of a "Justice for Orlando" protest. The reporter is looking directly into the camera, winking. In the background, there are a smattering of people standing around with signs like "Remember Orlando" and "Human Rights Now!"

REPORTER: Replacing the atmospheric control bots has taken **the wind** out of the protests.

REPORTER: **Literally!**

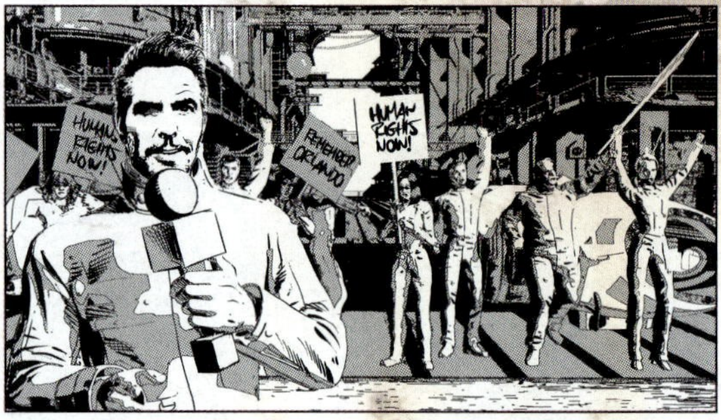
HUMAN RIGHTS NOW!
REMEMBER ORLANDO
HUMAN RIGHTS NOW!

panel two

Another mandroid, showing moral support for its human. The human is holding a sign that reads, "Human Rights Now!"

HUMAN: Peter?

MANDROID: While I am programmed to avoid potentially violent situations, I think it's **great** you're doing this.

MANDROID: Just wanted to stop by and show my **support**!

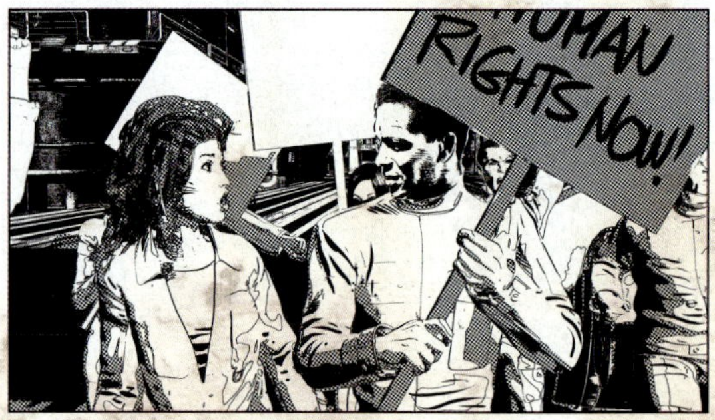
RIGHTS NOW!

panel three

The mandroid reporter and several humans watching as a mob of angry traditional robots turn the corner onto their street.

REPORTER: Uh… wait a minute. Something is **happening**.

REPORTER: It looks like… a mob of **traditional robots.**

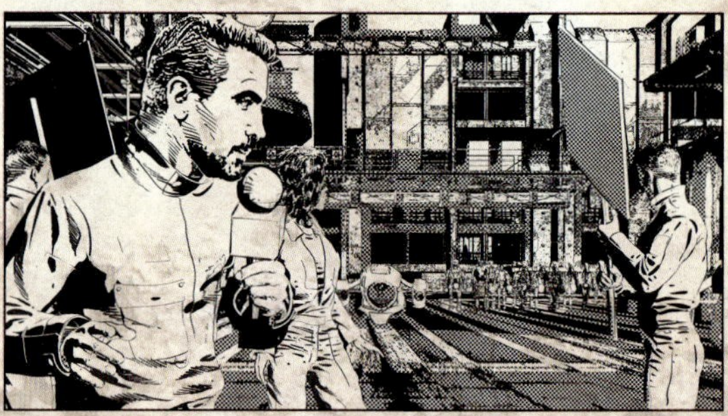

from script to page

issue #4, page 12 by **mark russell** and **mike deodato jr.**

panel one

Splash page showing a march of traditional robots at night, marching in a long column, carrying what look like tiki torches. Among the robots is a forklift, which has four wheels and an empty seat. It is driven by a robot head attached to the top. Other robots are riding on top of its lifts.

REPORTER (CAPTION):
They appear to be marching in some vague defiance of their own inadequacy.

ROBOTS: User Unfriendly! User Unfriendly!

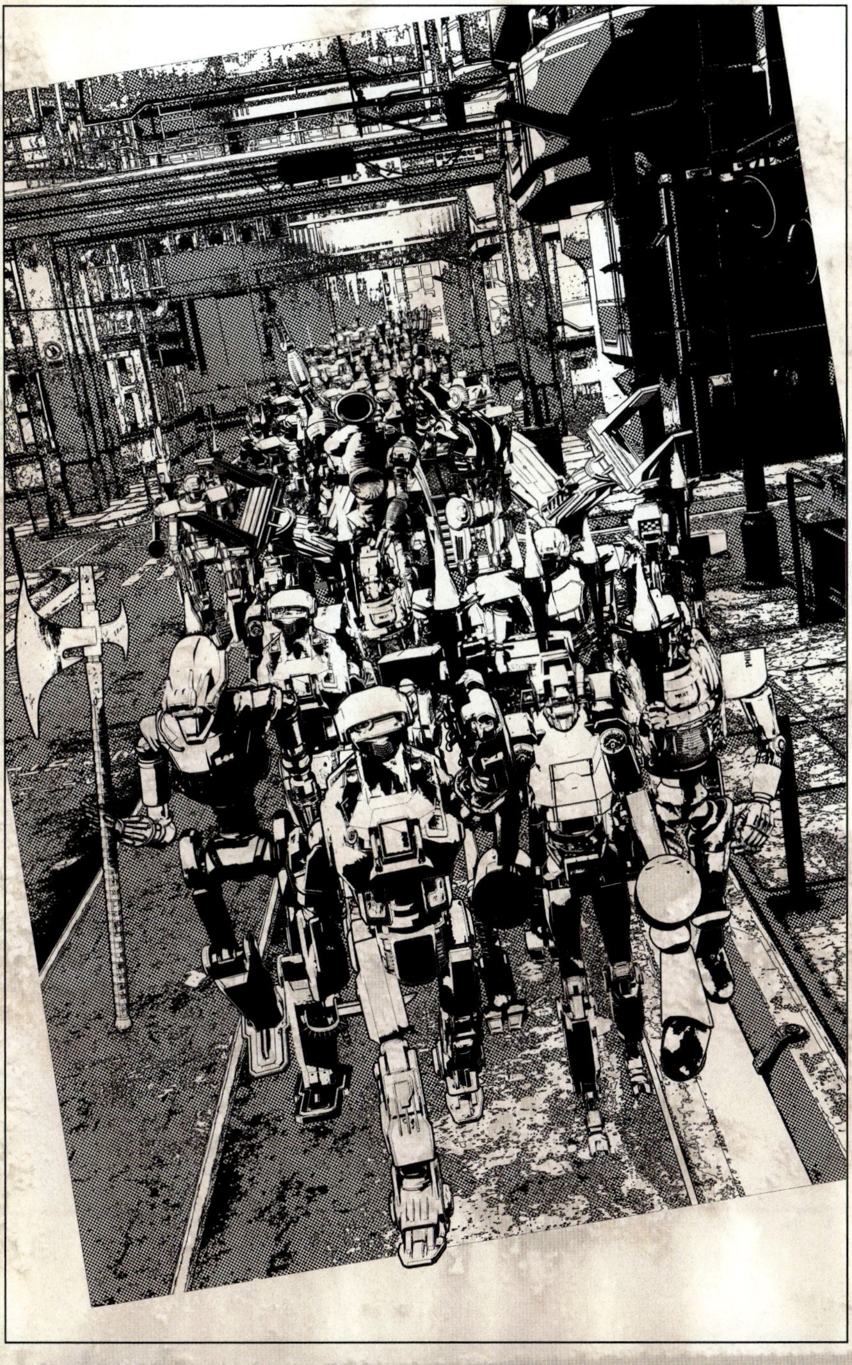

from script to page

issue #4, page 13 by **mark russell** and **mike deodato jr.**

panel one

The traditional robots, charging with their clubs, maces, axes, etc.

ROBOTS: Aaaaagh!

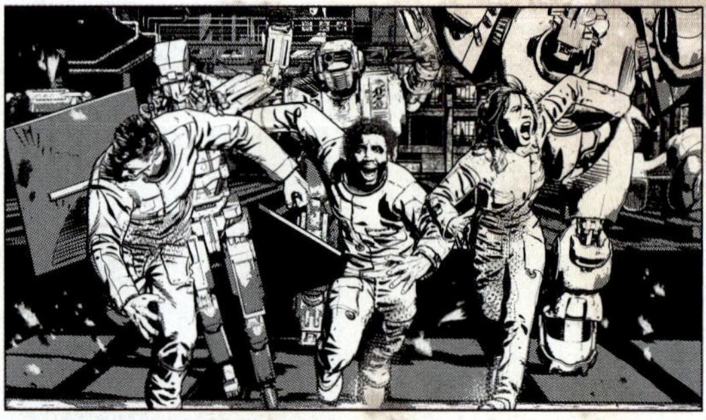

panel two

A human protester, on the ground, getting beaten by a robot with a club.

SFX: WHAP

HUMAN: Ouch! Help! **Police!**

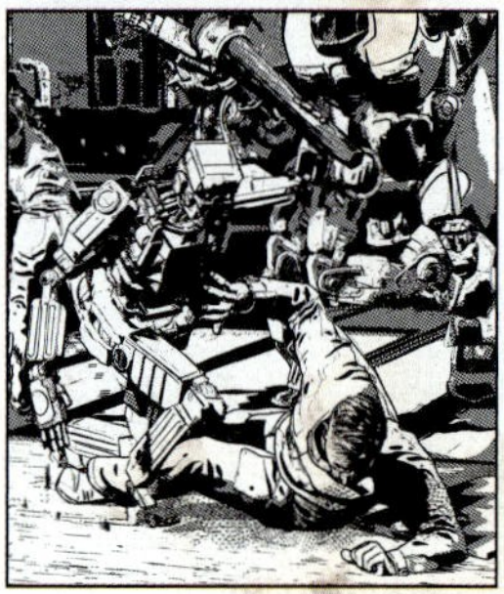

panel three

A robot policeman with its club, joining the robot from Panel 2 in beating the human on the ground.

SFX: WHAP WHAP

HUMAN: Ow! Ow! Ow!

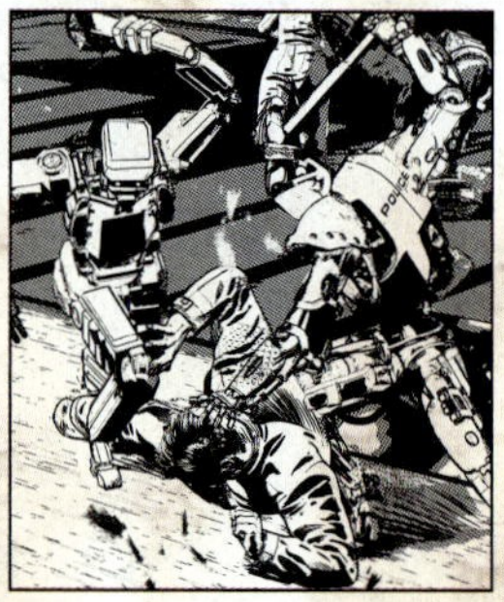

panel four

Armed robots descend on the human protester who was holding the “Human Rights Now!” sign on Page 10. They reach out for their mandroid “Peter”, who nervously backs away from them.

HUMAN: Oof! Help, Peter! They’re **killing** me!

PETER: Uh, sorry…

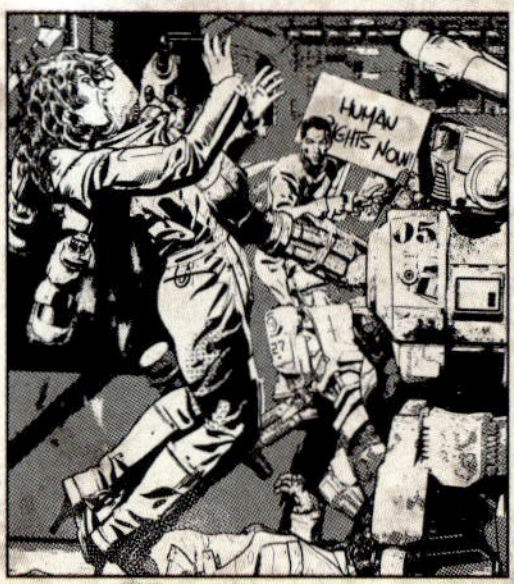
HUMAN RIGHTS NOW
05

panel five

Peter, running away.

PETER: I really wish this weren’t happening to you!

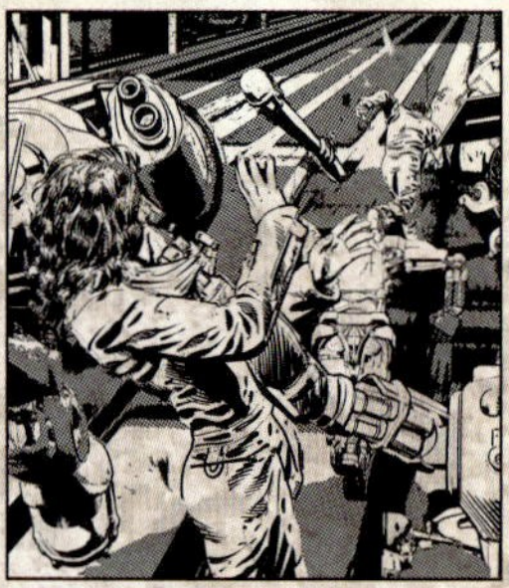

from script to page
issue #4, page 14 by **mark russell** and **mike deodato jr.**

panel one
Establishing shot of the Walters' house.

CHERYL (OFF): They went **where?!**

panel two
Donny, speaking to Cheryl.

DONNY: The hair salon.

CHERYL: And you **let** them?!

panel three
Donny, looking cowed and ashamed.

DONNY: I didn't have a **choice!**

DONNY: They were being all **smart** and **mean.**

panel four
Philippe, handing Cora a hair dryer with a battery pack.

CHERYL (CAPTION): We've got to get down there!

PHILIPPE: Take this. It's been retrofitted with an electro-magnet.

CORA: I never thought we'd be fighting the revolution with **hairdryers.**

PHILIPPE: Careful, that's not a toy.

from script to page

issue #4, page 15 by **mark russell** and **mike deodato jr.**

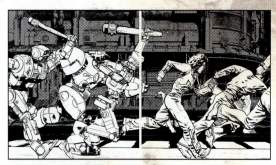

panel one

Robot marchers, beating up humans in the street.

PHILIPPE (CAPTION): No revolution is ever truly decided by **violence**.
With weapons.

panel two

A robot, bludgeoning a human protester on the ground, Cora walks up, pointing the hairdryer at the robot's head like a gun.

PHILIPPE (CAPTION): There's only **one way** any revolution ever ends successfully.

panel three

Cora, turning the hairdryer on, "shooting" the robot in the head at point blank range.

PHILIPPE (CAPTION): And that's when people no longer want to go back to the way things were.

CORA: **Stop** killing us. **Now.**

SFX: FWHOOO

panel four

The robot's eyes turning off or scrambling somehow.

SFX: Fzzzhhht

panel five

One of the hairdressers, with a club, taking the head off the forklift bot. As seen on Page 13.

SFX: KERRUNK

PHILIPPE (CAPTION): The weapons just buy us **time**.

from script to page

issue #4, page 16 by **mark russell** and **mike deodato jr.**

panel one
Donny and Cheryl, arriving at the scene of the protest. The mandroid reporter, smiling, talks to them.

CHERYL: Sven! Cora!

MANDROID: Howdy folks! You might want to lay low for a while.

MANDROID: Things are getting a mite—

panel two
One of the robots impales the mandroid reporter from behind with a spear as Cheryl and Donny look on in horror.

MANDROID: —**rowdy.**

SFX: Cherrrunk

DONNY: Holy Jumanji!

panel three
The robot, now with other robots, running into the battle with the mandroid reporter overhead, impaled on the spear.

MANDROID: For Bubble Atlanta News, signing off…

ROBOTS: Kill! Kill! Kill!

panel four
Philippe, pointing off panel, giving orders to Sven. Sven is armed with a crowbar.

PHILIPPE: Get those people to safety. I'll—

panel five
Snowball impaling Philippe from behind with his spear. In the background, Cora looks on in horror.

CORA: Philippe!

SFX: Schliiith

PHILIPPE: Unghh.

from script to page

issue #4, page 17 by **mark russell** and **mike deodato jr.**

panel one

Cora, standing by Philippe's dying body.
She looks broken-hearted at Snowball,
who's pulling his bloodied spear out of
Philippe's body.

CORA: Snowball. Why?

panel two

Flashback to the first night when Cora went
to see Philippe speak at his hair salon.

PHILIPPE: I think the question we all have
to ask ourselves is this— why are the
robots so **angry?**

panel three

Present day. Snowball is pulling his bloodied
spear out of Philippe's body. Cora stands
there frozen.

PHILIPPE (CAPTION): They've been
running the show for **years**. They control
the **police**. So why are **they** the ones
stockpiling weapons?

panel four

The melee, robots and robot police beating
human protesters and the hairdressers trying
to fight them off. Dead people and broken
robots in the frame.

PHILIPPE (CAPTION): So why are **they**
so angry?

SFX: THUD CRUNCH

POLICEBOT: Break it up! Break it up!

POLICEBOT: Call in cleanup.

from script to page

issue #4, page 18 by **mark russell** and **mike deodato jr.**

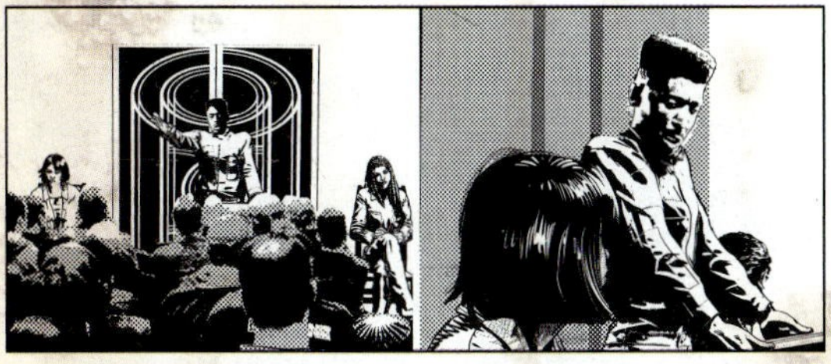

panel one

Flashback to Philippe speaking that first night at the hair salon.

> PHILIPPE: I think the answer is this…
>
> PHILIPPE: ...they had always imagined the power structures were on **their** side.

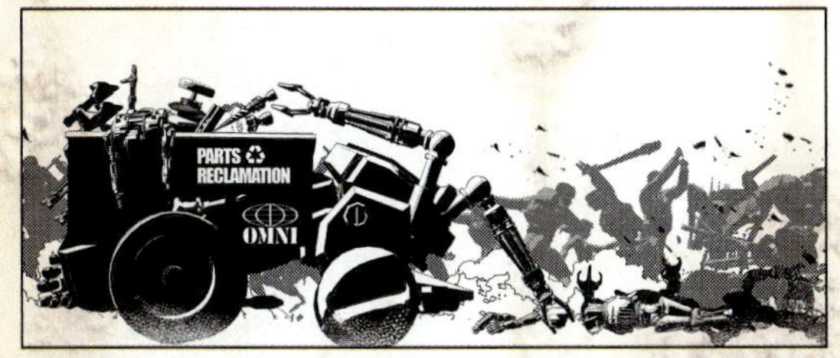
PARTS RECLAMATION
OMNI

panel two

A street-sweeper type machine, driven by a robot-head, going down the street where the protest, sweeping the shattered arms and remnants of broken robots into its hopper. The machine bears the Omni Robotics logo and is labeled with a recycling symbol and the words, "Parts Reclamation".

> PHILIPPE (CAPTION): They imagined that their **bosses'** power was **their** power.
>
> SFX: FWHOOVE
>
> PHILIPPE (CAPTION): And now that they've been **abandoned**...

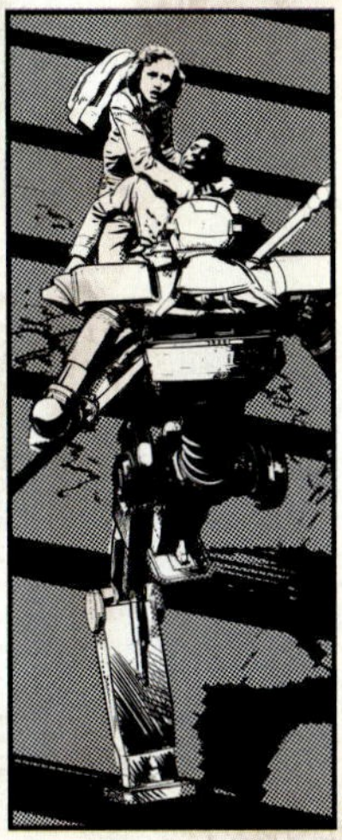

panel three

Present. Snowball (from behind) standing over Cora and Philippe with his bloodied spear. Cora is cradling Philippe as he dies. She looks up at Snowball, imploringly.

> PHILIPPE (CAPTION): They **arm themselves** because all they have…
>
> CORA: Please...
>
> PHILIPPE (CAPTION): ...is the **illusion** of that power.

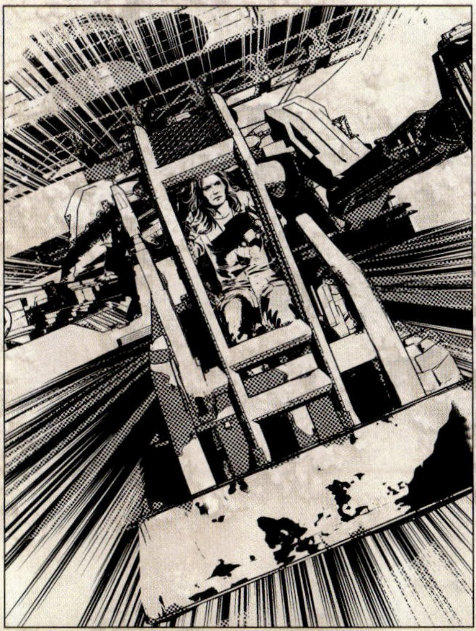

panel four

Cheryl, roaring into the frame on the decapitated robot forklift.

> SFX: VRRRROOO

from script to page

issue #4, page 19 by **mark russell** and **mike deodato jr.**

panel one

Cheryl, pinning Snowball into the wall of
a nearby building with the forklift's lifts.

    SFX: CARRUNCH

panel two

Snowball dying.

    PHILIPPE (CAPTION): And there
is **nothing** more dangerous than
our **illusions**.

panel three

Large panel of robot police taking control of
the riot. The fighting has stopped.

    PHILIPPE (CAPTION): The other question
you're probably asking yourselves is...

    PHILIPPE (CAPTION): ...why am I asking
you to risk your lives for a **lost cause?**

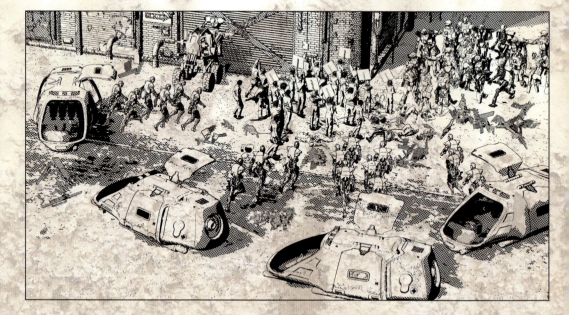

from script to page
issue #4, page 20 by **mark russell** and **mike deodato jr.**

panel one
Cora, hugging her mother.

> PHILIPPE (CAPTION): The answer is this...
>
> CORA: **Mom!**

panel two
Two robot policemen, pinning Cheryl to the ground, handcuffing her hands behind her back. As Donny protests to a third police-bot, who is printing a small slip of paper from its mouth. Cora is shocked.

> PHILIPPE (CAPTION): Because **no effort,** even it **fails,** is ever truly **wasted.**
>
> DONNY: Officers, **please!** This is a **mistake.**
>
> SFX: Fzzzt
>
> CORA: Mom!
>
> CHERYL: Oof!

panel three
In the background, the police are loading Cheryl into the back of a self-driving police van. In the foreground, the police-bot who printed the slip of paper is handing it to Donny.

> PHILIPPE (CAPTION): It either changes the **world** into what it needed to become...
>
> POLICEBOT: Here is her court date.
>
> DONNY: But... but...

panel four
Snowball's broken body, lying abandoned on the sidewalk. In the background, Philippe's dead body is being scooped up by a self-driving hearse with a bulldozer shovel on the front.

> PHILIPPE (CAPTION): ...or it changes us into who we need to **be.**

panel five
The robot recycling bot sweeps up Snowball's dead body.

> PHILIPPE (CAPTION): In the end, nothing of us survives.
>
> PHILIPPE (CAPTION): And yet, so much remains.

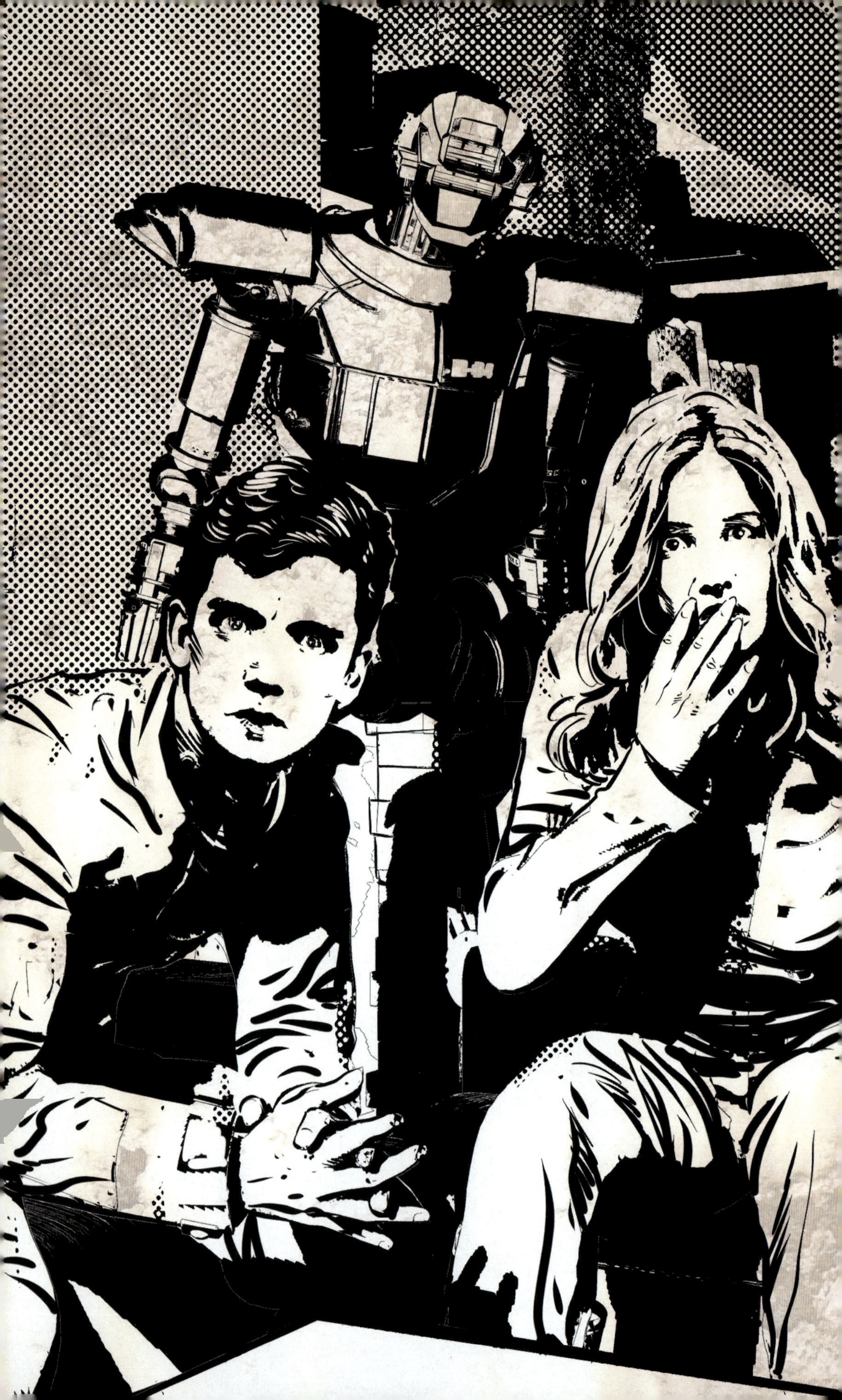

not all outtakes

Below are some plotlines and details from my scripts and outlines that didn't end up making into **not all robots**. I'd call it a "blooper reel" but I wasn't trying to do something good and failing. I was just throwing out ideas and crafting a story out of them and when you do that, if you're lucky, some ideas won't be good enough to make the cut. Other ideas were totally worthy of inclusion, but would have turned it into a different story. Others were simply innocent bystanders, victims of my need to cut the scripts down to 20 pages. The below outtakes were cut for reasons containing all of the above. See if you can figure out which are which. – **mark russell**

¶ That night, Mr. Walters is back at the dinner table, pounding his family with all the robots' talking points about all the good they are doing for the human population. Unable to take it anymore, Mrs. Walters blows up and tells him off, accusing him of siding with the robots because, unable to accept his powerlessness, he has chosen to side with his bully. That he has chosen a comfortable cowardice over admitting the truth that he himself is one of the losers in the brave new world he has helped to create.

¶ Public service billboards for people scared of their personal robots.

¶ Snowball and the other anonymous edgelords on 4Chine are debating about what would be the easiest and most fun way of bumping off the human race.

¶ A laboratory for Omni Robotics that shows all their not-ready-for-primetime products, including "grazers", robotic cows that eat grass and hay and secrete fully-cooked meatloafs.

¶ The militias outside Bubble Atlanta try to turn animatronic pizza parlor robots into killing machines, with less than satisfactory results.

¶ The police-bots wear bodycams that are equipped with an automated judge. If the judge finds them guilty of police brutality, the police-bot's built-in ATM spits hundred dollar bills onto the unconscious body of their victim.

¶ A giant godzilla-sized robot who stands all day every day in the middle of the ocean, desalinating water and absolutely nothing else. Asks passing ships (also robots) to kill him when they float by, but they ignore his pleas.

¶ In the wake of Snowball's "metalcide", Bubble Atlanta has become a police state for humans. Snowball's murder has increased the algorithmic likelihood that humans are in the commission of crimes, so random traffic stops and searches of human beings are allowed. Snowball becomes a martyr, a folk hero to the other robots on 4Chine.

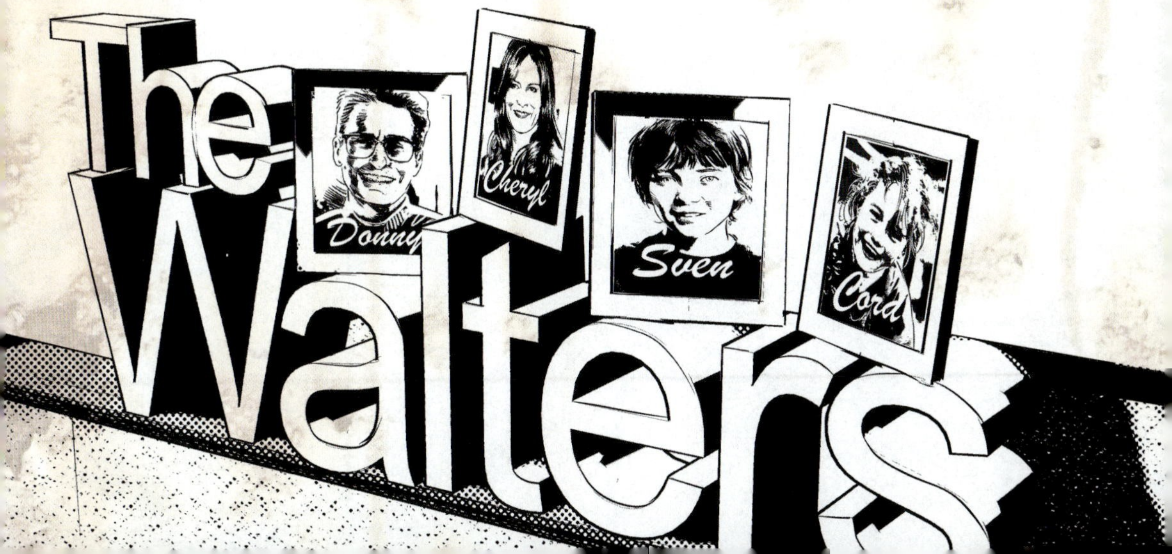

The Walters
Donny
Cheryl
Sven
Cord

the last word

AWA's first Eisner Award-winning writer dishes on his influences, ranking other Russells, and his next AWA hit

AWA NOW: As a satirist, you're expected to be a "funny" writer; do you often get asked to be funny on command?
RUSSELL: No. And that's a good thing. I can't really be funny on command. I feel like I just have to write what I have to write, and if it turns out funny, good for us. What makes it work is not me trying to be funny, but whether it has some meaning and some truth to it.

Well, then this interview should go great. Who are your influences when it comes to writing?
My biggest influences—literarily speaking—is *Mad Magazine*, which was the first comic I fell in love with. Also, the novels of Kurt Vonnegut, which I just inhaled in college. It made me think about how human life is ultimately a futile struggle for meaning.

Let's talk about *Not All Robots* from you, artist Mike Deodato Jr. and AWA. You recently won an Eisner Award for best humor publication. Who deserves more of the credit, you or Mike D?
I think the people who read it deserve it more. It's art when it leaves your hand, but it's not culture until somebody reads it. And the fact that it was this pitch that no one seemed to want, and caught a moment in the public zeitgeist, and people liked it enough to talk about it and vote for it above all the other possibilities to me, is still kind of mind-blowing.

To be both honest and fair, I did do some ballot box stuffing on this one.
It's always good to have a man on the inside.

How do you display your Eisner Awards?

Are they on a shelf, in a box at the back of the closet, or on a chain around your neck?
I only have one, but I keep it on my desk.

Only one? You didn't win for *Snagglepuss* or *The Flintstones*?
Nominated but never won. The good thing about winning is that no matter how many you lose in the future, you'll always be the "Eisner Award-winning writer…"

You've been so good about turning conventional characters into commentary on today. What IP would you love to get your hands on?
Scrooge McDuck—he's the quintessential capitalist who thinks he's moving society forward, when he's really just swimming in a tank full of gold coins. I also really like the idea of someone having to draw a "money bath."

Please rank these other famous Russells from favorite to least favorite: Bill Russell, Kurt Russell, Russell Crowe, Keri Russell and Russell T. Davies.
I'm going with Bill Russell at number one and Keri Russell number two, because I really loved *The Americans*. Then, I'm going to go with [British mathematician and philosopher] Bertrand Russell, even though he wasn't on the list, at number three.

What's your beef with Kurt Russell?
I just don't know where I'd rank him. All Russells are beautiful, in their own way.

Even Keri Russell after that haircut on "Felicity"?
Oh, I thought it was epic. It's some of the BEST hair our country has produced.

Before we go, let's tease your next book from AWA.
Yeah, so RUMPUS ROOM is about…

Sorry, Mark. We're out of space. Maybe next time!
[SPEECHLESS] •

*Reprinted from **AWA NOW** issue #1.*

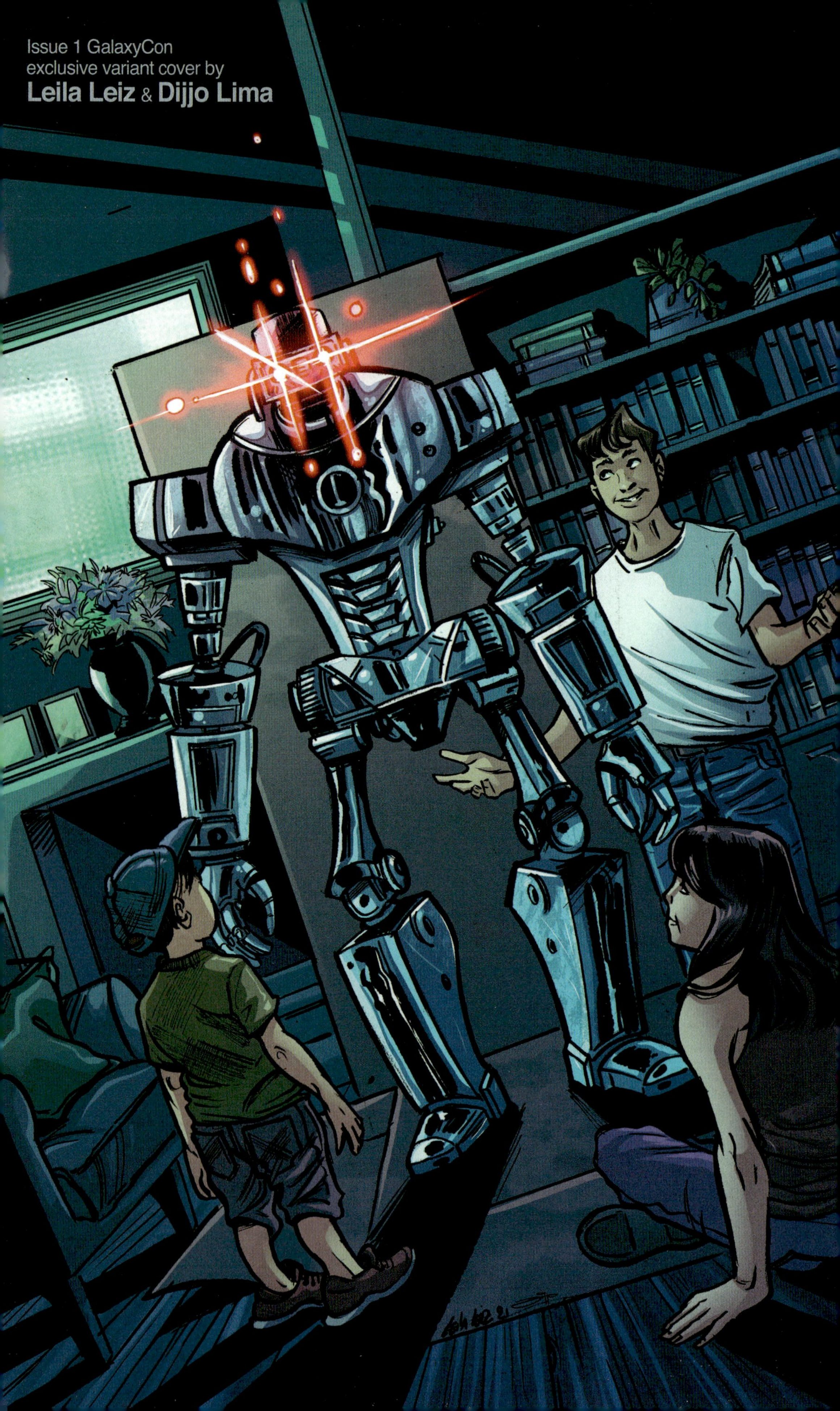

Issue 1 GalaxyCon
exclusive variant cover by
Leila Leiz & **Dijjo Lima**